Academic Freedom and Tenure

ISSUES IN ACADEMIC ETHICS

General Editor: Steven M. Cahn

Campus Rules and Moral Community: In Place of *In Loco Parentis*
  by David A. Hoekema, Calvin College

University-Business Partnerships: An Assessment
  by Norman E. Bowie, University of Minnesota, Twin Cities

A Professor's Duties: Ethical Issues in College Teaching
  by Peter J. Markie, University of Missouri–Columbia

Neutrality and the Academic Ethic
  by Robert L. Simon, Hamilton College

Academic Freedom and Tenure: Ethical Issues

Richard T. De George

ROWMAN & LITTLEFIELD PUBLISHERS, INC.
Lanham • New York • Boulder • Oxford

ROWMAN & LITTLEFIELD PUBLISHERS, INC.

Published in the United States of America
by Rowman & Littlefield Publishers, Inc.
4720 Boston Way, Lanham, Maryland 20706

12 Hid's Copse Road
Cummor Hill, Oxford OX2 9JJ, England

British Cataloging in Publication Information Available

Library of Congress Cataloging-in-Publication Data
De George, Richard T.
    Academic freedom and tenure : ethical issues / Richard T. De
George.
        p.   cm.
    Includes bibliographical references (p.   ) and index.
    ISBN 0-8476-8331-1 (alk. paper).—ISBN 0-8476-8332-X (pbk. :
alk. paper)
        1. College teachers—Tenure—United States.   2. Academic freedom—
Moral and ethical aspects—United States.   3. College teachers—
Professional ethics—United States.   I. Title.
LB2335.7.D4   1997
378.1′21—dc21   96-39513
                                                            CIP

Printed in the United States of America

∞ ™ The paper used in this publication meets the minimum requirements of
American National Standard for Information Sciences—Permanence of Paper for
Printed Library Materials, ANSI Z39.48–1984.

Issues in Academic Ethics

Academic life generates a variety of moral issues. These may be faced by students, staff, administrators, or trustees, but most often revolve around the rights and responsibilities of the faculty. In my 1986 book *Saints and Scamps: Ethics in Academia* (Rowman & Littlefield), I set out to enumerate, explain, and emphasize the most fundamental of these professorial obligations. To do justice to the complexities of academic ethics, however, requires the work of many scholars focused on numerous areas of investigation. The results of such an effort are embodied in this series.

Each volume concentrates on one set of connected issues and combines a single-authored monograph with reprinted sources chosen by the author to exemplify or amplify materials in the text. This format is intended to guide readers while encouraging them to develop and defend their own beliefs.

In recent years philosophers have examined the appropriate standards of conduct for physicians, nurses, lawyers, journalists, business managers, and government policymakers but have not given equal attention to formulating guidelines for their own profession. The time has come to observe the Delphic motto "Know thyself." Granted, the issues in need of critical examination are not exotic, but as the history of philosophy demonstrates, self-knowledge is often the most important to seek and the most difficult to attain.

Steven M. Cahn

Contents

Preface

Academic freedom and tenure are such entrenched parts of American academic life that many faculty members take them for granted. Tenure is often seen as a prize that a faculty member gets after six years of probation and that one then has for the rest of one's career. The granting of tenure is seldom, if ever, coupled with a list of responsibilities that go with it, and few people think of those responsibilities upon receiving tenure. But a little thought will lead one to realize that for a college or university to bestow tenure with no concomitant responsibilities on the part of the recipient would make little sense.

Similarly, most faculty members pursue their research and teaching and give little thought to academic freedom. Their experience tells them that there is really little cause for concern, and that if there is any real threat, then steps can be taken to protect it. Every now and then there is an incident precipitated by a controversial invited speaker. But by and large, university officials and outside bodies do not dictate what or how faculty members are to teach or what they may or may not pursue in their research. The claim that individual faculty members have responsibilities with respect to academic freedom would come as a surprise to many faculty members, who, if they give academic freedom any thought, consider it a right they have that others should respect and if necessary protect.

This quasi-idyllic approach to academic tenure and academic freedom has in recent years been shaken, although certainly not shattered. Academic tenure has come under attack from various quarters, and the downsizing that has griped the corporate world has led some governing bodies to ask why, in a time of fewer available tax dollars, universities should not also be made leaner and meaner. Some legislatures and some boards of trustees have become interested in the nuts-and-bolts operation of the institutions of higher education that they oversee and have called for increased accountability on terms that the former set, with negative consequences to those institutions that do not measure up or do not cooperate.

Within some colleges and universities the traditional great books have been successfully challenged, much to the displeasure of some alumni. Topics such as postmodernism and political correctness have crept into the conversations of ordinary citizens, columnists, and cartoonists. The result has not been salutary for some institutions and for their academic autonomy.

These conditions form the background of this book. What I have attempted is to see if a case can still be made for academic tenure and academic freedom as they have more or less been found in American colleges and universities in the past three or four decades. Central to the current conception of both is their formulation in statements by the American Association of University Professors (AAUP). Those statements have sometimes been the result of compromises, and some parts of the statements could very well have been other than they are—for instance the seven-year probationary period for tenure. The particular formulations are not ethically or morally mandatory. But that does not mean they are not justifiable. I have attempted to see to what extent they are justifiable. The tentative conclusion to which I came is that they are justifiable, providing that they are construed as carrying with them certain responsibilities, and their justification is contingent on these responsibilities being met. I have not attempted to ascertain whether in particular cases they have been or are being met.

In looking at arguments in support of academic tenure and academic freedom I had also to look at arguments against them. I made no attempt to be exhaustive in my presentation or discussion of arguments either for or against academic tenure and freedom. Rather I have tried to develop a general approach and to review the most frequently raised objections to each. Along the way I have kept my eye on the responsibilities and obligations that go along with both, because they seem to be so frequently ignored. I have argued in terms of rights, where that seemed appropriate. But I have not adopted any particular ethical position—for example, Utilitarianism or Kantianism—from which to argue. I believe the moral claims that I make are defensible from several positions and are not narrowly tied to a given ethical perspective. Sometimes the language of consequences and of producing more good than harm seemed appropriate, sometimes the concept of rights, sometimes the notion of fairness or justice appeared most appropriate and natural, and those are the terms and approaches that I used.

Part II of the volume consists of documents and articles by others. In Part I, did not repeat much of what is contained in the 1940 Statement of Principles on Academic Freedom and Tenure, but I have included it in Part II for easy reference. I did not develop at length or reply at length to any particular attack on academic freedom and tenure, and so I have included some representative articles in Part II. I did not attempt to settle the debate between postmodernists and those whom they attack, although I refer to the debate and try to assess its importance for academic tenure and academic freedom. So I have included some sample papers dealing with this topic. A bibliography at the end includes selected articles and books that I found useful and that I think others might find useful as well.

It is difficult to draw the boundaries between one's responsibilities vis-à-vis academic tenure and academic freedom and other areas of academic life. Other volumes in this series deal with many of these other aspects, and I have tried to keep my focus narrow enough so as not to repeat what others in this series have said at length and in detail.

My hope is not that this volume will give the last word on any of the topics it touches but that it will help provoke greater discussion among faculty members about their responsibilities with respect to academic tenure and academic freedom, and that this discussion in turn will lead to the actions necessary to justify the continuation and strengthening of both.

Richard T. De George

Acknowledgments

The readings in Part II are reprinted with permission, as follows.

"1940 Statement of Principles on Academic Freedom and Tenure With 1970 Interpretive Comments," pp. 3–7 [without list of endorsers], *AAUP Policy Documents & Reports,* Washington, D.C.: AAUP, 1995. Reprinted with the permission of the American Association of University Professors.

"Statement on Professional Ethics (1987)," pp. 105–6, *AAUP Policy Documents & Reports,* Washington, D.C.: AAUP, 1995. Reprinted with the permission of the American Association of University Professors.

"A Statement of the Association's Council: Freedom and Responsibility (1970)," pp. 107–8, *AAUP Policy Documents & Reports,* Washington, D.C.: AAUP, 1995. Reprinted with the permission of the American Association of University Professors.

"On Freedom of Expression and Campus Speech Codes (1992)," pp. 37–38, *AAUP Policy Documents & Reports,* Washington, D.C.: AAUP, 1995. Reprinted with the permission of the American Association of University Professors.

Ralph F. Fuchs, "Academic Freedom—Its Basic Philosophy, Function, and History," *Law and Contemporary Problems,* 28 (Summer 1963), pp. 431–46. Reprinted with the permission of *Law and Contemporary Problems.*

Robert W. McGee and Walter E. Block, "Academic Tenure: An Economic Critique," *Harvard Journal of Law & Public Policy,* 14, 2, pp. 545–63. Reprinted with the permission of *Harvard Journal of Law & Public Policy.*

Richard Rorty, "Does Academic Freedom Have Philosophical Presuppositions?" as published in adapted form in *Academe* (November–December 1994), pp. 52–63, from a longer essay by same from *The Future of Academic Freedom,* Louis Menand. Reprinted with the permission of *Academe* and The University of Chicago Press.

John R. Searle, "Rationality and Realism, What Is at Stake?" Reprinted with the permission of *Daedalus* from issue entitled "The American Research University" (Fall 1993), 122, 4, pp. 55–84.

Part I

The Justification of Academic Tenure and Academic Freedom

Chapter One

The Justification of Academic Tenure

Universities can exist without academic freedom and tenure, as they have done in many countries and for many years. Academic tenure as understood in the United States is of relatively recent origin when considered in the light of the history of the university as an institution.[1] Nonetheless, academic tenure as it has developed in the United States is a crucial part of the American academic scene, and its demise would be an enormous loss to colleges and universities as we have come to know them and as they now exist. This claim is not only not self-evident but it is being questioned increasingly by some powerful and influential voices both outside and, perhaps surprisingly, inside the walls of academe. The role, function, and justification of academic tenure are often simply equated with unnecessary, undeserved, and counterproductive job security for an elitist, self-serving group of overpaid and underworked college and university professors.

Because academic tenure has come under attack from both inside and outside the academy, I shall evaluate it to the extent possible on its merits, and see what sort of and how strong a case can be made for it. After providing an initial definition, I shall argue first that academic tenure is appropriate for a certain kind of university in a certain kind of society; second, that its justification in that sort of setting is based on the good of society, not of individual faculty members; and third, that even in that setting there are certain norms to which the process must conform if it is to be justified. Attacks on academic tenure are based explicitly or implicitly on academic tenure's failure on one of these three counts.

I. What Is Academic Tenure?

The first task is to make clear what academic tenure is. Calling it *academic* tenure puts emphasis on the fact that it is a special kind of tenure, tied to a

3

special rationale. Academic tenure in the United States is traditionally linked with institutions of higher education. Teachers on the primary and secondary levels of education may have job security or guaranteed reappointment or something else comparable either contractually negotiated or simply bestowed by the local school board or governing officials, but that is not the same as academic tenure.

Academic tenure, as the American Association of University Professors (AAUP) uses the term, and as I shall use it, is tenure held by members of a faculty at an institution of higher education, where this is defined as postsecondary education. The typical case is tenure held by a faculty member at a university or four-year college.

Academic tenure is explicitly tied to the academic function of faculty members. We can compare it to and distinguish it from other types of tenure. Judicial tenure is held by federal court judges. This is a guarantee that unless they fail to perform their functions, they have a guarantee of continued employment in their position as judges until they die or retire. The purpose of judicial tenure is to prevent the threat of dismissal from influencing their judicial decisions. Briefly stated, the argument is that for judges to make impartial judgments, they must feel free to make them on the basis of evidence, the arguments, and their best insights. If they could be fired for making unpopular judgments or if they had to worry about whether members of the executive branch of government liked or did not like their decisions, they would not be as free to render impartial decisions as otherwise.

Faculty members do not render judgments in the way judges do. Yet the kind of tenure appropriate to academics is tied to what they do in a way comparable to the way that judicial tenure is tied to what judges do. The claims of impartiality, of objectivity, and of lack of extraneous pressure are analogous in both cases.

Academic tenure is not the same as a guarantee of continuous employment, even though academic tenure may functionally be a guarantee of continuous employment. A guarantee of continuous employment may come about in many ways, for many reasons, in many different kinds of firms, organizations, or enterprises, and for many different reasons. It might be negotiated by a union for its members, or it might be bestowed by an employer on certain employees as a matter of principle or out of gratitude for long and excellent service. Usually the guarantee, just as with academic tenure, is contingent upon the financial viability of the entity guaranteeing the continuous employment and on the continued acceptable performance of the worker. Some civil service positions have the equivalent of guaranteed continuous employment as long as one's performance stays minimally satisfactory. Even though in some ways functionally equivalent to guaranteed continuous employment, academic tenure differs from these other cases by virtue of the ground on which it is bestowed and the function it is expected to play.

Academic tenure, considered as guaranteed continuous employment, was traditionally granted until the faculty member reached the mandatory retirement age set by the institution. With the demise of mandatory retirement ages, how long an institution guarantees continuous employment is no longer clear. Presumably it is until the faculty member dies, voluntarily retires, or is fired or otherwise relieved of his or her duties because of incompetence or failure to perform at an acceptable level.

Whether academic tenure is a right, and if so, what kind of right it is, are debated questions. As an approach to an answer, we can start by noting that no one has a right to any particular position. The doctrine of employment-at-will[2] still holds insofar as an institution has the right to hire certain individuals and not hire others. An institution may not ethically or legally discriminate against any candidate for a position on the basis of characteristics not related to the job, such as gender, race, national origin, and age. But an institution may describe its open positions as it wishes, and it may choose from among those applicants who satisfy the job requirements by any nondiscriminatory job-related criteria it wishes. No candidate can claim that he or she has a right to be hired by any given institution because of being the best or most qualified or for any other reason. The institution retains the right to hire whom it chooses, for the nondiscriminatory job-related reasons it chooses.

Initial hiring does not obligate the institution to grant continuous or even renewed annual employment. What ethics requires is that an institution make known to the applicant and to the newly hired faculty member the conditions of employment, including the terms and conditions of the initial contract, the possibility of a renewed appointment, the possibility of eventual tenure if that is the case, other conditions of employment, and the criteria that will be used in judging performance. Included in full disclosure of conditions of employment are the criteria that must be met for renewed appointment and, if appropriate, for academic tenure. Unless all this is clear upon the initial appointment, the agreement between the new appointee and the hiring institution is difficult to defend from an ethical point of view because the contract lacks the complete disclosure that is required if the contract is to be entered into and agreed upon knowingly and willingly. A binding contract from an ethical point of view requires that the contract be entered freely by both parties, and it requires that appropriate knowledge at least be available to both parties. For either party to hide something relevant to the contract is to knowingly deceive the other party, and so to undermine the ethical force of the agreement.

Tenure becomes a legitimate expectation when it is presented to a faculty member as something that may be earned and the conditions under which it may be earned are specified. To call tenure a right is to say that a faculty member who satisfies the stated criteria has a legitimate claim on it. But most institutions do not guarantee tenure or see it as something a faculty member can legitimately claim. Rather they see tenure as something bestowed by the institution and legitimately withheld by the institution for a wide variety of reasons. Tenure is rarely given automatically by an institution. It is usually granted only after an extensive review of the faculty member's performance by one or more committees and/or administrators. Some institutions have a formal or informal rule about the percentage of the faculty who may be tenured or who may be tenured in a given department. If such limits exist, that is pertinent information that affects the conditions of employment and that should be made known to faculty members upon initial appointment. An institution may also change its tenure policy, making it more or less strict because of growth or attrition in the number of students or because of financial reasons. This is permissible, as long as the policies are not ad hoc and are publicly defensible, and the affected faculty members are given adequate time to meet the new requirements.

If a right is a justifiable normative claim or entitlement, and if what we have said is correct, then untenured faculty members have no right to be granted tenure. What they have a right to is fair consideration for tenure in accordance with the criteria they have been told will apply. If they are refused tenure, they have a right to know why, providing they had a legitimate expectation that it would be awarded.

Just as no individual faculty member has a right to be awarded tenure, so no institution has an obligation to award tenure in a particular case or to have the practice of awarding academic tenure. It may be shortsighted of the institution not to have academic tenure, it may identify the institution as being of a certain kind or quality, and it may open it up to censure by the AAUP and other similar organizations or to boycott by potential faculty and by faculty elsewhere. But as long as the conditions of employment are clearly stated, those accepting appointment in such an institution cannot claim that they have a right to tenure since they were told from the start that the institution does not grant academic tenure.

Although tenure is not a right that one can claim, the granting of tenure confers certain rights on the faculty member, the principal one of which is guaranteed continuous employment, providing certain conditions are met on both sides. Once tenure is granted, the institution commits itself to certain conditions to which the faculty member has a legitimate claim or entitlement and so to which the faculty member has a right. The right is alienable, in that the faculty member may freely give up the claim. An institution that wished to phase out tenure, for instance, might offer large salary increases guaranteed for a specified number of years to faculty members who agree to give up any claim to tenure after the specified number of years. Faculty members at such an institution would be free to accept or reject such an offer. On the face of it, there is nothing unethical in either making or accepting such an offer, providing there is nothing unethical in undermining the institution of academic tenure once it has been established—a topic we shall discuss later.

Academic tenure is by definition academic. This means not only that it is held by people at postsecondary academic institutions, but that it is related directly and importantly to the academic mission and function of such institutions. Typically, academic tenure is not conferred by a college or university on administrators—not even the chief administrator or president or chancellor. Nor is it conferred on nonacademic appointees, such as clerical and support staff. It is restricted to those who teach and/or do research, although it is sometimes extended also to certain other classes of faculty-equivalent positions, such as librarians. These are the academic functions of the university, and it is to safeguard these that tenure was instituted and that it receives its clearest justification.

Although teachers in primary and secondary schools may be given guarantees of continuous employment, they do not usually receive academic tenure. The reason is that their relation to knowledge and to what they teach is considered importantly different from that of faculty at institutions of higher education. They are typically not expected to engage in research, or publish, or advance knowledge in the way that faculty members in postsecondary schools are expected to do. It may well be objected that what and how some high school teachers teach and what and how some junior college or college or university teachers teach is identical. Although this is true, the nature of the institutions in question and their function and role in society are different, and that difference makes the decisive difference with respect to academic tenure. What that difference is, we shall discuss shortly.

Academic tenure is defined by the AAUP as follows:

> After the expiration of a probationary period, teachers or investigators should have permanent or continuous tenure, and their service should be terminated only for adequate cause, except in case of retirement for age, or under extraordinary circumstances because of financial exigencies.[3]

The 1940 document allows moral turpitude as a legitimate cause for dismissal. This is defined by the 1970 Interpretative Comments as violating a standard of "behavior that would evoke condemnation by the academic community generally."[4] Also generally included under adequate cause would be academic incompetence and failure to meet one's professional obligations.

Academic incompetence is often difficult to substantiate. Any faculty member who has earned a doctorate and successfully passed the requirements for tenure was at least at that time considered competent. Failure to keep up with developments in one's field does not constitute incompetence, much less does failure to contribute to the developments in one's field. Nor does failure to communicate effectively one's knowledge to students. Perhaps with the elimination of mandatory retirement ages senility might become a basis for declaring a faculty member incompetent. But incompetence is a seldom used justification for terminating a tenured faculty member, and this is understandably the case.

On the other hand, failure to meet one's professional obligations is in some cases clear. For instance, repeated failure to go to one's classes or to teach the subject of the course during one's classes or to grade one's students' work constitute quite clear failure to meet one's professional obligations. Yet failure to publish in one's field after attaining tenure is not clear evidence of failure to meet one's professional obligations, for many colleges consider publication an extra, deserving reward, but not a deficiency to be penalized.

The 1940 Statement of Principles does not specify what constitutes failure to meet one's professional obligations, nor should it, since obligations vary widely among departments, fields, and institutions. This does not mean that the faculty within an institution, together with the administrators, cannot agree on broad guidelines of what constitutes failure to meet one's professional obligations. Having such guidelines both informs the faculty of what is expected and provides criteria for possible dismissal of tenured faculty members.

The possibility of dismissal for cause is a legitimate part of the practice of academic tenure, and it is a necessary part of academic tenure, if it is to be justified. Nonetheless, academic tenure is difficult to attain and is awarded by an institution upon the evaluation and recommendation of one's peers. The onus of proving one's worth is on the faculty member. Academic tenure should be commensurably difficult to lose, if it is to have meaning and serve its function. A tenured faculty member should be fired only upon the evaluation and recommendation of one's peers, and the onus is on the institution to prove adequate cause. Dismissal of tenured faculty is appropriately rare and exceptional and difficult, but not impossible.

II. The Justification of Academic Tenure

One of the arguments sometimes given for tenure is that it is justified in part because of the relatively poor salaries of most professors, given the years of study necessary for them to attain their positions.[5] It implies that relatively low salaries are justified for faculty members because they have tenure. That is, it implies that at some point faculty members traded job security for low salaries. This is historically inaccurate. Faculty salaries were low before academic tenure came on the scene. The other implication is that if faculty salaries were commensurate with the amount of study required to hold such a position, tenure would not be justified. But if, as I shall argue, and as the AAUP has consistently maintained, academic tenure is justified primarily because of its relation to academic freedom, then whether faculty members are well paid is beside the point. Academic tenure would be justified, if it is justified, even if faculty were relatively or even very well paid. If pay were a serious basis for tenure, then it is not clear why faculty should not be given a choice of either higher salaries without tenure or lower salaries with tenure. However, to offer any such choice is to imply that academic tenure is primarily a financial issue. It is not.

At best the financial argument is a justification given to some outside constituencies who do not understand the real basis for academic tenure, and to whom the claim that there is a trade-off between tenure and low salaries seems to make economic sense. There is an economic relation between job security and lower salaries. But this relation also serves as justification for keeping faculty salaries relatively low. To this extent academic tenure might well seem to some faculty members to be a disadvantage rather than an advantage. And certainly to some extent they would be correct. The argument for academic tenure is strengthened, not weakened, if accepting it brings with it a lower salary than faculty members would otherwise receive. For then the real reason for academic tenure becomes basic and overriding. What is that justification?

The justification is that academic tenure is the best means our society has devised to secure and preserve academic freedom.

In the former Soviet Union professors had job security, just as all workers did. The Soviet Constitution called for full employment and the government was the sole employer. Discharging any worker was very difficult under this system. Even though the professors in effect had guaranteed employment they did not have academic tenure because they could lose their positions if they attempted to publish or teach what was ideologically unacceptable. In 1924 over a hundred philosophers were removed from their positions and exiled. The only philosophers allowed to teach were Marxists. Some freedom of discussion among them was allowed until 1929. Then the leaders of the country stepped in and ruled against one of two competing factions. The winners in turn were replaced by a decree of the Central Committee of the Communist Party in 1931 for a list of ideological offenses. Thereafter, the leaders of the Communist Party were the ultimate authorities on what could and could not be taught. They were the defenders of the purity of Marxism and, in their minds, of the truth. Not without reason, they held that only the truth should and would be taught in all schools and universities.

In such a society the notion of academic freedom has no place. Since some group—in this case the leaders of the Communist Party—had both the truth and control over all the institutions of society, the task of those institutions was to promulgate the truth as defined by the leaders. Not only in philosophy, but in all other areas, these leaders—at least through 1951—were the final authority. Quantum mechanics and relativity theory were prohibited because they were bourgeois; Mendelian genetics was prohibited in favor of Lysenko's theories; non-Marxist philosophy could not be taught; only Marxist versions of history could be presented.[6]

Academic freedom involves the freedom to pursue one's research independent of outside political powers and pressures. Academic freedom loses its central meaning in a society in which the external powers that control the university decide what is true and what is not, and so what may be taught or published, and what may not be. In this situation, academic tenure also loses its meaning. At best what is provided is job security. But that is not academic tenure, since it is precisely for one's work in the academic area that one is most likely to lose one's position.

Academic tenure is closely linked to academic freedom. The main purpose of academic tenure is to prevent the possibility of a faculty member's being dismissed because what he or she teaches or writes about is considered by either administrators or some people outside the institution to be wrong or offensive. This is the basic claim in defense of academic tenure. The full argument requires spelling out and involves a discussion of academic freedom. But this rough statement suffices to see that academic tenure makes little sense in a society that does not allow academic freedom.

There are various models of a university. Only some of them are compatible with academic freedom, and hence only some of them are compatible with academic tenure.

One traditional model of a university goes back to its origins at the University of Paris in the thirteenth century. That model consists of a group of scholars banding together and gathering around them students interested in learning from the masters. The university claimed autonomy in the sense that it ran its own affairs and often even claimed independence from local authorities in the enforcement of laws and the punishment of student offenders. Debates and discussions proceeded without outside interference, even though sometimes certain theological doctrines would be condemned by the Catholic Church. As a model, however, the University of Paris was an autonomous faculty-run institution.

A second model is the student-run institution. Here students wish to be instructed in certain subjects in preparation for jobs of various sorts—law and medicine being the paradigms. The students hire faculty to teach them what they need to know. The faculty may have a voice in what they teach. But the students decide whether to retain the faculty, usually by whether they find their classes interesting enough to enroll in. The faculty in this model is not paid to do research, except insofar as they are expected to keep up with their field so that they can teach their students the latest knowledge.

A third model is the ideological model of the former Soviet Union in which the task of the faculty is to transmit the official state ideology as well as prepare students to fill the jobs society needs done. Here there is no autonomy of the university and it is completely subservient to the state.

A fourth model is the entrepreneurial model. Someone starts a university, hires administrators and faculty members, and pays them to teach students in such a way that students will pay to take their courses. The point is to make a profit, and the faculty are a means to that end.

A fifth model is the state university, which is a mixture of several of the above models. Typically the state university has some autonomy. Although the state supports the institution through tax dollars (and students support the institution through tuition) both the state officials and the students realize that they are not competent to decide what should be taught or how, and the academic part of the university is left primarily to the faculty, who are expected to have knowledge of their fields and of how to educate and train students for various kinds of work, including how to provide a liberal education.

Academic freedom may not be of much concern in models two and four and is of no concern in model three. Academic freedom is of central concern in model one, and it should be of central concern in model five, providing that society is of a certain type, the university is of a certain kind, and academic freedom is understood in a certain way. If the three are of the appropriate sort, then academic tenure is an important ingredient in the university, providing it is carried out in an appropriate manner. What are these types, and what is this manner?

A society should be interested in having a university to which it grants autonomy if the society receives something of benefit in return. The reason for granting autonomy is that those who wish to have a university and are not part of it believe that some people, whom they will hire as faculty, have specialized, systematic, and advanced knowledge. Unless the faculty have this specialized knowledge that others do not have, there would be little reason for letting them have much autonomy. It would make more sense simply to hire those willing and able to teach what they are told to teach. Typically that is what happens at the primary levels. Parents know they want their children to learn to read, write, calculate, and to know something about history, geography, their country, and a little about other parts of the world. School boards have a hand in developing and approving curricula.

Parents of would-be doctors, on the other hand, do not know what doctors should know, except generally that they should know anatomy and medicine. They must trust people trained in medicine to know what to prescribe for a curriculum and to teach the material and evaluate and certify the students. The same is true in law, engineering, mathematics, history, psychology, and the other areas covered at a university.

A society gives a university autonomy in the belief that the institution can achieve its results better if those who are competent in their fields run it than if people from outside with less knowledge try to run it. Primary among the tasks of a university are the education and training of students in their respective fields and professions. Not only do well-educated graduates fill the available jobs and keep the society functioning and productive, but they also make up an educated electorate, capable of voting intelligently, and of running government and keeping it from becoming a dictatorship, no matter how benign.

A second reason for granting a university autonomy is the belief that knowledge is not yet complete and that no one inside or outside the university knows all there is to know. If some group—a state, a political party, religious leaders—know the truth, then they would have little reason to grant autonomy to a university. At least in those domains in which they knew the truth, they would reasonably wish to ensure that the truth which they knew was taught accurately, that is, as they know it. On the other hand, if those who set up and fund a university believe that not all truth is known, then they would do well, if they also believed that it is worthwhile to pursue the truth and to learn more, to provide a place and to pay competent people to seek that truth. Since no one can say what will be discovered, no one can predict what will be discovered. Hence it would be a mistake to try to restrict the search for truth by establishing procedures or rules that might result in preventing investigators from finding the truth.

A third reason a society might wish to grant a university autonomy is if the society wished to have a place in which all aspects of the society could be freely examined and critiqued, without that examination and critique being expressed in a violent or destructive manner. If a society believes that it can be improved by having a place where debate takes place without immediate application in practice—as it is in a legislature, for instance—and where some distance from immediate results and politically motivated research can be carried on, then it would be reasonable to fund such an institution. Since it wants the investigations to be free of political partisanship, and at least to that extent to be objective, it can best achieve that result by granting the institution autonomy.

It is within a society such as this that a relatively autonomous university makes sense. The autonomy granted the university is justified not by the good of those within the university but by the good of the rest of society.

Within such an institution, the ends for which the university is given autonomy can in turn best be achieved by granting those within the university academic freedom. The same beliefs and arguments hold within the university as hold for the university. It is only if they do hold that the university can achieve the ends for which it is granted autonomy.

The final claim is that the best way to guarantee that faculty will pursue truth in their areas of competence freely and objectively is if they have no fear that they will be penalized if they break with tradition, try new approaches, or turn up unpopular results. One way to eliminate that fear and to reinforce the social and institutional desire for the advancement of knowledge is to guarantee that the teachers and researchers do not place their jobs in jeopardy by pursuing and reporting the truth as they discover it. That guarantee is what academic tenure provides, at least for those who have served a period of time to demonstrate their competence and their ability to pursue and advance knowledge and to communicate that to students and to pertinent others (colleagues, the general public, other specialists, as the case may be).

III. Academic Tenure and Academic Freedom

Given the above analysis, it is primarily the good of society, not the good of individual faculty members, that is of greatest concern. The argument maintains that society is the loser if the practice of tenure disappears. Without tenure, the faculty members have no guarantee that they will not be penalized for presenting new ideas, for challenging accepted truths or ways of doing things, or for criticizing existing institutions, governments, mores, and morals. Without this guarantee some faculty members will still do all these things, and run the risk of being fired because of it. But many others will not, and will practice self-censorship. The chilling effect of the firing of just a few professors who present their views will be considerable on many, many others.

The result will be a less dynamic and bold faculty, with less in the way of new truths or techniques being developed. Without a free forum for critique and discussion the community and so the state as a whole become impoverished. Without the example and encouragement of teachers who are bold and seek the truth wherever it may lead them, students will in turn be taught by example to be conservative and safe. The detriment to society is a less critical citizenry. Some societies and some political leaders may relish these results. But a free, open society will not.

Although a society may grant a university autonomy based on the belief that it will get commensurable goods in return and that it will achieve more of what it wants by granting the institution autonomy than by not doing so, it does not and need not operate completely on blind trust. It can legitimately exercise some oversight and expect a certain accountability.

Students can tell whether they are learning something. Employers can tell whether their new hires are competent and whether they have learned in their college or university education enough to perform adequately in the positions for which they are presumably qualified because of their education. The members of society can tell whether the younger generation that emerges from college has learned to think clearly and critically. All these assessments are rough and do not imply that those making them have the knowledge or expertise that members of the faculty have. But they do not need that expertise to make their assessments. Patients can tell whether they are benefiting from their doctor's care without knowing medicine in the way that doctors do. People can assess results without knowing how to produce them. This is as true with respect to education as with a great many other areas in which expertise and knowledge are important in producing certain results.

This is not to say that education is a commodity or to be treated as if it were. The university is not a factory or business. Nonetheless, the university exists not primarily for the good of the faculty, but for the good of society.

The argument that I presented for academic tenure hinged on academic freedom. I argued that academic freedom was important to society, and that if academic tenure is the best way to protect academic freedom, then academic tenure is important to society. Yet academic freedom and hence academic tenure are defensible only if the good of society can be achieved thereby. And that means only if there is knowledge that is not yet known that can be pursued and found, and if the university is the place where this is done. If truth is already known, then it has only to be preserved, and those who know it can rightly demand that it be preserved and passed on in the universities over which they exercise control. Academic freedom makes sense only if those outside the university who fund and control it do not have any privileged access to the truth and stand to gain by its being pursued in a university.

If there is no truth to be pursued, if there is no knowledge to be gained, then once again there is little reason to grant faculty members academic tenure. If all that universities have is the opinion or personal belief of faculty members, none of which is demonstrably preferable to any other, then there is little sense in granting them academic tenure or in believing there is any benefit to society in granting academic freedom. Freedom of speech may benefit a society, but that is not the same as academic freedom.

IV. Academic Tenure and the American University

I have argued that academic tenure makes sense only in a certain kind of society and only under certain conditions. The United States is the kind of society in which academic tenure makes sense—it is a relatively free and open society, and one in which there is a widespread belief that knowledge is useful, and that not everything is known. It is a democracy in which an educated and critical citizenry can play an effective role. And it is a developed society in which creativity and originality have an important function. In such a society academic freedom can be and has been a crucial component in its college and university system. It has gone hand-in-hand with academic tenure.

If, as critics claim, academic tenure is an institution whose time has passed, is the same to be said of academic freedom? Might academic tenure be feasibly applied to only some faculty or restricted to only some departments or only to some colleges and universities?

Consider an institution that gives academic tenure only to some professors but not to others. Of course, this is already the case. Only some faculty members have tenure. Tenure is not held by beginning instructors or assistant professors who work full-time, nor by full-time faculty members who are on limited-term appointments, nor by part-time faculty. There can be no objection in principle, then, in advocating a system of selective tenure. The justification for tenure under the present system, however, is that those with tenure should guarantee the academic freedom of the institution as a whole and so the academic freedom of those who do not have or who do not yet have tenure. The test of whether selective academic tenure is justifiable is whether under such a system those with tenure will be both able and willing to guarantee the academic freedom of the institution and of those without tenure. There would be little reason to expect those with tenure to defend the academic freedom of those who might have opted for tenure but who, for instance, chose higher-paying term contracts. By choosing such contracts over tenured positions they have in fact indicated either that they do not care for or about academic freedom, or that, if they do, they expect those with tenure to protect them. The latter is an unreasonable expectation. Hence a system of this sort is unlikely to protect the academic freedom of the institution and of all those in it. And since it does not, the reason for granting academic tenure to any faculty would not exist.

Some faculty may claim that they would prefer to take higher-paying term contracts than lower-paying tenured appointments because they feel either that they work in areas in which academic freedom is not crucial or that their work is in an area or field in which knowledge is secure and unlikely to need challenge of the type for which academic freedom is important. They may also feel that if they are unjustly fired from one position they are talented enough to be able to find another position. They assume that there are other colleges or universities in which their views will be tolerated, even though not tolerated in their former institution. That is to assume more than may be justified if the attitude such people adopt toward tenure becomes widespread. Their view considers academic tenure a personal protection and one that they feel they can do without. They fail to understand that tenure exists and is conferred on individual faculty members not for the benefit primarily of that individual but for the benefit of the institution and of the larger society.

There is no area in a university that does not need academic freedom. If it deserves to be in a university, there is knowledge to be preserved and transmitted, critically developed, and potentially challenged. If academic freedom is not critical to it, it does not belong in a college or university. It is an accepted body of knowledge, developed by others, that needs only to be transmitted to students. That is characteristic of the knowledge taught on the primary and secondary levels, and that is one of the reasons why tenure is not typically given in such educational institutions, even though some sort of guaranteed renewable contracts may be given. Hence there is no academic area of the university to which tenure is not appropriate. And if the purpose of academic tenure is to protect academic freedom, then it is best protected if there are some tenured faculty in every area, the better to safeguard it.

Academic freedom cannot be given to some part of the university and not to other parts. To attempt to do so is to misunderstand that the institution as a whole is autonomous, not just parts of it. What is true from the outside is true as well from the inside.

That leaves us with the question of whether some institutions of higher education might claim autonomy, defend academic freedom, and grant their faculty tenure, while others do not. We have already seen that primary and secondary schools do not typically grant tenure. For an institution of higher education not to grant tenure is implicitly to say that it does not value academic freedom. To the extent that academic freedom benefits society, society is better off by having all or almost all of these institutions guaranteeing academic freedom. If only some do, then there is less chance of developing creative, new knowledge, and there are fewer students trained in the critical thinking fostered by the institutions that defend academic freedom. Just as the tenured faculty in an institution have the obligation to protect the academic freedom of all the faculty at their institution, so the tenured faculty members at each institution that values academic freedom should do what they can to protect academic freedom at all institutions. One institution typically does not put pressure on others. But it could do so. And faculty could apply pressure. That is the reason for the AAUP's censuring of institutions. The obligation of tenured faculty to support academic freedom in institutions other than their own is less strong than in their own institution. But since the reason for their tenure is the benefit not only of their own institution but of society as a whole, then they also have some obligation to do what they can to protect academic freedom wherever it is violated in the society.

Tenure has been misrepresented and misperceived both within and without the university. If understood as I have suggested, it is both defensible and of such benefit to society that it deserves to be continued.

V. Some Attacks on Academic Tenure

The attacks on tenure that have received the most public attention rarely mention academic freedom. Rather, the primary arguments are economic. I have already indicated that the economic arguments in favor of tenure are secondary and that the major line of defense is and should be the defense of academic freedom. But since the economic arguments get so much attention, they should be explored.

The most frequently heard argument is the "deadwood argument." There are various versions. The most extreme is that faculty members may work hard during their first six years in order to get tenure. But once they have attained tenure, they have little incentive to continue to work hard, and consequently do not. They tend to do as little as possible. They may teach, but they do not publish. They do not keep up in their fields. They spend as little time as possible in their offices or working with students. This is the claim. The basis for it is primarily imaginary, the result of the imaginations of those who are not in academe and assume that this is what must take place. There is no evidence that those who achieve tenure suddenly and en masse stop acting as they did before they got tenure. Any such broad claim is without substance. But the variation is that over the years after receiving tenure, some faculty members, perhaps a considerable number, find that they have little new to say and stop publishing, that they lose some of their energy and interest in teaching, that they perform at an adequate level but not more. And then they cannot be replaced because they have tenure.

Even this more modest charge is usually made without any evidence. But it would be equally unreasonable to claim this never happens. It happens in every profession and every area of work. And it is typical for burned-out employees to be kept on as long as they perform adequately. Those with civil service positions or union contracts usually cannot be fired. And even in areas where people can be fired they often are not. In cases of true incompetence, we have already seen that a college or university can fire a tenured faculty member. But in all these circumstances, whether at a university or in business, the proper first recourse is not termination but counseling and attention to rekindling the flame that once existed. Moreover, in the case of college and university faculty members, they have undergone longer periods of both training and probation than people in most other areas, and the chance of their becoming deadwood is correspondingly less than in other areas. Nonetheless, institutions do make mistakes, especially if they do not exercise the care they should in granting tenure. In such cases, the institution suffers the result of its mistake, just as in other cases. These bad effects are not a result of tenure. In fact the tenure process, with its requirement that one either get tenure or leave, is more likely than otherwise to help institutions terminate those who are not likely to continue to be productive. Without such a system it is very likely that marginal people would be kept on, perhaps indefinitely, one more year at a time. They become friends whom one does not want to hurt, and then they have been around so long that it feels unethical to dismiss them for acting as they have been acting for years.

The deadwood argument is exaggerated, and true deadwood can be terminated for incompetence or for failure to perform adequately. The problem, to the extent that it exists, is not with tenure but with the failure of institutions to counsel and help, and if necessary ultimately dismiss those deserving of dismissal.

The next charge is one of inefficiency. Corporations are engaged in downsizing and, in the process, getting rid of excess workers—executives as well as those in the ranks. The rationale is that the firms are becoming more efficient by becoming lean and mean. They can thus remain competitive. By contrast, it is claimed, universities are saddled with tenured faculty—perhaps too many or in the wrong areas as needs have changed. But because of tenure they are not able to get rid of them. They cannot become lean and mean. The institutions cannot become efficient. Because they are overwhelmingly not-for-profit organizations, they face no competition and have no incentive to cut costs or change with the times. Even if they wanted to, tenure makes it impossible for them to do so.

This charge is really multiple. The general charge of inefficiency is a difficult one to evaluate, because it is not entirely clear what efficiency means when applied to an institution of higher learning. "Efficiency" should not be equated simply with the number of degrees awarded or the number of courses or students taught. And in fact there is competition among colleges and universities. The costs of running a research institution are higher than those of running a primarily teaching institution. Tuition at prestigious institutions of higher education is typically much higher than tuition at a state-supported institution. Yet it is not clear that a school with a lower student/faculty ratio is more efficient than the reverse. American colleges and universities are still the envy of most countries, and these institutions attract students from around the globe, showing that they are competitive in the worldwide educational arena.

However, the important point is that the criterion of efficiency is not the appropriate one to apply. Universities should not be compared to factories, and the education of students is inappropriately considered comparable to the products turned out by factories. This does not mean that colleges and universities cannot be held accountable for what they do and how they use the funds they have or receive. But the criteria should be suitable to their mission, which is not the production of goods but the preservation, transmission, and development of knowledge.

The claim is rarely made that tenure makes it impossible or difficult or unlikely for universities and colleges to be run in such a way that when evaluated by the proper criteria they cannot or do not measure up. If it were made, then the difficulty would be to show that tenure is the culprit. But this is unlikely. It is in part tenure that helps keep the salaries of faculty members low in comparison to the training required. The economic value of tenure is factored into the salary structure. Since tenure is not something that a faculty member can opt out of, all faculty members pay in lower salaries for the job protection that tenure provides. Moreover, tenure provides a relatively stable faculty for an institution. It cuts down on the costs of constant recruiting and the training that takes place in the initial period on a new job.

Finally, unlike in many other positions, as faculty members grow older they can also grow in insight in their disciplines and they may gain wisdom with maturity. Wisdom is different from knowledge. It involves knowing not only a great deal but also how such knowledge fits together within a broader perspective. It also involves understanding the value of what is known and its place in a grander order of things. It involves as well the ability to make sound judgments that do not depend only on knowledge. Wisdom involves knowing not only what to do and how to do it but knowing what is worth doing. In a business in which the end is profit and the means available to a company are fairly well circumscribed, wisdom may play no important role. In a college or university setting in which the purpose is to train young minds, prepare them for the well functioning of a society, and counsel them in how to live, wisdom is an essential ingredient in the faculty. Older faculty are not the same drag on an institution that they might be considered in a business environment.

There are many other differences between a university and a business. A business arguably exists to make a profit. It downsizes in part to make it more likely to do so, and usually with an eye toward raising the value of its stock. Not only is a university usually a not-for-profit organization, but it has no unique end or bottom line by which it can be evaluated. It is multifaceted, and it exists to educate students, to increase knowledge, to preserve and interpret that knowledge, and to serve a number of different complex needs of the state or society in which it exists. Downsizing does not necessarily make the university more efficient (the same is true of corporations); nor does downsizing raise its value. On the contrary, downsizing faculty tends to diminish the university.

Corporations tend to be managed hierarchically. The CEO with or without the board of directors and with or without other senior managers can decide what or who is to go and what restructuring is to take place. A university is not typically structured in this way. Faculty members are not told what to do but help decide what to do. They are the authorities in their own area and they usually and appropriately have a strong voice in what the institution does and how. The president or board is not competent to direct the university as a CEO can, at least in theory, direct the corporation. In fact many companies are moving to a structure of shared responsibility and empowerment of lower-level managers and employees in order to improve morale, efficiency, and productivity. Such a structure of shared responsibility and empowerment is already present in the university and does not require that it be achieved by downsizing. Downsizing without faculty consultation is more likely to have precisely the opposite effect—lower morale, less efficiency, and decreased productivity. Loyalty to any institution on the part of those who work there is not automatically deserved or given but is appropriately the result of reciprocal consideration on both sides.

Finally, although some fields go out of favor and new ones emerge, such transitions take many years, and a well-managed institution will not find itself with faculty whose expertise is no longer needed. Before that happens the institution can help faculty members to retrain and move to neighboring fields to teach.

A third argument is not so much an economic one as it is an argument from supposed inequity, and more properly from a concealed sense of jealousy. Because many ordinary citizens live and work in an environment in which people are laid off due to no fault of their own—to downsizing or to technological changes—they ask why faculty members at colleges and universities should be treated differently from the mass of workers. When budgets become tight at universities the same question is often raised by those employed by the university who are not faculty or civil service or union-protected. These people are vulnerable in a way that tenured faculty are not. The reason is that they are not necessary to guarantee academic freedom. Once again the justification for academic tenure is not the good of the individual faculty member or even of the individual institution but the good of society as a whole. Those who attack tenure in this way ignore the fact that others, such as federal judges, also have tenure and that civil servants enjoy greater job security than those employed in the private sector. They also ignore the fact that faculty face a crucial period in which they either get tenure or are terminated, unlike those in other areas. The issue is not whether faculty with tenure are treated differently from other workers but whether such differential treatment is justified—an issue that the argument ignores.

In recent times a fourth argument against tenure has come from some medical schools. The salaries of clinical faculties at some medical schools have been extremely high even in comparison with the salaries of faculty members in medical schools who are not clinicians, much less with faculty not in a medical school.[7] The reason for the high salaries is that the faculty members, through clinical practices—especially expensive operations—bring in much more than the salary they receive. As HMOs became more competitive and other factors led to curbs on the income such faculty members were able to bring in, some of the schools proposed cutting the salaries of such doctors accordingly.[8] This seems like a reasonable proposal. But many faculty both in and out of the medical schools see this as a threat to tenure. If an institution can cut the salary of any tenured professor, and if this is not a violation of tenure, then what does tenure mean? Tenure ceases to have much meaning if the institution may cut one's pay to any level it chooses, and so force out those whose views someone in or out of the university disapprove of.

Some of the medical schools, conscious of this view, have proposed first that the salaries of those who already have tenure not be affected, and second that those who will receive tenure in the future be paid in two parts. One part of their salary will be comparable to that received by other nonclinical members of the medical school. This would be considered the regular salary and would not be subject to cuts except in cases of financial exigency. The other portion of the salary, in some cases the larger portion, would be tied to the income that the faculty member generates through clinical practice. The proposal has been condemned by some. It does create a dual salary structure for the time that two different salary systems are in place, and understandably new faculty members would prefer the old system. But it is arguably not unfair to new faculty members who come into the new system freely and completely informed. If they compare their positions not with senior clinical faculty but with all the other faculty, they would see they are not only being treated equitably but have the opportunity for much higher total salaries than most others. The solution respects the tenure system, and recognizes the importance of tenure and the principle of not cutting salaries, since that can rightly be seen as a means of undermining tenure. The proposal may have other defects. But from the point of view of tenure, it seems unlikely that the procedure would carry over into other areas. If it did, then it would make sense only in those areas in which faculty members generated large incomes for their institutions. And in those cases, granting tenure with a competitive guaranteed salary and additions based on income generated does not seem unreasonable.

At the present time it is not unusual for a tenured faculty member to be given a salary supplement when he or she takes on an administrative position in the university. Sometimes this is the change in appointment from nine months to twelve months. Since faculty members do not have tenure in administrative positions, when they leave administration and return to full-time teaching, they revert from a twelve-month appointment to a nine-month appointment, with the loss of two or three months' salary. This is not unusual or unfair, nor does it affect academic tenure in any way. A comparable case can be made for variable pay beyond a reasonable base in other cases with a comparably null effect on tenure.

Although the economic arguments receive the most attention, they are far from decisive, especially since I have argued that academic tenure is best justified as being beneficial to society rather than as being primarily beneficial to individual faculty members, even though individual faculty members who have academic tenure have guaranteed continuous employment. I have argued that the rationale for academic tenure is academic freedom. Once academic tenure is seen in this way, it is not something that is simply conferred on faculty members. It is conferred for certain reasons and carries with it certain obligations. When the obligations are not met, then the point of continuing the practice is correctly open to question.

Since the point of academic tenure is to allow faculty members to pursue the truth in their disciplines wherever it leads them, those who have tenure have the concomitant obligation in fact to pursue truth in their areas to the best of their ability. They have the obligation to be as objective as they can be, to be as critical as appropriate in their field, and to follow arguments and their data wherever they may take them. This is not a right they have because of their tenure, but an obligation that goes with tenure.

Similarly, since the point of academic tenure is the preservation of academic freedom, a second obligation of the tenured faculty is to protect academic freedom throughout the university. This means that they have the obligation to protect and promote academic freedom for their untenured faculty as well as for their students. Academic freedom solely for tenured faculty makes little sense. All members of the college or university must have academic freedom if the institution is to fulfill its mission. Since not all faculty are tenured, those who have tenure and hence cannot be fired except for cause—understood as incompetence or moral turpitude—are in a strong position to defend the academic freedom of those without tenure. This is another consequence of seeing that tenure is not solely or even primarily for the benefit of those to whom it is given but for the institution as a whole, and ultimately for the benefit of society. It is this perspective that allows us to develop the ethics of tenure, that is, not the ethical justification for tenure, but the ethical conditions that tenure imposes on institutions and on those members to whom it is given.

Academic tenure so understood allows us to evaluate and answer some of the noneconomic attacks on tenure. We shall look at four of the more prominent of them: (1) the deadwood argument, again; (2) the six-year conformity-training argument; (3) the postmodernist attack; and (4) the politicization attack.

(1) The deadwood argument, again. This version is noneconomic but also claims that some of those who get tenure use it as an excuse to do little, and eventually turn into deadwood. That is certainly an abuse of tenure, but there is little evidence that this is a widespread abuse. Academic tenure provides protection for faculty to pursue the truth. The guarantee of employment that is part of it is circumscribed and is not absolute. We have already noted that if a faculty member fails to perform his or her academic tasks, that is grounds for dismissal. Tenure does not prohibit continuous review for purpose of promotion and of salary increases. It does not relieve departmental chairpersons and deans and other university administrators from evaluating tenured faculty or from encouraging, counseling, and helping those who are not as productive as they once were or as the institution feels they should be. Tenure should not be an excuse for tolerating incompetence, laziness, or failure to perform at an acceptable level. If it is so used, then both the faculty member who so uses it and the institution that allows that abuse are at fault. But such failures do not show any intrinsic failure or weakness in the practice of awarding academic tenure.

(2) The six-year conformity-training argument. The second attack claims that young faculty are inculturated by the system to be safe rather than bold during their six or so years as faculty members without tenure. They spend six years conforming to the desires and views of their senior colleagues, who hold the tenure decision in their hands. These senior colleagues are unlikely to vote tenure for new faculty who will challenge their views or undermine their authority with students. Hence the young faculty member conforms, perhaps thinking that after six years he or she will be free to be creative and really express individual views. But six years of repressed or constrained thought yield a habit of so thinking, and the habit of routine research takes over and typically replaces more creative tendencies. The result is a habit of safe research. Those who do not conform are weeded out prior to or in their sixth year.

This argument describes not the result of a tenure system but an abuse of the tenure system. If tenure is understood as I have portrayed it, then those with tenure have the obligation to protect the academic freedom of those without tenure. If their academic freedom is protected, then untenured faculty members will have little reason not to pursue truth and to follow their pursuit wherever it leads them. A university should in fact expect this in its new faculty members, and unless they do pursue truth in this way, they may not be deserving of receiving tenure. Hence tenure should not act as a deterrent to pursuing truth, but just the opposite. To the extent that this is not the case, those who have tenure can be faulted for not promoting the proper atmosphere of academic freedom in their institutions and for not demanding such pursuit of their new faculty.

(3) The postmodernist attack. According to postmodernists and others within the university, there is no such thing as objective truth, and all there is are opinions, points of view, and different stories. I argued that the rationale for academic tenure is academic freedom and that this presupposes that there is still knowledge to be developed and truth to be pursued. If there is no such truth and if there is only opinion, then the basis for academic tenure and academic freedom seems to disappear. This would indeed be the case if all one had was opinion and there were no objective criteria for deciding that one opinion is better than another. A complete answer to this objection is a long story.[9] The short answer is that in some fields—most clearly in the sciences—there is ample evidence that some theories are better than others because of the impressive results that are possible as a consequence of accepting those theories. Even in the humanities, which are most prone to the attack, sophisticated versions of the attack on objectivity redefine it and redefine truth so that not everything within the various disciplines is equally defensible or acceptable.[10] But if there were in fact no way to discern valid from invalid or true from false or better from worse claims, then it is not clear why those subjects are pursued at the university. The claim is not so much damaging to tenure as it is to the disciplines themselves. And if the disciplines are removed from the university, then those who teach them would have little claim on tenure. But even defenders of the attack are reluctant to draw this conclusion. What they wish is not the abolition of the university or of certain departments within it, but an effective—preferably a dominant—voice within them.

(4) The politicization attack. The fourth attack is somewhat similar to the third. If universities are not places that search for truth but are the repository of positions of power in which certain political views are pressed on students, then academic freedom loses its rationale. And if academic freedom loses its rationale, so does academic tenure. Political correctness, some claim, is nothing new, but simply a new name given to the fact that the university is and always has been politicized.[11] The politicization of the university is inimical

to academic freedom whether the politicization comes from without or from within—whether it is the tool of politicians or the tool of politicized faculty members.

The proper answer is that if the universities are politicized, they should be depoliticized. But if they cannot be, then the rationale for academic tenure dissolves.

In all these cases I have conceded that if the attacks are justified, then academic freedom is not justified. But in each case I have maintained that the charge is not an attack on the principle of academic tenure itself, but on some of the abuses to which it is amenable. Those who oppose academic tenure on these grounds do a service to academic tenure by pointing out abuses where they exist. Faculty and institutions interested in academic tenure have the obligation to use it properly and to police abuses. But abuses, unless they cannot be corrected, are not sufficient justification for eliminating tenure. And some of the objections we have briefly looked at have made this clear.

VI. Colleges and Universities Without Tenure

The attacks on tenure have so far not seriously undermined the practice of tenure, although they have raised concern in many faculties and have led to increased attention on accountability. If the result of the attacks is a renewal of respect for the institutional and individual obligations that accompany tenure, they will have served a valuable function. But if they succeed in undermining tenure, they may achieve both less and more than their proponents intend.

What would happen if tenure were eliminated in all colleges and universities? The proper answer is that no one really knows what would happen. Tenure was eliminated in all English universities, and according to one commentator "English academic life so far appears unchanged."[12] He adds that the academic tradition in England is longer and different from that in the United States. So one guess is that little, if anything, would change immediately in academic life in the United States. It seems unlikely that many colleges or universities would suddenly fire their deadwood and replace them with bright, eager new faculty members. If those institutions have done nothing about faculty members the administration actually considers deadwood, it does not seem likely they have the nerve or inclination to take any drastic action if tenure were no longer required. If they had the nerve or inclination to do anything, they could have and would have done something about such faculty members—however few or many there are—under the tenure rules. Moreover, if tenure were abolished it is unlikely that it could legally or ethically be abolished retroactively. Those who were hired under conditions of tenure are entitled to tenure, even if it is abolished for those who start without any such expectation. Those on tenure-track appointments who have not been granted tenure had no assurance they would be granted it, and hence the institution's obligation to them is very different from those to whom it has granted tenure.

Without tenure would the pay of professors increase? This is difficult to predict. Since in the past decade or so there have been many more people applying for positions at colleges and universities than there have been openings, we can expect that the supply is still sufficient not to require any raise in pay. The abolition of tenure would not create any new positions. It would only make easier some reallocation of positions.

If there were no tenure, would young assistant professors be under pressure to publish and perform the way they are when on a tenure track, facing the requirement of receiving tenure or being dismissed? Would colleges and universities keep faculty on longer, and postpone any decisions about poor or mediocre performers, reappointing them year after year because the institution is not forced to make any decision? This would certainly happen at some institutions. It is not possible to guess whether it would happen at the majority of them. The abolition of tenure will not automatically produce better college or university administrators than we presently have, nor would it make any easier the kinds of value judgments required with respect to retaining faculty.

Would it mean a difference in the number or treatment of part-time faculty? Once again this is difficult to predict, but there seems to be little reason why the abolition of tenure would produce a change here. If part-time faculty are hired because they are paid less and do not have to be paid many fringe benefits, the presence or absence of tenure will not change this.

Would faculty change institutions more often? Once again there seems little reason to believe so. The number of openings will not change because of changes in tenure. Faculty members presently move, and if they have tenure they typically get it or get some assurance of it as a condition of their moving. If it is easier to fire faculty members, as it would be, more might be fired. But since the up-or-out requirement would no longer exist, it is not clear that more faculty on the whole in any given year would be let go from their positions.

The economic changes that would result are thus speculative. Those who attack tenure claim that the changes would be great, and those who defend tenure claim it would make little difference in the areas I have mentioned. The changes will probably on the whole be less than those who seek to abolish tenure envisage.

The big difference the abolition of tenure would make is the impact on academic freedom. And this is a loss that many of those who attack tenure fail to consider. I have argued that academic freedom is the central justification for tenure, and without tenure the status of academic freedom would certainly change. How quickly and how drastically, it is difficult to say. Tenure was abolished for new faculty at Bennington College in 1994 when the institution declared financial exigency and sent dismissal notices to twenty-seven faculty members, about two-thirds of them tenured. An AAUP investigating committee concludes its report by saying "Academic freedom is insecure and academic tenure is nonexistent today at Bennington College."[13] Tenure was evidently perceived as a hindrance not only to restructuring but to restructuring by the administration without faculty consultation. Without a tenure system there is a strong likelihood that safeguards for academic freedom will be seriously diminished. The university as a business, with authority coming from the top and faculty serving at the sufferance of the administration, is a model that some, perhaps many, colleges and universities would adopt. Once a college or university follows the model of business, it is likely that the movement toward faculty unionization would gain a momentum it has not yet had as the faculty members would attempt to provide some job security to make up for the tenure they had lost.

If not required to provide tenure, some institutions might still do so and might still commit themselves to something very much like academic tenure. But without the system's being widespread, there would almost certainly be a chilling effect on faculty teaching, research, and publication with respect to any area or topic that is at all controversial or possibly unpopular. And this will result in less critical students and less innovative and critical workers and citizens.

The major cost of the loss of tenure would not be to faculty members who would for the most part learn to protect themselves, to conform, and to secure their positions. The greatest loss would be to the fabric and quality of the society as a whole.

Notes

1. For a history of the university, see Hastings Rashdall, *Universities of Europe in the Middle Ages*, F. M. Powicke, ed., and A. B. Emden, new ed. (Oxford: Clarendon Press, 1987), 3 vols. For a history of academic tenure in the United States, see Walter P. Metzger, "The 1940 Statement of Principles on Academic Freedom and Tenure," *Law and Contemporary Problems* 53, 2 (1990), pp. 2–77. Academic tenure as we know it is based on the 1940 Statement, coauthored by representatives of the American Association of University Professors (AAUP) and the Association of American Colleges (AAU). Interpretive comments were added in 1970.

2. The legal doctrine of employment-at-will states that an employer may hire whomever he or she wishes and fire that person whenever the employer wishes for any reason or even for no reason. An employee may accept any offered position he or she wishes and may quit whenever he or she wishes for any reason or even for no reason. The doctrine still applies in law, although it has been circumscribed in various ways by antidiscrimination, plant-closing, and other legislation.

3. "1940 Statement of Principles on Academic Freedom and Tenure With 1970 Interpretive Comments," *AAUP Policy Documents and Reports* (Washington, D.C.: American Association of University Professors, 1995), p. 4 (reprinted in this volume).

4. Ibid., p. 7.

5. The 1940 Statement states: "Tenure is a means to certain ends; specifically: (1) freedom of teaching and research and of extramural activities; and (2) a sufficient degree of economic security to make the profession attractive to men and women of ability" (ibid., p. 3).

6. See Richard T. De George, *Patterns of Soviet Thought* (Ann Arbor: University of Michigan Press, 1966), ch. X–XII.

7. The highest-paid professors are most often in medical schools, with some receiving salaries of over $400,000. *The Chronicle of Higher Education* (September 14, 1994, p. A25) lists a professor of cardiothoracic surgery at Cornell University Medical School as the highest paid for 1992–93, with a salary of $1,762,083. The average full professor's salary in a Category I institution in 1995–96 was $73,610 (*Academe*, March–April 1996, p. 26).

8. See for example, the report on the University of Minnesota: "A Parlous Time for Tenure," *Chronicle of Higher Education* (May 17, 1996), A21–23.

9. For two arguments against this objection, see Ronald Dworkin, "Objectivity and Truth: You'd Better Believe It," *Philosophy and Public Affairs* 25, 2 (1996), 87–139, and John R. Searle, "Rationality and Realism, What Is at Stake?" *Daedalus* 122, 4 (1992), 55–84 (reprinted in this volume).

10. See Richard Rorty, "Does Academic Freedom Have Philosophical Presuppositions?" *Academe* (November–December 1994), 52–63 (reprinted in this volume), and Stanley Fish, *There's No Such Thing as Free Speech and It's a Good Thing, Too* (New York: Oxford University Press, 1994), 102–19.

11. "Political correctness" is the most recent version of the politicization argument. See "Two Views: Debating Political Correctness," by Elizabeth Fox-Genovese and Larry Scanlon, *Academe* (May–June, 1995), 8–15.

12. Ernest van den Haag, "Academic Freedom and Tenure," *Pace Law Review* 15, 1 (Fall 1994), 7.

13. "Report: Academic Freedom and Tenure: Bennington College," *Academe* (March–April 1995), 103.

Chapter Two

Ethical Issues in Tenure

The justification of academic tenure is its role in promoting and defending academic freedom. But the justification depends on a conception of academic tenure that involves responsibilities as well as benefits. Unless those responsibilities are met by institutions, administrators, and faculty members, the justification does not hold. The slippage between academic tenure as justified and academic tenure as it is found functioning at too many institutions of higher education is the primary reason for the attacks on it. Hence the need to look carefully at the responsibilities of academic tenure.

I. The Obligation to Defend Autonomy

Since the justification for tenure depends ultimately on academic freedom, considerations of academic freedom form the basis for a discussion of the ethical obligations of institutions, departments, and individuals with respect to academic tenure.

An academic institution of higher learning that seeks autonomy in its academic functions can reasonably be held accountable for preserving the academic freedom for which it is granted autonomy. Colleges and universities sometimes seek and defend academic autonomy as if it is a right that they possess, independent of their actions. Rather, it is a right granted to them under certain conditions, and its continuance is appropriately contingent on its continuous satisfaction of certain obligations. The paramount obligation is the preservation within its walls of academic freedom.

A college or university that is run autocratically by a president or chancellor or advisory board and that fails not only to grant but to guarantee the academic freedom of its faculty and students has little legitimate claim on autonomy. Such an institution cannot fulfill the social role of objective critic, challenger

29

of accepted doctrine, or teacher of independent-minded students and future citizens. Academic autonomy is not conferred on administrators but on the institution as a whole, and essential to achieving the purposes of academic autonomy is the guaranteeing of academic freedom of faculty and students.

As a result, the typical college or university entrusts to the faculty the setting of graduation criteria, and it entrusts to the various departments or divisions the setting of requirements for degrees in those respective areas. The faculty in a discipline are the best qualified to know what students must learn and master to advance academically in that discipline. They are the best qualified to examine and certify the students in that discipline. Such judgments can no more be made by the institution's administration than they can by the governing board or by any group outside the institution.

The right to set requirements and determine criteria carries with it the obligation to set these as impartially and as objectively as possible. This means that those who set requirements should be able to defend them, if called upon to do so by others inside or outside the university. They should have some relation to what is generally accepted as the discipline and requirements elsewhere, and serious deviations from the discipline's norms should be defensible. To its students the college or university has an obligation to offer such instruction in their field of study that they can pursue further study elsewhere. Hence they have an obligation not to be idiosyncratic in their requirements and in the course of study offered, unless this is clearly made known to students. Faculty are not given the right to set requirements to benefit themselves; the requirements must benefit the students, and more broadly society.

We have already seen that institutions can be held accountable. Departments, divisions, and schools within a university can similarly be held accountable by the administration, by other parts of the university, and by the students. Departments that set very low standards, that require very little work, that award all students the highest grades no matter how much or little the students do, can rightly be called to account. Claiming disciplinary expertise or departmental autonomy does not cover such actions, which do not require disciplinary expertise to question validly.

An institution that does not guarantee the academic freedom of its faculty and the academic freedom of its students does not deserve the autonomy that it has been given. The obligation of the institution is to protect that academic freedom, which must involve the officers of the institution actively doing so, and the faculty similarly taking active part in making sure that it exists for all. Failure to do so is a failure to meet an obligation, and undermines the autonomy the institution has been granted. The proper course of action by those who grant the institution autonomy is to see to it that those in charge do protect academic freedom, and to replace them if they fail in this regard.

This is very different from the way most institutions are judged. But most institutions have done a poor job of educating their outside constituencies about the nature and function of academic autonomy and academic freedom. The result is that the institutions are often evaluated from the outside on the wrong—sometimes on diametrically opposite grounds—from those by which they should appropriately be judged.

Moreover, since autonomy is given not only for the sake of the institution and those in it, but also for the sake of society, it becomes the obligation of autonomous institutions of higher learning to promote and protect academic freedom at other such institutions when it is threatened. Just as the members of the institution are in the best position to judge violations of academic freedom within its confines, so they are best qualified to judge violations elsewhere. Autonomy does not mean insulation from criticism or insulation from other institutions. Either through associations of which the institution is a member—such as the Association of American Colleges—or through institutions of which faculty are members—such as the American Association of University Professors—pressure can be brought to bear on institutions that violate academic freedom, and the light of publicity can be shone on outside bodies that violate the academic autonomy of colleges or universities. The AAUP has been the model in this regard and the body to which faculty have often turned. Professional organizations also have a responsibility in this regard, and the members of these associations have the responsibility to exert such pressure as they can. The American Philosophical Association's publication *Jobs for Philosophers*, for instance, flags openings in departments that are under AAUP censure.

Far from being inappropriate or unwarranted outside interference, such action is an appropriate and important part of academic autonomy and academic freedom.

II. The Obligation to Evaluate Faculty

A second ethical obligation of institutions is to evaluate its faculty in terms of the degree to which they exemplify academic freedom in their own areas and the extent to which they defend it within the university. This means in part to evaluate them in their pursuit of truth. Do they seek it? Do they exemplify that search in their teaching and research or scholarship? This is an important ingredient in the evaluation of research, which is all too often simply a counting of articles or other publications. Taking tenure seriously means taking academic freedom seriously. And that means taking the pursuit of truth seriously.

Not every faculty member breaks totally new ground. But dissertations are supposed to be additions to knowledge, as published articles and books should also be. As additions to knowledge they involve pursuing the truth as appropriate to the discipline in which one works. In many cases the additions to knowledge will be small and relatively safe and uncontroversial. Nonetheless, as additions, they come under the search for truth and academic freedom. Simply because they are not controversial does not mean that they do not exemplify academic freedom.

Of course the contributions that raise problems are those that are new and different, that provoke new interpretations and force rethinking or new defenses, or that threaten established positions, held beliefs, or ways of thinking. Deciding when these are well founded and when they are not is part of the process of discussion and debate that takes place within each discipline. It cannot be decided from outside. A university dedicated to academic freedom protects such debate rather than stifles it. How those not in a discipline are to judge whether faculty members are making a true contribution to knowledge is a question we cannot settle here and will discuss later under academic freedom. The present point is that taking tenure decisions seriously leads to making judgments about whether the faculty member does pursue truth and make additions to existing knowledge. For those institutions in which research is of less or little importance, the same criterion can be applied in teaching. Does the faculty member pursue truth in his or her preparation for teaching and does he or she encourage the pursuit of truth in students? If not, then the granting of tenure loses much of the justification I have developed earlier and seems to amount simply to job security.

III. Choosing Departments

The choosing and recommending of a faculty member for tenure is typically the task, at least initially, of the members of a department. At small institutions it may be the task of the dean. But at those institutions which are large enough to have departments and in which the departments exercise some relative autonomy, the decision starts with them.

Yet from an institution's point of view the question of which departments or schools or disciplines are represented at an institution is one that usually does not fall to any particular department. The decision might be made by a dean or a president, by a committee, or by a senate or governing body. Wherever the responsibility falls, there is an obligation on that person or body to face and raise the question of the allocation of new faculty. For simplicity of discussion, I shall refer to this as a dean's decision, even though in many cases the responsibility will fall elsewhere. Where it falls does not essentially change the nature of the responsibility.

No institution can represent all areas of learning, and hence no institution has the obligation to do so. Every institution must choose which ones to include. Having done so, it is not bound to keep the ones it initially chooses. But if it does eliminate a department it has to justify that decision to the faculty members in that department, and it should do what it can to transfer them to another department. Unless its reason is financial exigency, it has a continuing obligation to those whom it has tenured to keep them. Otherwise tenure becomes meaningless, and any faculty member who teaches or espouses some unpopular opinion may be terminated by terminating the department or area in which he or she teaches.

Academic disciplines rise and fall. It was only in the twentieth century that business became an accepted academic discipline. Other more recent departments and programs include women's studies, black or African American studies, and critical legal studies. Colleges and universities have no obligation to introduce these subjects. But members of the faculty or students may make a case for including them. That case should be considered carefully by whoever makes the decision, and it should be weighed against other competing demands on the funds that a new program or department requires. If such a program or department is started, it cannot go more than seven years without the faculty members hired for it having a claim on tenure. Hence those in the position to make such decisions must determine whether a given area is a fad or a bona fide area of study with a body of knowledge to be taught and mastered and in which research is possible for the indefinite future. To start a department only to close it after a small number of years is unfair to those hired, unless they know that both the future of the department and their tenure status are uncertain.

The responsibility to decide on new faculty in existing departments, to reallocate positions among departments, or to create new departments or programs all involve considerations that impinge on tenure and that affect academic freedom. In all these cases the faculty typically has an important say, if not the last word. If there are new trends in a field or discipline, those already in a department may reject the new trends. They remain the best judges of their fields, unless a dean or a governing body determines by a study or the use of consultants or by some other means that the department is below par.

Nonetheless, the faculty remain the best judges of the needs of a department or field or program. They should not be closed to new developments. They may respond to pressures from students or peers in other departments. But in the final analysis the faculty in each department are the best judges of the needs of the department. A dean or other administrator must judge between the cases made out by the various departments as to where to allocate positions. Such an administrator may also on good grounds reject candidates proposed by a department. None of this violates academic freedom or tenure. Mistakes may be made. There is a danger that some departments or administrators may make poor decisions. But there is no outside body better qualified to make them. Those who make the decisions have the obligation to make them as well as they can, keeping in mind the good of the institution and its mission to seek and advance the truth.

IV. Procedures for Tenure

Faculty members serve a certain amount of time, a probationary period, before receiving tenure. An institution may commit itself to early tenure in a given case. AAUP requires that tenure be given to those who have served seven years at the institution (or have accumulated seven years at that and other institutions). The seven-year rule is, of course, an arbitrary one. It is longer than required to gain job security in a civil service position. And a few select institutions require a probationary period of up to ten years. There is no magic number. Seven years was decided by the AAUP and the AAC. It might have been shorter or longer. But it is appropriate that a definite period is specified and agreed upon, lest probation turn out to be half a lifetime of work, which is unfair to those who are eventually turned down. What is essential is that the procedure adopted be fair, publicized, and known. There should be no hidden caveats or terms. It would be unfair to have a cap of a certain percent of the faculty that are allowed to receive tenure or are allowed to be tenured in any given year. Such a cap violates the notion of tenure, which means that if the individual in question satisfies the stated criteria of teaching, research, and service, the person is eligible for tenure. If there is a cap, then no matter how outstanding a person is, he or she may be turned down for tenure because there are not enough tenure slots available. That means that the person was not really eligible for tenure based on his or her performance.

All faculty members should know whether they are in a tenure-track position. If in one, they should know what the expectations are for achieving tenure. The expectations should not be a moving target that grows more severe year after year.

Tenure-track professors have the right to know the criteria they have to meet to attain tenure, the rough probability of their getting tenure, and a candid appraisal of their progress toward tenure as they go along. They have the right to be evaluated on the published or expressed or agreed upon criteria. This should be stated at the time they are hired. If the conditions change over the years as they progress toward tenure, they should be so informed. But fairness requires that the changes be such that the candidate can meet them in the time remaining. The changes, moreover, cannot be ad hoc or simply for a given candidate. Even for a given department there must be some legitimate rationale for changing the conditions for tenure, such as complying with institution-wide requirements or some comparable reason. Otherwise departments might change their requirements as a tenure-track faculty member nears the tenure decision precisely to prevent that person from getting tenure. Any such action would be clearly unfair.

Tenure-track faculty have the right to be judged on the stated criteria and to be judged on the basis of their professional performance. Their personal lives, unless they give grounds for charges of moral turpitude, should not be used as a basis for denying tenure. This means that their political views, or their religious views, or their private consensual sexual behavior, for instance, are not appropriate considerations in deciding on tenure. Nor, in general, is their collegiality or lack thereof, unless this negatively affects their professional relations with colleagues or staff or students. Whether or not they perform their academic responsibilities—their teaching, research and publication, and service—are the usual and appropriate criteria.

Not only should faculty know what is required for achieving tenure, they should also be appraised of their progress and prospects as they go along. It is the responsibility of the chair of the department, the dean or the evaluation committee to carry on periodic evaluations and to inform the candidates of their progress, or of their necessity to improve if that is the case, or of the likelihood that they will not get tenure unless they improve dramatically, if that is the case. It is unfair for candidates to be told during a six-year period that they are doing well, and then turn them down for tenure at the end of their sixth year. If they have been doing well, then the burden is on those who deny tenure to justify the denial in the light of the earlier evaluations. If a candidate is told that he or she may or may not get tenure, for example, because the quantity or quality of publications is marginal, then that should come as no surprise at decision time. The candidate should have been warned of this fact as the years went by and counseled as to what was necessary to achieve tenure.

It is obvious that the committee or committees granting tenure must look at the dossiers provided and judge as impartially and objectively as possible, based on the material provided, and the written requirements for tenure developed and published by the school and/or department. Since granting tenure commits an institution for a long period of time to the person given tenure, the committee owes the institution the best decision it can make. It has the obligation to deny tenure to those who are not qualified or who do not measure up to the required standards. The committee's ethical obligations look both ways: to the institution and to the candidate. Both deserve their best judgment. Both deserve careful and fair treatment.

Academic tenure as a practice imposes serious obligations on all those connected with it. It involves the rights of candidates to accurate information about their status and to fair evaluation on the basis of stated criteria. It imposes on the institution at various levels and so on individual administrators and faculty members the obligation to respect the rights of candidates at the same time that they protect the institution against committing itself to granting tenure to those who have not clearly earned it.

Borderline cases will always arise. In such cases ethics cannot mandate either always in favor of granting tenure out of respect for the candidate or refusing it out of concern for the institution. Difficult cases are difficult because they do not fall clearly under a specific rule or generalization. The most that can be expected is that all those involved in the decision make the best judgment they can and that they be ready to give an account defending that judgment, if necessary.

V. Tenure Review and Confidentiality

Confidentiality was long considered appropriate in tenure decisions, just as it was considered appropriate in many other personnel decisions in the university. When beginning teachers are initially appointed, the unsuccessful candidates are not usually critiqued or allowed access to their dossiers or to the department or school discussions about them. Their dossiers often contain letters of recommendation, and usually when candidates ask for such letters they indicate whether the letters are confidential and whether they waive any right to see them. They may decide not to waive that right. But they are usually counseled by their advisers to waive it on the assumption that those reading the letter are more likely to think them truthful and accurate if the candidate has waived the right. I do not know whether this assumption has ever been tested. But it is a poor one to make. If what one says in a letter is true, the writer should not fear repercussions from the person evaluated if that person reads the letter. The latter may be surprised if the referee has given the candidate reason to believe he or she thought highly of the candidate's work or potential, and then says otherwise in the letter. But we can question the ethics of leading students to believe one thinks highly of their work when this is not the case. Typically one asks for letters only from those for whom one has done good work, and from whom one expects a reasonably good letter.

The situation is somewhat different in soliciting letters of recommendation or of an evaluation of a faculty member being considered for tenure. The department or institution may ask the faculty member for a list of possible referees. But often the department or school will write to members at other institutions who are fairly well known in their fields and ask if the referee is willing to give an assessment of the faculty member's published material. The requesting letter may or may not mention confidentiality. Since the letter is not solicited by the individual, the individual cannot sign away any right to see the letter. To what extent should such letters be confidential? To what extent can and should the deliberations of the committee be confidential? And what rights, if any, does the faculty member have to knowledge about the dossier and about the deliberations?

Gender, racial, and other kinds of discrimination have brought the U.S. courts, including the Supreme Court, into the picture. In a case that received much publicity, Professor James A. Dinnan of the University of Georgia refused to reveal how he had voted on a tenure decision for a female professor. He was fined $3,000 and given ninety days in jail for his refusal. He claimed that his vote was confidential and that he was not required to reveal it. The court disagreed. In *University of Pennsylvania v. EEOC*,[1] the Supreme Court unanimously ruled that the University of Pennsylvania had to turn over to the EEOC all the tenure files requested because they might contain evidence substantiating discrimination. The Court did not take upon itself the question of whether the University of Pennsylvania should have awarded tenure to the faculty member in question, Rosalie Tung. But it did place upon the university the obligation to reveal its review process so that the Court could determine whether the charge of discrimination on the basis of sex or race might be substantiated.

Can this decision be justified on ethical grounds? The answer seems to be yes. The Court held that to deny access to the files is tantamount to saying that the institution should not be held accountable to show that it does not engage in illegal discriminatory practices when challenged. If it does not engage in such practices, it should be able to demonstrate this by revealing the bases on which it makes its decisions, and by showing that the documents and discussions follow the procedures and apply the criteria for tenure equitably. In order to do so, it should have clear procedures and clear criteria, and it should adhere to both. Committees should not be arbitrary in making their decisions, and they should be able to back up their decisions with the reasons for the decisions they make. These should be such that they can present them to the candidates who are turned down for promotion. If such reasons are sound, the committee need not fear their being revealed in a court of law, even though committees would clearly prefer that complaints never get to that stage.

The moral obligation of the faculty member being considered is not to attempt to influence members of the committee or the university prior to a decision, nor to harass them after the decision, if there is reasonable evidence that the decision is fair, even though negative. A nuisance suit may make the rejected faculty member feel better, but that is not sufficient justification for bringing it.

Might the possibility that one's letter of recommendation or one's evaluation will be made public in court have a "chilling effect" on letter writers, such that they will say only positive things about any faculty member's work or such that they will not give truthful evaluations? That is possible. But it is the responsibility of faculty members generally not to succumb to this temptation. When one agrees to give an evaluation one agrees to give a fair evaluation—fair to the person whose work is reviewed and fair to the institution requesting it. If one cannot and will not do this, then the proper thing to do is to refuse. All evaluations are to some extent subjective. The better and more credible the evaluation, the more it will give reasons for the evaluation presented. A statement such as "This is poor scholarship" deserves a statement of at least the general basis for that judgment. Providing a basis, rather than simply making the statement, requires more time, thought, and care. Knowing that one's evaluation may appear in court may well make faculty members more careful in what they say, and it may make them take more seriously the evaluations they make of the work they are asked to review. That is a positive consequence, not a negative one, of accountability, whether or not required by law.

Faculty members who are under consideration for tenure should be able to find out, if they wish, what is contained in their tenure dossier. Since a very important decision about their careers will be made on the basis of what is contained in the dossier, fairness requires that it be accurate. Hence candidates at some point should have a chance to rebut negative information if they believe it is unfair or inaccurate. This means that if a department chairperson or a dean gives the faculty member an unfavorable evaluation, the faculty member would know it. But there is nothing wrong with that. The chairperson or dean should be able to give justification for the evaluation, just as any evaluating committee should be able to supply the reasons for its judgments. Candidates may disagree with the evaluations, but at least they will know the reasons for them. Perhaps some candidates would prefer not to know the reasons for an evaluation and can give themselves excuses for any negative judgment chairpersons, deans or committees make about them and for their failure to get tenure. There is no requirement that faculty members must ask to see their dossiers or must be forced to look at them. All that is required is that they have access if they desire it.

Candidates do not have a right to know the details of the deliberations about their case and about who said what. The purpose of closed deliberations is to enable the committee to arrive at a final decision through frank discussion. What is important is the final decision and the reasons for it. Some member of a tenure committee may be especially vocal or influential in certain decisions. It is the responsibility of the committee to be aware of this and not to be unduly swayed by any individual member. But there is certainly nothing wrong with members arguing for their evaulations and the reasons for them and convincing other committee members that their evaluations are correct.

Universities typically have appeals procedures, and if a faculty member feels he or she has been treated unfairly in a tenure decision, just as in any other decision, that faculty member should have recourse to an established appeals procedure. Such an appeal should have some credible basis, however, and should not be a means for another committee to award tenure when the tenure committee has voted against it. It is only right for all internal avenues of redress to be exhausted before going to the courts, since going to the courts imposes costs on an institution that it should only have to bear if it plausibly acted improperly.

VI. Post-Tenure Review

Tenure is not only compatible with continuous evaluation and performance review, but since tenure carries responsibilities with it, such a review is appropriate and should be expected. Tenure means that one cannot be discharged for what one teaches or professes. That is very different from saying either that one cannot be discharged or that any post-tenure evaluation is inappropriate. Nonetheless, while post-tenure reviews are appropriate, they should not be used in such a way as to undermine tenure or academic freedom by indirectly penalizing a faculty member for what he or she teaches or publishes.

The obligation on the part of the institution is to respect the faculty member's academic freedom. The faculty member's obligation is to continue to carry out his or her responsibilities in a professional manner.

An annual review of faculty members for purposes of determining salary increases is common at many institutions. At this time typically all faculty members are judged on the basis of their teaching, research, publication, and service during the previous year. This is often a time for informing nontenured faculty members of their progress or lack of progress toward tenure. For tenured faculty members it is appropriately a time for them to be evaluated as to the fulfillment of their duties. If faculty members perform in some way that is below expectations, this is a fitting time to let them know that fact and to discuss appropriate measures to remedy the deficiency. Repeated deficiencies may eventually amount to legitimate, documented, and appropriate claims of academic incompetence or of failure to perform at an acceptable level. Academic tenure does not preclude such judgments. Fairness to the institution and to its constituencies demands that institutions be willing and ready to make such judgments and to terminate incompetent or nonperforming faculty members when appropriate. If an institution has made its tenure decisions carefully and with due regard for standards, it may never have to dismiss a tenured member of the faculty. Such dismissal is appropriately rare. But it is probably less rare than it might or perhaps even should be.

Failure of institutions to make appropriate post-tenure evaluations and to follow up on them makes them and the system of tenure open to legitimate charges of protecting incompetence. If properly done, annual or periodic reviews will reveal faculty members who are not performing up to par, and will serve as a signal for them to be counseled, helped, and encouraged to improve. After a reasonable time, they can be warned that if they do not change their behavior they may be terminated. And finally, if they do not change, they should be terminated. Clear cases where action should be taken involve dereliction of duty, such as not showing up for classes, not grading assignments, or otherwise not teaching appropriately. More difficult cases are those in which a faculty member teaches at a minimally acceptable level but does not keep up with his or her field or, if at an institution that expects publication, in effect ceases to publish. In the case of failing to keep up, that determination is best made by the chairperson or appropriate members of the faculty member's department. It may be that the person can continue to be an effective teacher without keeping up with the latest literature. Some fields change rapidly; others change more slowly, and arguably teachers can be very effective, for example, teaching foreign languages or English composition, without keeping abreast of new techniques. The same thing might even be said for some of those in the sciences. Perhaps someone well trained in some of the sciences can teach introductory courses in an area without keeping up with the newest discoveries and theories, since available texts are usually revised and kept up-to-date. Whether this is the case is a determination to be made by those in the field, and hence by one's peers in the department in question.

Failure to continue to publish, where this is expected, is a more difficult matter. If faculty members cease publishing (assuming they had to publish a certain amount to get tenure), is this evidence of failure to perform adequately? It is almost certainly not a sufficient indication of incompetence. Some faculty members have argued with some reason that there is too much publication of insignificant work and that the expectation that all faculty members should publish is unreasonable and does not really advance the field. No blanket statement is possible on this count. If publication is expected, and if this is known, then it is the responsibility of the faculty member to live up to that expectation to the best of his or her ability. That is compatible with not publishing for a number of years while working on a large project such as a book, and with not publishing every year. If the expectation is to publish, then the onus of explaining a failure to publish falls on the faculty member. If the failure to publish extends for a number of years, then it is not unreasonable for the person's department or institution to seek some method of equalizing the workload of members within the institution. If teaching loads are assigned with the expectation that a faculty member is spending a certain percentage of time on research for publication, then if the faculty member is not engaged in such work, it is appropriate that he or she accept or be assigned other work to make up for that time. Such faculty members might teach more than other faculty members, or carry more administrative responsibilities, more student advising, or any number of other kinds of appropriate work. Such reallocation of time is not punitive and should not be seen as punitive. But for it not to be, there should be some clear understanding in the institution of what is expected and of what alternatives come into place if justifiable expectations are not met.

Faculty members expect salary increases, just as those in most other areas of work do. If an institution awards a certain percentage average raise to the faculty, then faculty have a right to know why they received more or less than the average—their evaluations and the basis for them. Neither salary nor assignments should be used as a means of controlling faculty with respect to their academic freedom and their exercise thereof. Such measures can be and have been used for this purpose, and are rightly condemned when so used. They should be condemned by the faculty at the institution as well as by those outside it, if the facts are known.

Tenure is fully compatible with evaluation. Failure to engage in post-tenure evaluation because of a claim that tenured faculty members cannot be fired except for incompetence, moral turpitude, or financial exigency is an abdication of the responsibility of an institution. It is unfair to faculty members who have to carry more than their share of the institution's load in order to make up for their colleagues' failure to perform; it is unfair to the institution, which gets less than its money's worth; and it is unfair to the general public, which loses confidence in the institutions, in the faculty, and in the tenure system.

The responsibility of the tenured faculty is to continue to keep up in their field; to continue to teach, carry on research, and publish to the extent expected at their institution; and to continue to pursue the truth and to defend academic freedom in their own institutions and other institutions as well. Failure on any of these is a failure for which they can and should be appropriately held accountable.

Discharge is the most serious of penalties, and tenure guarantees that it will not be undertaken lightly. The onus of proof is on the discharging institution. Unless the situation is one of clear dereliction of duty, incompetence is appropriately judged by those in the field, or in an institution, typically by those in a department. But academic incompetence can often be judged by those in neighboring fields as well. Incompetence in many cases, however, cannot adequately be judged by those outside the academy, and the judgment is most reliably made by one's peers. Asking one's peers to judge the competence of a fellow faculty member is an onerous and unpleasant task to impose on them. But unless they are willing to undertake such a task and to render honest and reasoned judgments on the basis of evidence presented by both sides, they implicitly cede such decisions to others less competent to make them. They have an obligation to make such judgments when called upon. That is part of their role in defending academic freedom and in justifying the continuation of academic tenure.

The end of mandatory retirement because of age has caused some worry, even though in the few years that have passed since retirement because of age was declared illegal, there is little evidence that a problem has emerged. Faculty continue to retire at about the same age as previously, and many have taken early retirement, often facilitated by early retirement packages offered by their institutions. The claim that faculty members have a moral obligation to retire in order to make room for younger faculty does not carry much weight. It is not clear on what basis such a claim could be sustained. If it were the case that the senior faculty member is able to support himself or herself on retirement pay, then whenever a faculty member is no longer dependent on salary, the faculty member would be obliged to retire. There is no such requirement, nor is there any good reason for there to be one. Providing that senior faculty continue to perform satisfactorily, there is no reason why they are less valuable to an institution than new faculty members. Although new faculty may bring new ideas, they probably got many of those ideas from older faculty, who can still help other students develop them. Senior faculty have had time to develop reputations, which may enhance the reputation of the institution and attract students. Senior faculty typically get paid more than junior faculty, and frequently an institution might hire two junior faculty members with the salary released by a retiring senior faculty member. But that is no reason to claim that the senior member has the moral obligation to retire at a certain age.

A more plausible claim is that senior faculty members have the obligation to retire when they are no longer able to perform their duties satisfactorily. The difficulty comes when they believe they are performing satisfactorily and others believe they are not. Counseling and frank evaluations are appropriate, just as with other instances of faculty evaluations. The situation in academia is not much different in this regard from the situation in corporations.

The change in the law affected the conditions of tenure. When there was a mandatory retirement age, tenure was granted until a faculty member reached that age. Would it be a violation of tenure to grant a faculty member tenure that extended until the faculty member reached age 65 or 68 or 70—whatever the rule was prior to the change in the law?

Since granting tenure until reaching retirement age was compatible with the concept of tenure, it would seem to be compatible with the concept to fix an age beyond which it is no longer guaranteed. But what would be the point of such an arrangement? It might be claimed that if faculty members had tenure only until, for example, age 70, thereafter, although they could not be fired because of age, they could be fired because of incompetence or failure to perform adequately. But that, of course, is true even if tenure continues indefinitely rather than ending at a certain age. An argument might be made that since dismissal of a faculty member who has tenure is so difficult, it would be easier for an institution to dismiss faculty members who stay on beyond the previous retirement age if they do not have tenure. But any such argument seems to have as a premise some belief about the incompetence of those older than a certain age—a premise that the age-discrimination law was passed to rebut.

Hence, there seems to be no good reason to grant tenure up to a certain age, since that is against the spirit and the intent of the legal abolition of retirement ages. Faculty members should no more be subject to dismissal because of their unpopular views or their scholarly positions when they are older than when they were younger. The basis of tenure is the protection of academic freedom, to which age is not relevant.

Age discrimination should not be confused with tenure. The two can and should be kept distinct. If colleges and universities face problems because faculty retain their positions beyond the former retirement age, that is not a function of their having tenure. If tenure did not exist, they would still have their positions and they could still not be fired simply because of their age. The law makes performance the appropriate criterion for retention or dismissal, as it should be.

VII. Financial Exigency and Moral Turpitude

Dismissing or firing tenured professors is not and should not be easy. That is the point of awarding tenure. But we have already seen that dismissing tenured faculty members is possible and appropriate when they fail to perform adequately or are incompetent. Two other grounds for dismissal are moral turpitude and institutional financial exigency. What are the rights and obligations of all parties in such cases?

"Moral turpitude" is defined by the AAUP as "behavior that would evoke condemnation by the academic community generally."[2] Sexually seducing one's students seems to qualify here. More blatantly, seducing them by promising and giving them better grades than they academically deserve is not only moral turpitude but also sexual harassment and academic fraud. Faculty members hold power in their institutions and can and should be held accountable for how they use it, especially with respect to students. They are also in positions of trust and are held as role models by many students, whether or not the individual faculty member wishes to be held as such. They should be conscious of this in their public activities and especially in their contacts with students. Yet this does not mean that they are not entitled to the privacy afforded to all members of society and that what they do off the job, providing it does not affect their performance and effectiveness on campus, should be considered in their roles as teachers and researchers. The AAUP standard is an admittedly vague one. It does not require unanimity in its condemnation. But it does mean that simply violating some community standard is not enough.

Financial exigency, according to the AAUP, consists of "an imminent financial crisis which threatens the survival of the institution as a whole and which cannot be alleviated by less drastic means" (other than terminating faculty with tenure or others before the end of the specified term).[3] The rationale is fairly straightforward. If an institution cannot survive without cutting faculty costs, if it were required to keep on all faculty, it would eventually have to close its doors, in effect firing all faculty as well as all other employees. AAUP regulations demand a "demonstrably *bona fide*" case and spell out a number of conditions, all of which are reasonable. The point is to prevent claims of financial exigency being used as a subterfuge to fire faculty members whom the administration cannot otherwise fire because of tenure.

Two points deserve special attention. The first is that for financial exigency to be bona fide it must be institution-wide. There is no bona fide financial exigency for a department or for only a portion of a college or university. As a result of financial exigency a department or program may be closed down. But that is different from declaring financial exigency of a department or program and closing it down. Moreover, the only way to be sure that financial exigency is not an excuse to fire tenured professors is to require that tenured professors be reassigned to the extent possible and that nontenured professors in an area be let go before tenured ones.

The second point to note is that the best way to make sure that financial exigency is not used as a subterfuge for undermining tenure or firing tenured faculty members is for each institution to draw up its plans for financial exigency together with the faculty or faculty representatives while it is in a financially viable condition. If such plans have been worked out prior to any danger of financial exigency, then there should be no complaints if and when the plans that have been agreed to by the faculty and the administration are put into effect. Failure to develop such plans may be a sign of bad faith, and failure to include the faculty is ground for possible charges of improper behavior after the fact. In no case does financial exigency develop overnight. There is always some period of danger and warning. If financial exigency plans have not been developed prior to such times, they should be developed as early as possible after signs of possible serious financial difficulty have begun to appear.

VIII. Undermining Tenure: Part-Timers

The use of part-time faculty has become controversial in some instances, and some people have correctly seen it as an attempt to undermine tenure. We can distinguish three different kinds of part-timers: graduate teaching assistants (TAs), non-Ph.D. teachers, and Ph.D. or terminal degree holders.

The first group is heavily used at some Ph.D.-granting universities. Those in this group are graduate students, working toward their graduate degrees, who during this period are paid to teach courses or to assist in teaching courses. Their proportional pay is usually well below that of a full-time beginning faculty member. But the faculty member typically has finished his graduate degree, and is expected to do research and contribute to both the institution and the profession through service of various kinds. (Whether the pay of TAs is exploitive is a separate issue.) Hiring TAs certainly costs less than hiring full-time equivalent teachers, both because the cost per credit hour paid is less and because the fringe benefits of TAs—if they get any—are typically much less than those given to full-time faculty. Hence an institution might find it cost-effective to use TAs instead of full-time faculty, especially in staffing introductory courses.

As more and more full-time equivalent positions at an institution are turned into TA positions, the number of full-time faculty decreases, and so the number of tenurable positions. The justification for using TAs is not only economic; there is also the claim that such teaching gives them good preparation for the teaching they will do after they get their degrees and become faculty members. If their teaching is done under the supervision of experienced faculty they can learn from that faculty member, they can correct their teaching mistakes, and they can get the teaching experience that will help them obtain full-time teaching jobs. Moreover, although their pay is low compared to that of regular faculty members, they are still students. If they did not have employment of this type, many of them would be forced to work part-time in a variety of nonteaching jobs, which often would not pay them any more and from which they would not learn as much about their fields and about teaching as they do with teaching assistantships.

Part-timers in the second category are those who do not have terminal graduate degrees, or if they do, have other jobs. Some part-time teachers in professional schools are people who have jobs in the profession in question and who teach because they love doing so, and not necessarily or primarily for the money they are paid. As with TAs, part-time teachers of this sort are usually not paid proportionately as well as full-time faculty, receive few if any fringe benefits, and usually do not have any voice or part in the institution other than teaching their assigned courses.

The third group, those with Ph.D.s or other appropriate terminal degrees, would like to have full-time, tenure-track or tenured positions, but because of market forces, lack of openings, or other reasons they have not been able to get such a position. Like the other two groups, these teachers are poorly paid, usually by the course, receive few if any fringe benefits, and have little place in the institution other than teaching their assigned courses. Not infrequently such people teach part-time at more than one institution in order to make ends meet. They may teach much more per week than full-time faculty members, and must in addition travel to different institutions.

Members of all three groups are usually hired year by year or semester by semester. Hence by the heavy use of such teachers an institution may staff many of its introductory and some of its other courses with comparatively inexpensive staff, who receive few or no fringe benefits, who are renewed at the pleasure of the institution, and who have no say in how the institution is governed. What the institution does not get from such people is research or service of the nonteaching variety. But many institutions see this as a plus rather than a minus.

What are we to say about the ethics of such practices, and what effect do such practices have on tenure? Is tenure really undermined by them?

It is theoretically possible to combine hiring such teachers with hiring full-time faculty members for three-year terms, renewable for another three years, and with no possibility of renewal thereafter. Such an institution would by design have no tenured faculty members and no tenure-track positions. But if it were to do this, it would be just as easy to declare that it did not give tenure and then hire as many full-time faculty members as it wished who would accept positions under those conditions. It need not engage in subterfuges to undermine tenure. But if it does abolish tenure—as Bennington College has done—or if it does not wish to give tenure, it declares something about itself and its position on academic freedom. It then limits the number and possibly the quality of the faculty members whom it can hope to attract and keep. If its policy is known publicly, it cannot be faulted for misrepresentation. And if it is faulted by some for being the kind of institution it is, that may not worry it at all.

What can be faulted is an institution that presents itself as a bona fide institution of higher learning that is committed to academic freedom and that at the same time does all it can to restrict that freedom by severely limiting the number of tenured faculty it has. We have seen that one of the obligations of the tenured faculty is to guarantee the academic freedom not only of themselves but of all members of the institution of which they are a part, and to the extent possible of those institutions of which they are not a part.

The heavy use of part-time employers raises three kinds of ethical charges against institutions. The first is one of exploitation, the second is one of restricting academic freedom, and the third is the deliberate undermining of tenure in order to be able to carry on the other two with relative impunity.

The charge of exploitation is a difficult one to determine in the abstract and is often difficult to sustain even in the concrete. Workers should be paid at least enough to sustain themselves and their families at a decent level of life, given the general standard of living of the society in which they live. Beyond that they typically get what the market allows or demands. The difficulty with applying such criteria to part-time teachers is that they are fairly well or very well educated and capable of getting decent-paying nonteaching jobs. They are not illiterates or unskilled laborers. But they choose to take part-time teaching jobs because they are students or they have hopes of getting full-time teaching jobs or they want to teach or they would rather have such jobs than other jobs that might be available. They are not forced to take such jobs and they take them well informed about their pay and the benefits or lack thereof. They are not the typical exploited workers, even though they receive less for similar kinds of work than full-time faculty receive for teaching, and even though they are poorly paid given the amount of education, training, and experience they have. If colleges and universities did not hire such people, they would have to hire full-time faculty who would cost a great deal more in order to get their courses taught. If they could not afford to do that, then an alternative would be to cut back on the size of their student bodies. If this were the general practice, the result would be that many fewer students would have the opportunity for a college education. Alternatively, institutions could raise their tuition or legislatures could increase the amounts given to state educational institutions. The increased costs of operating with only full-time faculty would raise the expenses of such institutions, which would have to be covered somehow. So if there is exploitation, the beneficiaries are the students and the taxpayers, whose costs are less than they would otherwise be. The third alternative would be to lower the wages and fringe benefits of the full-time faculty and use the saving to hire more full-time faculty, or to make the full-time faculty teach more courses or more students. To lower the faculty salaries sufficiently to make up the difference would lead to the similar charge of exploitation made for part-timers, and would decrease the number of bright and productive faculty who would be attracted to such positions. Increasing faculty teaching loads might be possible to some extent, but if the demands on research and service remain constant, it is doubtful the necessary amount of teaching can be secured in this way.

The charge that using part-time faculty is a device that enables an institution to restrict academic freedom is possibly, but not necessarily, true. If the full-time and especially the tenured faculty members of the institution take seriously their responsibility to protect the academic freedom of all, this will not happen. But generally full-time faculty are little aware of the part-time nongraduate-student faculty, whom they typically have little contact with or knowledge of. That is a failure of the system or of the faculty's willingness to take their responsibilities in this regard seriously. If faculty did take their responsibilities seriously, they would organize and devise the means to ensure the academic freedom of all the faculty, part-time as well as full-time. An administration that purposely hires part-time faculty in order not to have to worry about academic freedom sins against academic freedom and is guilty to that extent. It can easily fire or not renew any faculty member who teaches ideas that the administration does not want to have taught, who questions the authority or administration of the institution, or who in any other way is a bother or is perceived as a troublemaker. The defect is not so much in the use of part-time teachers as in the reason for their use.

This is precisely the point of the third charge. If the intent of using part-time teachers is to preclude academic freedom, then it undermines part of the fabric of the institution, which turns itself into something different from what it typically pretends to be. It seeks to achieve by indirect means what it is reluctant to say publicly, namely, that as an institution it does not care about academic freedom and is run by the administration in such a way that only those views approved by the administration can be taught. This deception and this failure to live up to its purported ideals are where its faults lie. The undermining of tenure that its actions involves is not the major issue, although it is a symptom of the same defect.

A similar analysis applies to other practices that colleges and universities adopt that indirectly undermine and weaken tenure. Such practices also and most importantly undermine and weaken academic freedom. Most often they are tactics adopted to lower economic costs by finding substitutes for full-time faculty. The use of electronic teaching—courses and degrees offered by closed circuit or "open university" TV programming, and courses through the Internet—are all means of increasing enrollment relatively inexpensively. The quality of instruction cannot equal that offered on the home campus even if the electronic courses are taught by master teachers. The teachers or assistants needed to facilitate the course through on-site discussion sections, grading, and similar functions are rarely full-time faculty. Carried to the extreme a university could offer only such courses with a skeletal faculty and a very large number of part-time and nontenure-track faculty. Such an institution should dubiously be called a university. It would no longer have as a primary function the development of knowledge and the institution's commitment to preserving it as well.

The trend to cut full-time faculty has an important effect not only on tenure but also on academic freedom. The administration of a university should not place its administrative goals ahead of the academic mission of the university and of its responsibility to protect and foster knowledge and so to protect and foster academic freedom and hence academic tenure as well.

IX. The Ethical Obligations of Departments

The ethical responsibilities of departments are comparable on the departmental level to the responsibilities of the college or university or school at their levels. Usually departments do not have full autonomy, and they are assigned positions or openings by the institution depending on the student demand for the department's courses or the function it plays in the overall institution. In deciding on which positions to request and fill, it should consider the good not only of the department but also of the institution as a whole. The good of the department does not mean the good of the faculty members, but of the students and of the wider commitments of the department as well. The obligation of the department and so of the members of the department is to hire the best people available for the positions it has available.

In practice, weak departments are composed of weak faculty members, and there is a tendency of such department members to eschew candidates who are brighter or more talented than they are, for fear that they will suffer by the inevitable comparison that will take place by the administrators, students, and other faculty members. This tendency is an ethical as well as intellectual failure and a failure of character. A strong administration interested in the quality of its institution will be aware of its weak departments and of this tendency and will do what it can to offset the perpetuation of mediocrity. In some extreme cases, it will appoint a chair from outside the department or will require members outside the department to serve on the department's recruitment committee.

The department, as the institution, has the obligation to make known to its new faculty members their duties and prospects, and what they must do to be kept on, renewed, or granted tenure, if they are on a tenure-track appointment. It also has the responsibility to evaluate them fairly and objectively and to inform them annually whether they are performing satisfactorily, whether they are making acceptable progress, and if they are not what they must do to be kept on and eventually be awarded tenure. The department should also guarantee the academic freedom of its junior members—a function that falls in large part on its tenured members.

The department is usually the initiator of a tenure recommendation. Its responsibility is to prepare as strong and fair a dossier as possible. Its responsibility to the candidate is to present all the candidate's good points as strongly as possible. To the institution, its evaluation must be honest, without exaggerated praise and with no attempt to hide difficulties that are pertinent to the tenure decision. The awarding of tenure is one of the most important decisions an institution makes, because it commits itself to the faculty member for possibly thirty or more years. A department has the obligation to be honest in its evaluation. It would break its faith with the institution if it were reluctant to make a negative decision on tenure and forwarded a recommendation to the next higher unit with the hope that it will be turned down. It may feel that it owes that in friendship to its faculty member. But that would be a misperception of its responsibilities.

The collegiality of departments is in several ways the greatest threat to its members fulfilling their responsibilities with respect to tenure. Some departments maintain a sharp distinction between tenured and nontenured members to prevent the formation of friendships that cloud objective judgments about the qualifications of junior faculty members. This is not ethically mandatory and most departments accept junior faculty as fully participating members. Friendships often develop and not infrequently one's departmental colleagues constitute an important group for one's social life on and off campus. Senior faculty are thus aware of the difficulties of junior faculty, of how hard they work, of their successes and failures in research and publishing, and of the difficulties they and their families will suffer if they do not get tenure. Friendship may cause them to be kind and unwilling to hurt them with harsh criticism or warnings of poor progress. Senior colleagues may give their junior colleagues false hope and may judge their work more favorably than others would. They may recommend tenure when they know it has not been earned.

To do so is to fail in their responsibility to their institution. And if those above the departmental level defer to a department's judgment, the institution grants tenure to someone who on objective grounds should not have received it. The result is a long-term commitment that should not have been made and a mistake that will be very difficult to remedy.

A variation on the friendship theme from the other side occurs when one senior faculty member befriends or champions the case of a junior colleague. Other senior colleagues, unwilling to cause internal dissent, say that they too support the candidate, despite their private serious reservations or negative judgment. Then either they vote in favor of the candidate despite that judgment—which violates their responsibility to the institution—or they vote against the candidate, much to the surprise of the faculty member championing the candidate, and in the case of a departmental vote against granting tenure, much to the surprise of the candidate. This scenario is most likely in departments that vote on tenure by secret ballot. To lead on one's colleagues in this way is unfair both to the colleague and to the candidate. But the temptation to do so is obvious. This fact presents a reason for arguing against secret ballots and for holding those who vote for or against tenure accountable in the sense that they state and defend the reasons for their vote. It is not morally mandatory that such votes be made public and it is probably preferable that they be kept confidential unless a challenge is made concerning fairness or discrimination and an investigation of some sort is demanded and approved on the basis of probable cause. Clearly, if votes are confidential, leaking information about votes or any other confidential material is a breach of ethics.

The obligation of the individual departmental faculty member in voting for or against tenure is to ensure fairness both to the institution and to the candidate. The temptation to vote in favor in the hope that others will vote against the candidate so the faculty member can report his or her favorable vote to the candidate should be resisted. At each level the system imposes an obligation of fairness that should not be ignored in the hope or expectation that the next level of review will remedy the situation by making the correct decision.

Failures based on friendship may be understandable, but they are failures nonetheless.

The attacks on academic tenure that carry most weight stem from failures of institutions and faculty members to fulfill the responsibilities that the tenure process imposes. It is not tenure as a practice that is defective but its implementation that comes negatively from failure of nerve to deny it when appropriate or positively from a failure of justice to grant it when appropriate. The ethics of tenure are too rarely mentioned or discussed both in and out of academe, yet they are at the center of its proper functioning.

Notes

1. 110 S.Ct. 577 (1990)(No. 88–493). See also William P. Galle Jr. and Clifford M. Koen Jr., "Tenure and Promotion after *Penn v. EEOC*," *Academe* (September–October 1993), 19–26, for two opposing views of the implications of that decision.

2. "1940 Statement of Principles on Academic Freedom and Tenure With 1970 Interpretive Comments," *AAUP Policy Documents and Reports* (Washington, D.C.: American Association of University Professors, 1995), p. 7 (reprinted in this volume).

3. Ibid., p. 23.

Chapter Three

The Justification of Academic Freedom

Academic tenure is justified by its relation to academic freedom. How is academic freedom justified? Although academic freedom is not necessary for a university, it is necessary for a university of a certain type in a certain kind of society. In discussing academic tenure I claimed that academic freedom is necessary for the kind of colleges and universities that have developed in the kind of open society we find in the United States. It is time now to take a closer look at what academic freedom is and the arguments in its defense.

I. The University and Society

Imagine that tomorrow all the colleges and universities would close their doors. What would society lose? We need not imagine that what happened in China during the Cultural Revolution would happen here. We can imagine not a change in the total system but only in the system of higher education. Faced with such a situation, would-be lawyers might well train, as they once did, as apprentices in law firms. Similarly, engineering firms would take over the training of engineers, and each business would screen the high school applicants and choose certain ones to train for whatever positions the firm required. They might make the condition of training contingent on the candidate's agreement to stay with the company for a certain number of years.

Presumably artists and writers who are now partially supported by teaching would either carry on their art in their spare time or try to support themselves from their art. We can imagine that business firms in need of research would increase their expenditure on research and development and might establish more research centers and institutes or increase their existing departments and facilities.

Some groups might establish institutions comparable to the former colleges in which these as well as the sciences and professions are pursued. Such groups might wish certain subjects taught—and taught in a certain way. They might wish to adopt certain ideological orientations or preach certain religious or political doctrines. Students attending such institutions would do so if they were adequately informed with full knowledge that this is the sort of training they would be paying for and receiving.

Most likely to fall by the wayside are general education, the humanities, some of the social sciences, and basic research. It is not clear whether business or the various professions would see it in their immediate interest to provide these in-house; nor it is clear who would provide them. The results of basic research would undoubtedly be considered proprietary. Hence these are areas that would most suffer from lack of support. Society would lose these, and probably the most serious loss would be the general higher education of its citizenry. Society would also lose the places where ideas are discussed freely and openly, where new ideas are pursued, where new knowledge is shared instead of being treated as proprietary, and where students can be exposed to many fields without committing themselves immediately to any.

To imagine colleges and universities as simply places where students are prepared for jobs or the professions is to exclude a great deal that these institutions provide. It is because they provide these as well as preparing students to take jobs or positions in the workplace that society supports colleges and universities.

If the aim of a society is to support basic research, to make sure that knowledge is preserved for succeeding generations, and that it is subject to constant critical evaluation as it is passed on to the next generation, society will want and will support colleges and universities. If it is an open society that believes that its leaders do not possess infallible truth, and if it believes that knowledge is good for human beings—and so its citizens—to have available, and that knowledge is useful for the multiple ends that society and its members have, then it will provide a place where such knowledge can be developed.

We have the history of many countries in which the government did not support free inquiry and we know the price those societies paid. As we already noted, the former Soviet Union provides a fairly recent example. After Joseph Stalin's ideological watchdogs decreed that quantum mechanics and relativity theory were bourgeois, the Communist Party reversed its position in the 1950s only after it learned that these were essential for contemporary science and for such practical tasks as building an atomic bomb. The Soviet government for a number of years similarly prevented for ideological reasons the development of cybernetics and certain kinds of psychology. The same was true in many areas in the humanities and social sciences in which only Marxist interpretations and approaches were allowed. It paid a price for being a closed society in part by hindering its own development.

John Stuart Mill in *On Liberty* gave the classical defense for allowing freedom of inquiry, arguing that truth had nothing to fear from criticism, and that one's belief in what is true is strengthened, not weakened, by challenging it, and by providing responses to doubts and objections. This view implies that there are truths or true statements that can be known, and that knowing them can make a difference in what people do and what they are able to achieve. We could never have reached the moon without knowledge about gravity, celestial mechanics, heat shields, atmosphere, and so on.

It is in this setting that academic freedom comes into play. Universities of various sorts have existed in which academic freedom was severely circumscribed. We find this historically in the Middle Ages, in which the Church determined orthodoxy in theology and in areas in which theology had implications. We find it in Germany at various periods in the eighteenth, nineteenth, and twentieth centuries. We find it in the Soviet Union, in universities in Eastern Europe during the Soviet period, in China, and elsewhere. In each case we find the lack of academic freedom going hand in hand with a repressive government. But the repressive governments restricted not only universities and faculty members but usually the media as well, and often its citizens. Is academic freedom, then, anything special, or is it reducible to the freedom of speech that a free society guarantees to all its citizens?

I shall argue for a distinction between academic freedom and freedom of speech, even though the two are often conflated by the courts and by those both in and out of academe. Academic freedom is a term that is used in many ways and for many purposes. Some have claimed that if freedom of speech were truly available to all, there would be no need for academic freedom.[1] Academic freedom according to this view is simply a subset of free speech.

Since academic freedom and freedom of speech both embody the word "freedom" it might be useful to note first that freedom in both cases does not equal license or complete lack of restraint. The kinds of restraints applicable to each are different. The correlative responsibilities of each are different, just as the purposes and justifications for each are different. It is for these reasons that it is useful to distinguish them, even though the two are related, to some extent overlapping, and both are properly part of an open and free society.

Academic freedom has three aspects: institutional autonomy, student freedom to learn, and faculty freedom to teach and research. Each is restricted and each carries with it responsibilities. All three receive their ultimate justification from the society of which they are a part and which they are expected to benefit.

A society that supports a college or university does so with the expectation that it will receive something in return. It grants these institutions autonomy only if it believes that it can achieve more of what it desires by so doing than it can otherwise. If this were not the case, then it is not clear why any society should support these institutions or grant them autonomy. If this is the case, the society rightfully can expect that the colleges and universities to which it grants autonomy can nonetheless be held accountable. Otherwise the society would never know whether it was achieving what it desired.

The society expects that the college or university that it supports will educate young adults who will be prepared to take an active and fruitful place as contributing members of society. The society expects that the students will fill jobs requiring skills that they would not receive in secondary schools and technical training schools, and that they will be trained in the kind of analytical and disciplined thinking that a free society requires. Society also realizes or hopes that a college education will make the students who receive it capable of the greater range of human experience that cultivation of the mind produces and that is worthwhile for itself. Since such benefits accrue mainly to the individual student, it is not inappropriate that the student bear part of the cost of education in the form of tuition. Students also invest in their future and in what they expect will be enhanced earning power.

A society will also expect that a college or university will preserve knowledge in its libraries and archives, in its museums and databases. Its criteria are not industry- or corporation-specific, but general. Moreover, through the research of the faculty the society expects that the base of knowledge will be increased, and that the new knowledge will be passed on to its students and to others in the society through publication. Once again, it expects that developed knowledge will not be proprietary or industry-specific but general and available to all areas of society.

It is to the extent that society's legitimate expectations are met that the academic freedom it grants colleges and universities is justified.

II. Institutional Autonomy

We saw in Chapter 1 that the reason for granting the institution autonomy is that the members of a society realize that those best equipped for determining a course of study for students, for deciding what a student should know in a certain field, for realizing what knowledge needs reexamination, and for gauging what knowledge might be developed are those especially trained in the various disciplines. A legislature or a group of businesspeople or a random sample of society are not competent to decide these things and are smart enough to know this. Hence, if a society wishes the development of knowledge and the proper advanced education of its young population, it knows that it can best achieve these by turning such issues over to those most competent. This means that the society grants the institutions a good deal of autonomy in deciding what should be taught and researched and how. If any other portion of society knew better than those entrusted with these tasks—ultimately the faculty—then it would be proper to have them instruct the faculty on what to do and how to do it. But if these people or this body know better than the faculty, it should be clear how they achieved this knowledge, and it would have to be by some special means, for example, divine revelation. For the demonstrated way knowledge is typically attained is through the means developed and followed at colleges and universities.

Nonetheless, society grants to the college or university only a limited amount of autonomy, namely that autonomy necessary for it to achieve its purpose. If its purpose were the inculcation of a political ideology, then the society would grant the university very little autonomy. Society would dictate what has to be taught, and it might also dictate how it is to be taught. But if the society believes that the university is a place in which knowledge should be pursued, developed, preserved, augmented, and taught, then the society must provide the institution with the means to do so. If the society believes that there is knowledge that is worth pursuing, then it should grant to the institution the right or authority to pursue it. This authority has its basis in knowledge. The authority that knowledge gives extends to the means by which it can best be discovered or found, preserved, and transmitted. Hence authority based on knowledge or epistemic authority is vested in those with the appropriate knowledge. The development and presentation of courses, the requirements for the various degrees, the academic evaluation of prospective faculty and their professional evaluation after their initial appointment, the grading and certification of students, the development of a curriculum, the requirements for effective research—all of these are based on knowledge and are appropriately issues that should be decided by those with the requisite knowledge. The autonomy of the university consists in its having the right to determine these and other issues that are based on knowledge. In some cases, as with course content, the decision may be made by one or more faculty members. With respect to general curricula requirements, many within the institution may and most often should play a part. No one member of the university has special knowledge in this area, but the best determination of what requirements should be comes from the faculty acting as a group and arriving at a joint decision. There is no one single best answer to requirements. But there is no group other than the faculty better equipped by training and experience to make this decision. Similarly, requirements for a particular discipline are best decided by those who have gone through the training proc-ess, have mastery of the field, and jointly decide on requirements. These are typically reviewed in the light of experience and changing times and circum-stances. But once again the faculty members are the best judges of what the requirements should be.

The assumption in granting the institution autonomy and in allowing de-partments or other subdivisions within the institution to set requirements is that they do so conscientiously, keeping in mind, in the case of degree require-ments, the good and needs of the students, rather than the good or needs of the faculty. The faculty has the responsibility to act in the best interests of the students.

There may well be disagreements among faculty members on any number of issues, from degree requirements to what knowledge is worth pursuing and how. But these are debates that appropriately take place within the university, not outside of it, and that are decided by those with knowledge and training, not by those lacking these.

With respect to the pursuit of knowledge through research, the faculty are once again the most qualified to decide what to pursue and how.

Because new knowledge and discoveries cannot be predicted, they cannot be commanded or dictated. We have learned from the experience of the former Soviet Union that a dynamic economy cannot be centrally planned. The same is true of the development of knowledge. Special projects may be planned— such as the atom bomb project during the World War II in which the govern-ment hired appropriate specialists and funded them with the mandate to produce such a weapon. But even then the government could not tell the group of scientists how to do this. That had to be determined by the group.

The same is even more true when it comes to the areas that are generally called the humanities—philosophy, literature, art and literary history and criti-cism, history, classics, and related studies—and to a large extent the social sciences—anthropology, sociology, and political science. The arts and letters have flourished outside of universities. But their preservation, their critical study, and their transmission to a new generation have been most effectively carried on in and by the college and university, which have the obligation to do so.

There are disputes within these disciplines, and the disputes may carry over into the media, where they are sometimes reported as if they were a sporting event. But the disputes are appropriately academic disputes best settled by those engaged in them, providing they observe the basic rules of evidence and argument appropriate to a field. If these rules are themselves in debate, then the parties to the debate must fall back on logic or reason or whatever is agreed to by the disputants. If the decision comes down to a matter of power, other than the power of discourse and reason (however defined), then the dispute is no longer one in which epistemic authority rules and so no longer one that is best decided by those engaged in the debate. Whether this is a situation that colleges and universities are actually experiencing is a question we shall examine in the next chapter.

A university is a place where all ideas that can be rationally defended may have a voice. Not every position need be present or presented. But there is no authority either within or outside the university that can know and so can decide that a position for which there is a rational defense is wrong or mistaken until the arguments and evidence for it are examined.

It is in virtue of the knowledge that the university contains, especially in the minds of its faculty, that it is granted autonomy and that it is capable of exercising epistemic authority. But this authority lives side by side with other kinds of authority in a college or university.[2] Not everything is a function of the specialized knowledge of the faculty. As an operating institution the university must be run—the buildings must be maintained, the paychecks issued, the books balanced, the grass cut. The faculty may take on the task of supervising the running of the institution, as is often the case in European universities in which a faculty member is elected to the position of chancellor for a limited term and faculty members rotate in the position of dean. The organization and administration of the university in the United States typically follows a different pattern. The authority to administer the university can be called operative or executive authority, which is different in its purpose and justification from epistemic authority.

In a state-supported university, the state—usually the legislature—establishes the institution and the government appoints a board of directors. These in turn have the responsibility and authority to hire a chancellor or president. The president in turn hires deans, who in turn hire faculty. There is a hierarchical administration and operative structure. The president hires other administrators who hire people to do maintenance, keep the books, run the physical plant, and provide secretarial and support services to the faculty. From an administrative point of view the university resembles a business in many respects. But a key difference is that the faculty maintains epistemic authority, which is the dominant factor in the institution. In the realm of knowledge, and so in the realm of epistemic authority, the legislature, the board of directors, the chancellor, and deans hold no legitimate sway, unless they possess the requisite knowledge in question.

This dual authority structure—the epistemic authority of the faculty based on its knowledge, and the operative or executive authority of the legislature, board of governors, and administrators based on the legal status of the institution—causes a tension within the institution and between the institution and some of its outside constituents and the general public. Who, after all, is in charge? The answer is that it depends on what is at issue. No one, no executive authority, no administrator can make true a statement that is false. Of course, neither can a faculty member. Faculty members may be expert in their field and considered authorities in their field by others in virtue of their expertise. But each of them is fallible. When it comes to matters of fact or knowledge, all are constrained by the way things are and/or by the best means we jointly have for determining the way they are.

The two kinds of authority also help create confusion in the minds of many over the autonomy of the university and what it means. The university is properly autonomous in the areas in which knowledge is appropriate and decisive. But in the functioning of the plant and the operation of the institution, knowledge is typically not decisive, and the university is not autonomous but very clearly dependent on those who support it.

The running of the university is in part an operative function involving legal and operative authority and in part an academic function, involving knowledge. Faculty members have the dual status of being those with the greatest epistemic authority, while at the same time being paid employees of the institution. The efficient running of the institution requires a melding of the two kinds of authority, with proper respect paid to each kind. A university is properly collegially run in determining academic matters, there are nonacademic areas in which the faculty appropriately can claim no expertise and so appropriately may have no voice, and there are areas in which both kinds of authority are pertinent. The presence of the two kinds of authority, and the direct impact on academic freedom that some administrative decisions have, make appropriate a strong faculty voice in a university's governance.

Faculty members have the right to pursue their research to its conclusion without fear of being prevented from doing so because of the possibly controversial nature of the results at which they will arrive. This is fundamental to research and discovery. But an institution may not be able to support all research, especially if it requires expensive equipment. Faculty members should be able to teach the truth as they see it in their area without fear of being fired. But how many courses they teach is not only or clearly a matter that they can settle. Typically the teaching load of an institution is decided by the administration and faculty jointly, and faculty members know their obligations in this regard before they take their positions. How much or how little voice a faculty has in issues of administrative detail varies greatly from institution to institution.

The dual authority structure, moreover, permeates the institution. A teacher in the classroom is and has epistemic authority. But the faculty member also exercises operative authority to structure the course, give assignments, mark papers and tests, and award grades. Because of his or her knowledge, the faculty member is given both the authority and the responsibility to give grades. Grades are not a necessary part of the learning process, and a student may learn just as much (some claim more) without being graded. Grades may be a teaching tool. But certification is part of an administrative process to help fulfill one of the functions that society has given the university, namely, the certification of students and of their having attained certain skills or levels of competence in certain areas.

As an academic institution the discipline of knowledge is the primary discipline, and judgments about what it is or is not appropriate to do should always have this aspect at their core. But other sorts of discipline, consisting of rules of behavior, are also necessary for a university, just as for any other kind of organization or society.

It is with this background that we can fruitfully approach the accountability of a college or university. If it were self-supporting, it could claim greater autonomy than if it were not. To the extent that it is not, it must justify the autonomy it is given and it can only do that effectively by holding itself accountable and being held accountable by those who support it. Accountability means being willing and able to give a satisfactory account of one's actions. This in turn requires that what constitutes a satisfactory account is based on the nature of the institution and the mission it is expected to fulfill. It should be held accountable for fulfilling that mission, rather than for doing other things that some of its critics or even some of its supporters wish or believe it should do. An important aspect of an institution's accountability is articulating its mission, explaining and defending that to those to whom it is accountable, and so in part helping to determine the criteria to which it is appropriately held.

In state-supported institutions the state provides a good deal of the support for the institution, the rest coming from tuition, research contracts, and grants of either public or private money. As the major supporter, the state decides how much support to provide, and it balances what it can afford against other needs and how much it and the citizens are willing and able to pay in taxes. As a result an individual state may support its institution at a higher or lower level, and it can expect returns roughly comparable to its expenditures. If it fails to provide much money for library acquisition and maintenance, it cannot expect to have a very strong library. If it fails to provide sufficient staff for the number of students enrolled, it cannot expect the quality of instruction to be very high. If it does not fund laboratories, it cannot expect its faculty to excel in laboratory sciences. It can, nonetheless, demand accountability. And this can be provided in rough form so that the results are intelligible to a layperson and such that the legislatures and the general public can make a rough determination about whether the institution is fulfilling its function. If the institution turns out graduates who cannot function in the professions for which they have supposedly been trained, this soon becomes obvious to their employers, to the graduates themselves, and before long to the general public.

The reason for supporting research is both to advance knowledge—which to some extent those outside a university can also judge—and in part to have something worthwhile to teach the students who attend the institution. Unless faculty members keep up with their fields, they teach old knowledge, which—while it may be as valid as ever—is no longer as applicable as it once was or no longer sufficient for the changing times. If the members of a faculty do not themselves do original research that contributes to the store of knowledge, then they must rely on what others have learned and produced and published. Obviously, if all faculty members relied on others at some point there would be no new knowledge created or produced.

The proper means of accountability that justify institutional autonomy varies, depending on the kind of institution, and its stated and perceived role in the society in question that supports it. If the institution is established to pursue knowledge, then it would be inconsistent to prevent it from doing so. And the way to prevent it from doing so would be to interfere in its pursuit, either by telling it what to pursue or preventing it from pursuing certain kinds or areas of knowledge. If those who establish and support the institution know better than the faculty whom they hire what knowledge is and how and where to find it, then they and not the faculty should pursue it.

The autonomy of the institution may be challenged from without by any of its supporters: the state (if it is a state-supported institution), its board of trustees or governors, its prospective students and their parents, alumni, government or nongovernment contractors, and donors. Each type of challenge is different.

The threat from the state is that legislators or other government officials who control the state's support of the institution will demand a say in what is taught or how it is taught or who is appointed or not appointed to the faculty. All of these controls are areas in which the competence of the institution comes into play and are areas in which the institution's autonomy should be respected. Yet the legislature may appropriately decide to fund the institution at a certain level, which may be less than the institution would like or needs to function at the level at which it is mandated to function by the state. If the state lowers its contribution, then it must expect lower performance on either a qualitative or quantitative scale. The state might expect some belt-tightening in difficult financial times and it might pressure the institution to do more with less or with the same amount. But at some point this becomes impossible and either quality or quantity will suffer. It would be counter to the state's mandate to the institution and so a breach of faith to withhold funding in order to pressure the institution to change its curriculum or fire a certain professor or do anything over which the institution has proper control. Acting in such a way would be to violate the autonomy that is at least implicitly conferred in establishing the institution and setting its mission.

The action of the board of trustees or governors is somewhat different. In a state setting such a board is usually set up as a buffer between the institution and the legislature. The point is to keep direct pressure away from the institution and to work through the board, whose function is both to oversee the institution in a nonpartisan way and to present and defend its needs to the legislature. Such a board typically approves new degree programs and may be the authority that formally awards faculty promotions, tenure, and sabbaticals. Yet its task is to oversee the institution as a whole and not to second-guess promotion and tenure recommendations or the addition or deletion of particular courses. It approves degree programs and other innovations that cost money, and part of its responsibility is to make sure that any program that is approved can in fact be adequately funded once it is introduced. It may demand that the costs be covered by reductions elsewhere, but it should not direct where the "elsewhere" is. The transfer of resources from one sector to another is an internal decision properly made within the institution and not directed from without. Because it has the dual function of oversight and advocacy, it must balance the two. It is not a tool of the state to enforce the state's wishes. Nor is its function to run the university. On the other hand, although properly an advocate of the university's needs, it appropriately holds the institution accountable and expects justification for the institution's requests. The temptation to which boards often succumb is to confuse their administrative authority with the academic authority that rests with the university and importantly with the faculty (e.g., setting academic standards, teaching loads, class size).

The pressure of parents and prospective students is usually indirect. Parents are often concerned about their children's progress and their eventual ability to get a good job after graduation. They may wish the institution to change its curriculum or develop different specialties or increase the number of places available in a particular division. But all such decisions are properly the domain of the institution, even though the institution should be open to suggestions and requests for change. And it should be aware of demographics and of changing demand for different fields. But that is different from being directed to make particular changes. In practice, the pressure from parents, except when they go though members of the legislature or board of directors, is not a major challenge.

Although alumni are usually supportive of their alma mater, the support can turn into a desire that it be run conservatively, without much change. Media reports of faculty actions or of curricula disputes, such as the debate over what books are to be considered great and to form part of the Great Books or Western Civilization reading course, not infrequently lead to alumni pressure on the institution's president and alumni office to "take action" so as to preserve the good name of the institution. The action requested is usually of a specific type, namely to settle the academic dispute by administrative authority in a certain direction, depending on the views of the alumni in question. Sometimes the requested action is the firing of a faculty member who is quoted as holding or teaching a certain view. Sometimes such requests are phrased as demands and are joined with threats to withhold future donations.

Alumni have a stake in the good name of the institutions from which they received their degrees. They are concerned about that good name, the value of their degrees, and the institutions to which they are often genuinely attached and about which they evince real concern. But any attempt to influence what is properly an academic decision by threats or pressures of a nonacademic kind misconceives the different kinds of authority in a university and the proper function of the university. To accede to such threats or pressures is most often to do serious damage to the institution and so to its reputation and the value of its degrees.

Alumni rightly wish to preserve the institution's honor and good name, but the institution has the responsibility to withstand even well-intentioned attacks on its academic autonomy.

The influence of government and private granting agencies and private donors, however, is a serious issue for any research institution. No outside party has the authority or the right to dictate what research will be done at a college or university. Yet research can certainly be skewed by the availability of funds. If research money is available for the cause of cancer but not for the cause of AIDS, research may well be skewed toward the one and not the other. Granting agencies and private foundations only rarely award grants for a faculty member to pursue any research the faculty member chooses. Most often funds are given for specific research projects. And the kinds of research projects that a specific agency or foundation will support is frequently stated at the time the competition is announced. If one's research requires outside funding, then the availability of funding will probably influence what one pursues. There is of course no requirement that anyone or any institution pursue the research that a government agency or a foundation decides to support. And within the broad guidelines set by the agency or foundation the faculty members and the institution develop their or its own specific proposal. But there is at least the danger of undue outside influence in the inner workings of the institution.

The danger becomes clearer when the grantor is not a government agency but a private corporation that wishes certain research done for which it will give grants. And it becomes even clearer when the corporation does not give grants but awards contracts for specific research that it wishes done and to which it may wish to claim a proprietary right.[3] No easy answer is possible here, but the danger to autonomy is one of which the university as whole as well as its individual faculty should be aware and especially careful. If outside agencies skew research in certain directions, the institution must be aware of what is happening and decide whether it is in the best interests of the university that it go in that direction. It would be unfair to the departments and programs within the university that suffered because of such a skewing, as well as to the students and perhaps to the society as a whole.

Private donors are the other source of potential threat to the autonomy of an institution if the donors give money with inappropriate strings attached. Donors frequently attach conditions to their grants, and give money for specific purposes. They may establish scholarships, for instance. But once they do, it is up to the institution to award them and not up to the donor. Similarly, they might endow a professorship. But it is the prerogative and responsibility of the institution to choose and appoint faculty members. It would be a violation of the institution's autonomy to accept a gift that stipulated that the donor had the right to select the holder of the chair or that the donor reserved the right to veto a proposed holder of a chair. These are academic decisions to which donors have no right. Any faculty member becomes a member of the institution and the institution is responsible for the appointment. The faculty member is in turn responsible to the university and should not be responsible or beholden for his or her position to an outside donor. Nor should the university accept funding for a chair except in an academic area where academic competence is the criterion for appointment and not whether the faculty member belongs to a certain political party or espouses a certain ideology. Chairs should not be accepted if their purpose is the spread of an ideological position. A college or university that accepts such a chair compromises its own integrity, as does the faculty member who agrees to any such terms placed on what he or she must teach or believe.

The academic freedom of the institution, and so its academic autonomy, is not only compatible with accountability, but a society is justified in granting an institution autonomy only on condition that society holds the institution accountable. The kind and degree of accountability, however, should be appropriate to the institution's mission. It should not be held accountable for failing to do what it was not intended to do, and it should be held accountable for what it was intended to do. If it was founded to seek knowledge, then it should not be faulted for doing so, even if the results are different from what the government or some other group thought the results would be. All too rarely are colleges and universities judged by whether they have added to the store of knowledge and by the validity and importance of that addition. The reason is that since those outside the university typically are not at the cutting edge of the knowledge of the disciplines in which the faculty does research, they are unable to judge, sometimes even to understand, the contributions that faculty members make to knowledge. They must rely on other experts who attest to the advances and their importance, or they must wait until the advances are applied, perhaps commercially developed, before they can come to see or judge the advances themselves. This is a difficulty to which there is no easy solution. Colleges and universities could, however, do much more to have their faculty members translate into lay terms, to the extent possible, the results and significance of their research. Too often the proxy for such evaluation is a glance at the number and value of external grants received or the number of publications the faculty has produced.

In the absence of proper evaluations of the development of knowledge, legislatures, boards of directors, and the general citizenry often seek measures they understand, and they seek quantitative measures with which they are familiar, whether or not such measures are proper instruments for measuring whether the institution is fulfilling its mission, and how well it is doing so.

The easiest measure is the number of students or credit hours taught or the number of degrees awarded. To this might be added student satisfaction, perhaps as measured in student evaluation of courses or in exit interviews or questionnaires. These may give some indication of the achievement or lack thereof of an institution, but not necessarily so. The desire on the part of legislators or boards of governors to expect accountability is understandable and proper. But the accountability should be appropriate. Since the legislators and members of the board are not the experts in the various fields, and would most often not pretend to be able to evaluate areas in which great expertise is needed, they must have access to measures that make sense, are valid and reliable, and measure the degree to which the institution fulfills its stated function. Anecdotal accounts from students or students' parents or stories told by third parties about faculty members inside the institution are not the proper sources for evaluation or accountability, even if they may be taken as starting points for investigation.

Since the faculty and the administration of the university are the experts in what they do and teach, it is they who should suggest, develop, and defend instruments and means of providing accountability. This is not a carte blanche to the institution to decide how it will act and then to provide information that it has so acted. Its responsibility is to devise ways by which it can be held accountable for its activities in such a manner that the account is intelligible to those outside the institution, who can be shown and convinced that the criteria being applied are appropriate and adequate. A frequent difficulty is that institutions do not do this, and by default find that inappropriate instruments, fashioned by those outside the institution, are thrust upon them. This, they appropriately feel, is a violation of their autonomy, since they are being asked to act in accordance with the measures used to evaluate them, whether or not they are appropriate. The proper response is to help develop appropriate measures.

For the different constituencies, the measures may well be different. Students may not be interested in how much new knowledge is developed, and some feel that faculty are at the college or university to teach students first and primarily, and only to do research in the faculty member's spare time, if at all. Such a view is not uncommon among students and parents, as well as among many ordinary citizens. What is appropriate is accountability showing that the students are getting a good education, using criteria that make sense and are understandable to all. The criteria cannot simply be that which is decided by the students. They are able to judge to some extent whether they are learning, the fairness of their professors, whether the professors communicate well, and whether they find themselves prepared to take the next level of study in a particular area. Hence their perceptions and evaluations have a place. But they are still in the learning process, and having not yet completed that process are not in a position to know as much as those who have completed the process and who know more of the field than the students do.

Accountability to granting agencies is usually determined in conjunction with the grant—the required reports or other measures having been specified at the time the grant was made. Accountability to donors consists perhaps of informing them how their money is being used. But if used as they intended, and frequently this is a legal requirement, reporting may not be necessary. If a donor is unhappy with how the money is being used, there is usually little recourse except to give no more. As already noted, donors have no right to interfere in the appointments made to positions they endow, although often those holding chairs come to know the donors and may establish some sort of professional relation with them.

Only in an institution that has relative autonomy with respect to its academic side does it make sense to speak about the academic freedom of those within the institution. Without autonomy in its academic affairs, those outside the college or university will be able to impose their will on the institution and thus on what and how it teaches, who teaches it, and what shall not be taught or learned. Unless institutional autonomy with respect to academic matters is secure, academic freedom within the institution cannot be. The threats to academic freedom from within the institution are serious enough for concern. The institution as a whole, its administrators, and its faculty, have the responsibility to protect the autonomy of the university from outside encroachment, and to do what they can to help other institutions do likewise. Typically they can only be effective by joining forces with other institutions and with those in other institutions to protect the autonomy of colleges and universities generally and in particular cases. One way in which this responsibility is discharged is by articulating the reasons for academic autonomy publicly and clearly and helping inform all the institution's constituencies as well as the general public.

Within the confines of an institution's academic autonomy we can distinguish two aspects of academic freedom, as derived from the German notions of *Lernfreiheit* and *Lehrfreiheit,* or freedom to learn and freedom to teach. Although most of the emphasis in the United States has been on the latter, it is worthwhile investigating the former as well.

III. The Freedom to Learn, or the Academic Freedom of Students

The academic freedom of students in the United States is considerably different from the academic freedom of students in nineteenth- and even twentieth-century German and other European universities.[4] The typical European university consists of lecture courses, which students are free to attend or not. No attendance is taken and the job of the teacher is to lecture, usually without questions from the students. Students are to learn, but there are no fixed assignments in a course. For a degree a student must pass a series of tests—often administered orally—over certain subject matter. How the student learns the subject matter is up to the free choice of the student. The rules governing what a student is to learn are often not rigidly prescribed. However, the price of such freedom is a very high failure rate, often exceeding more than half the students.

This approach has never been popular in the United States, especially at the undergraduate level. Most colleges and universities have a prescribed number of credit hours students must earn, and they earn them by taking courses. Courses are usually structured, with requirements to be met—papers, assignments, tests—throughout the course as well as a final requirement—a final examination or a term paper or both. Students must also satisfy a number of requirements such as course or competence requirements in math and English, a distribution requirement to ensure that they have taken at least a sampling from the humanities, physical sciences, and social sciences, and a major concentration requirement.

The freedom of students to learn is thus structured and restricted in many ways by requirements. The structuring, and so the restrictions, are usually justified on pedagogical grounds. In fact, these grounds seem the only legitimate grounds for requirements. Having requirements simply to make life difficult for students, building hurdles simply to have students jump over them, or structuring a curriculum simply to enable the faculty to teach what they want would be to abuse the academic authority the faculty has. The requirements set by the faculty for graduation and for acquiring a basic knowledge of a field—the student's major—must be for the benefit of the student.

Since any requirements limit a student's freedom to learn, they must be justified. The requirements of some schools and of some disciplines are more rigid and rigorous than of others. Often the graduation requirements in a school of engineering allow students almost no freedom in the choice of courses they take. The justification for the requirements is that there is a great deal that any engineer must master. The faculty knows what that subject matter is. And when divided into courses, the requirements take up most of the four years an undergraduate degree is expected to take. If engineering students were willing to spend five or six or more years full-time in college, of course they could have more freedom of choice in what they took. But to be certifiable as engineers they will have to master what engineers have to know, and will have to take the required courses at some time or another, often in a certain sequence, since one course builds on the knowledge attained in another.

The most rigorous requirements are usually in the professional schools and in some of the sciences. The humanities and social sciences usually have more leeway in choice of courses, if the institution is large enough to offer a wide array.

In the 1960s some students were very vocal in their claim that their freedom to learn was being restricted by requirements, and in some cases the faculty agreed and loosened them. At the extreme, some colleges allow students to take any courses they want as long as they earn the required number of credit hours for completed courses. Sometimes such unstructured curricula lead to a nontraditional degree, for instance, to a Bachelor of General Studies, rather than to a Bachelor of Arts or a Bachelor of Sciences. This is because one function of the university is accreditation, and the different degree indicates to any interested external party that the student has had a nonstructured education, whereas the traditional degrees indicate a certain breadth (from taking courses to satisfy distribution requirements) and some depth in a major field of study.

American students have not clamored for complete freedom in their choice of courses or curricula, nor has American society. What then does the freedom to learn mean in such a situation, and since it is circumscribed, how is it abridged?

As a general rule, I suggest that a student's freedom to learn is not abridged so long as the requirements and restrictions placed on his or her learning can be reasonably defended as being in the interest of the student's general desire to learn and to become educated. The setting of requirements and restrictions is not an exact science and the faculty has the obligation to do the most conscientious job that it can. It should be able to give a rationale for its requirements when called upon to do so either by administrators or faculty in other fields or by the students subject to the requirements. Freedom to learn at least implies that when students can muster good reasons to challenge the existing rules or requirements, they should have some way to get a hearing. Participation in governance and representation on committees or bodies that set requirements are ways that some colleges and universities make this possible. A beginning chemistry student cannot know what a chemist must know to carry on research and so appropriately initially acquiesces to what the faculty in chemistry requires. But at some stage advanced students may know enough to question some requirements or to propose helpful changes.

Nonetheless, the dual authority structure in the college or university leaves the final administrative decision mainly in the hands of the faculty because they are the ones with the greatest appropriate knowledge and experience.

Requirements will restrict the courses a student can take. Class size will frequently limit the number of students in a particular course, and most colleges and universities do not allow students freely to sit in on any lectures they feel like attending unless they are enrolled. This limitation is a function of size, costs, and functionality of courses in which students come or go, attend or not as they please. In some instances this may work well. In others in which the course is tightly structured, lab work is required, and space is limited, such a laissez-faire approach may be disruptive and counterproductive for the enrolled students.

The freedom of students to learn in a class at least implies that they should not be coerced into believing—if such were possible—what a teacher says, even though they may be held responsible for the content presented in the course. Freedom to learn means that students should without penalty be able to disagree with the teacher's views or with material or interpretations presented. This is usually easier to do in a course in literature, where part of what is to be learned is how to interpret and defend one's interpretations, than in a class in calculus, where one learns how to do calculus by mastering integration and differentiation. Nor does freedom to learn mean that all disagreement is equally valid. Each discipline has canons or criteria of what constitutes knowledge or of how the discipline works. These can only be validly challenged after they are learned and known. The challenging of the presuppositions of a discipline is not usually well done by those learning about the discipline in introductory courses, especially if they have little or no training in identifying and evaluating presuppositions.

Freedom to learn and hence freedom to dissent is compatible with teachers prescribing and enforcing requirements and maintaining order in the classroom or teaching environment so that all may learn. The freedom of each student is restricted not only by the rules set by the teacher, but by the logic or discipline of the material studied and by the freedom of the other students to learn. Disrupting a class or dominating it by asking questions and raising objections is not fair to the other students, and such action is appropriately limited by teachers.

Typically the scope of the student's freedom to learn increases as he or she learns more. Undergraduate major requirements are appropriately more specific than are Ph.D. program requirements, in which a student is usually expected to be able to demonstrate mastery of a broad body of knowledge within the given area. Whether that knowledge was acquired through course work or independent reading and research is irrelevant. Similarly, graduate students typically have a fair amount of leeway in choosing their dissertation topics, and they must be free to pursue their research where it carries them. The conclusions of original research cannot be known in advance, otherwise it is either not original or not research. This freedom is once again appropriately circumscribed by the methods and techniques accepted in a field or area, and if the research requires challenging these, that itself must be done in terms the student can defend. Hence the requirement that students defend their theses and dissertations. The written product of the research must be up to the professional standards of the field, and successful completion of the dissertation has this as one of its functions. The oral defense shows that the student can defend his or her work against objections and can fill in gaps and go beyond the presentation on the written page.

If education is a process in which students learn how to learn, the freedom to learn consists in learning how to be free. When one learns how to read, one must learn that skill. Once learned, one is free—in the sense of being able—to read anything in that language. Freedom to learn is compatible with restraints and limits. But these are best imposed by the subject matter and the very process of learning, and it is the task of the faculty to translate these implicit restraints into external requirements on both the general curricular level and the individual class level. The responsibility of students is to attempt to learn, to respect the rights of other students to learn, and to retain their individual common sense in evaluating what they are told or taught. The responsibility of the faculty is to help students learn, to respect their attempts to do so through questioning and challenging a teacher for explanations or more defense of a position, and to foster their creativity. This is compatible with their grading of student efforts. But in the grading they are responsible for being fair in their assignments, consistent in their evaluations of student work, and tolerant of differences of opinion in areas in which opinion and not fact are at issue.

I have said nothing so far about the student's right to free speech. The reason is that properly speaking this right has little to do with the freedom to learn. Every student has the civil right to free speech. Students also have the right to their beliefs—religious, political, and other. They should not be penalized by either faculty or their fellow students for holding their beliefs, and general rules against discrimination are appropriately applied. But freedom of speech is compatible with strictures on when students may speak in class and on the introduction of extraneous subject matter.

Freedom to learn means that the institution and the faculty in their classes have the obligation to provide an atmosphere conducive to learning. This means an environment in which students feel free to express their opinions in class without fear of ridicule, as well as an environment free of gender, racial, and other forms of discrimination or intimidation. The responsibility falls not only on the institution and the faculty but also on the students in their relations with each other and in their behavior in class and on campus.

Freedom to learn also means that students are expected to make mistakes in the learning process, and mistakes are not to be considered defects of character. Nonetheless, it is appropriate and consistent with freedom to learn to grade students on what they learn, accomplish, and produce, and not on how hard they try. Moreover, freedom to learn means that students should be graded and academically evaluated on their academic performance, not on their extracurricular or private activities.

The freedom of speech that students enjoy outside the academic area is not a matter of their freedom to learn and so not a matter of their academic freedom. There is a gray zone between the classroom and the street corner, and that is the area of university-related activities. If American colleges and universities, like some European universities, were concerned exclusively with academic matters, such concerns would not arise. But in U.S. settings students often run newspapers, sometimes through the journalism school, sometimes independent of any academic unit. Student activity fees are collected by the university and usually administered by students, who sometimes invite guest lecturers. Are limits placed on such quasi-official or campus activities covered by academic freedom, by freedom of speech, by both or by neither? No simple and easy answer is possible, because one must look in detail at what the activity is, whether and to what extent it is academic, and what rights are at issue or what good is to be achieved by the activity.

If a student newspaper is run as part of a class or program in journalism, then there is an obvious academic aspect to it. Students are to learn through practice, and that means they will make mistakes as part of the learning process. But mistakes of fact that damage a student or a faculty member's reputation when they appear in a newspaper are different from mistakes one makes on a paper one turns in to a professor. Libel laws apply to student newspapers as to other newspapers, and student reporters must learn that. What of investigative reports that damage the institution or its reputation? Can such reports be kept from publication? The students who successfully uncovered a story, for instance, have learned how to do so whether or not the story is printed. In many cases the decision of whether to publish is a judgment call. How much good will be done? How much harm and to whom? Does the good outweigh the bad? Is the presentation fair and are both sides of an issue presented? Is the point of view of the student a biased or uninformed one? Faculty appropriately raise these and other questions with the students who run the paper, and doing so is part of the learning process. Responsible students and faculty should be able to jointly arrive at reasonable answers. The paper should have policies about whether stories must be approved by faculty advisers or teachers of certain classes, for example, in reporting. If the paper is an official organ of the university, then perhaps legally the president has the right to prior approval, which he or she may delegate to some other administrator or faculty member.

Individual students have no right to invite speakers to campus, and the college or university has no obligation to provide a forum to any student who wishes to invite a speaker. But what of student groups? Does the students' freedom to learn include the right to invite any speakers they wish on any subject they wish? Is their freedom to learn infringed if some other group or some faculty or administrators are offended by the very presence of the speaker or by his or her views as expressed? If the ground is the students' right to learn and not the claim of the civil right to freedom of speech or assembly, then the criterion to be applied is whether the speaker's knowledge, background, and presentation are such as to expect that what the speaker says will lead to knowledge. If student fees are used, the question may be whether the fees are used as students desire and in accord with the rules they have set up for the invitation of speakers. Some speakers are invited for their entertainment value, in which case freedom to learn seems to have little place. Controversial speakers are of different kinds. If they are known ideologues, then a defense on the basis of freedom to learn seems shaky, even when a defense on freedom of speech grounds may prove legally sound. Hate speech may be defended on the basis of freedom of speech; it does not seem defensible on the basis of freedom to learn.

Freedom of speech is a civil right. I have not called freedom to learn a right. It can be considered one, but it is not a moral or human right and it is not a civil right. If considered a right, it is a special right that students have as members of an institution of learning, and a right that is appropriately limited by consideration of learning and by the comparable right of all the other members of the learning community. The criteria applied are different from those applied with respect to freedom of speech. Too often the two are confused. They can be kept distinct in many cases in which they are not.

IV. The Freedom to Research and Teach, or Faculty Academic Freedom

The core justification for academic freedom is the attainment of truth for the benefit of society. Without the belief and faith that there is truth that can be attained or at least approximated and that having the truth is good for society, there is no reason why society should grant educational institutions autonomy or those within it academic freedom. A democratic and liberal society might grant all its citizens the civil right of free speech. But academic freedom would make little sense.

If the core justification holds, then we can approach what academic freedom should mean and entail by looking carefully at how truth is attained in a university. The institutional setting is as important as the faculty, for only if they are part of the institution are they faculty. The search for truth is carried on not individually and in seclusion but at an institution in which openness and the sharing of knowledge is the rule and secrecy the exception. Hence the concern about carrying on classified and proprietary research at a university. Knowledge is communally held and it is by its nature shareable.

How then is new knowledge attained or discovered? The answer is by research, the very purpose of which is to systematically seek to discover new knowledge. It follows, then, that at the core of academic freedom is the freedom to pursue research.

Freedom of Research

Freedom of research means the freedom of faculty to pursue their research where it takes them, freedom from prior restraint and from hindrance along the way, and freedom from fear of punishment or dismissal for the publication or presentation of unpopular findings. This freedom is granted to faculty members, and the expectation is that they will pursue research in areas in which they are competent, for that is where they will most likely find or develop new knowledge. The area of competence of an individual faculty member may be very broad, and competence is not to be narrowly construed as the area of restricted specialization. It is often by breaking out of one's specialization that discoveries are made and new insights developed. Faculty members have been trained to learn and to teach themselves, and their interests may take them well beyond the traditional boundaries of their disciplines. There is no reason to limit their research by field or area or content, for they prove their competence by their research and its results. The main point is that because research is a primary way in which new knowledge is developed, if faculty are to develop or find new knowledge they can do so most effectively if they are free to pursue their research where it leads them.

From the point of view of knowledge, no one is in a position to know prior to original research that it should be prohibited. There are of course ethical boundaries as to how research is conducted, such as the rights and respect due human subjects in any research project. We cannot demand that faculty members find new knowledge, which is by its very nature unpredictable, and then deny them the freedom to pursue that knowledge as they see fit. At the same time, this does not mean that any institution has the obligation to supply all the equipment any of its faculty says he or she needs. In a world of limited resources choices have to be made. In this way the research of scientists is in fact more restricted by colleges and universities than is the research of philosophers who need little in the way of resources.

Freedom to pursue research involves not only doing one's research but also, equally important, submitting the results to the scrutiny of one's peers. Here too there is no reason for any restraint, and academic freedom means the freedom to present one's results openly with no fear of being penalized for conclusions that are unpopular or that some see as threatening. Whether the results or conclusions are sound is best determined by open and free scrutiny, replication, and discussion by those competent in the area. Hence, to attain society's aim of the increase in knowledge, educational institutions should allow the greatest freedom of discussion in scholarly journals, in professional association meetings, and in faculty forums on campus. Because these are the places where those with the most knowledge can debate controversial ideas, test them, and present objections and have them answered, it would be counterproductive for those not involved to in any way try to control what takes place in these arenas. In fact, unless there is controversy in these scholarly outlets, one can wonder whether those involved are in any way testing the boundaries of what is known and so developing new knowledge.

The argument for academic freedom limited only by ethical considerations of the rights of those directly involved in or affected by the research is most compelling in the areas of research and publication and discussion in professional scholarly contexts. Here faculty members deal with knowledgeable peers. Free debate is the way ideas are tested, corrected, and refined. That the popular press or media may pick up new ideas presented in scholarly outlets and exploit, distort, or oversimplify them, and may draw implications that go beyond the data or the theory as developed, should in no way restrict or restrain what goes on in the scholarly and professional discussions. The academic freedom of faculty with respect to research should protect them from popular repercussions of their findings that may lead some people to call for their dismissal or removal from the faculty.

The responsibility of the scholar is to pursue his or her research wherever it leads, draw the conclusions justified, and present them accurately. The responsibility of the scholar's peers is to protect each faculty member's academic freedom, being receptive to change and innovation while at the same time verifying suspicious results and challenging new ideas. The first step in such a process is peer review of papers submitted for publication or presentation at a meeting.[5] The more original and different the ideas in a paper, the more difficult it usually is to pass peer review. This seems lamentable but it is actually appropriate. Peer review is the best means we have come up with to get fair evaluations of submitted material and to separate what is publishable from what is not. While it is true that new perspectives or views in any area have difficulty gaining acceptance, at the present time this is probably truer of the humanities and social sciences than of the hard sciences. The implications of the humanities and social sciences are often easier for the general public to understand than the discoveries in the sciences, and they are sometimes unpopular. The need to protect scholars' academic freedom is all the greater in such circumstances because the pressure to silence them is greater, and hence the danger of losing what truth or knowledge they may have. The danger within the academy is that scholars, secure in their positions and dominant in their fields, may unethically attempt to block attacks on them and their methods and conclusions. They may also feel ethically justified if their appraisal of submitted material does not satisfy their academic criteria. This may well be the case when those submitting material adopt different criteria or methods, at odds with the dominant mode. But the present system in the United States with its many universities and its large number of faculties and of scholarly publications is sufficiently diverse that those who challenge the academic establishment have been able to do so in a great many fields within the academic framework. The challengers may find their efforts more difficult than they would like. But the emergence of radical legal theory, critical theory, a variety of versions of feminism, deconstruction, and antiscience is evidence that the system works. It would not work as well if all or at least most parties did not respect academic freedom as well as academic tenure.

Research and publication are at the heart of academic freedom.

Freedom to Teach

Publication, of course, is one form of teaching. It is the means by which a scholar communicates what he or she has found to colleagues and to the general public. But what is generally considered the teaching covered by academic freedom is the freedom to teach students what one knows and believes in one's area of competence without fear of punishment or dismissal for doing so.

For the most part teaching is not a means of attaining new knowledge. It involves the attempt to attain new knowledge when a faculty member includes students in his or her research project as part of their courses. This is more frequent in the hard sciences than in the humanities or social sciences, and involves students in the research process as apprentices. The result is sometimes joint publication.

Most teaching is not of this type, and is not so much a search for knowledge as the presentation of what the faculty member sees as knowledge or truth, even if presented tentatively, sometimes using students as a sounding board and possible source of criticism as the faculty member works out his or her ideas. Teaching most often is not so much a search for knowledge as the transmission of knowledge as pursued and perceived by the faculty member.

Although research is often considered by students and by many outside the university as opposed to teaching, this rests on a misconception of both as approached on the college and university level. In order to teach, the faculty member must have something to teach, namely a body of knowledge. At the advanced level of university education, that knowledge is most often not simply factual. Someone had to develop and organize, systematize, and evaluate the subject matter. Who does this? Obviously it is done by those faculty members working in a field, usually at the college and university level. They write the articles, the books, and the texts that are used in classes and that faculty members assign their students. Those doing the research and publishing teach in their classes to the extent appropriate what they have developed. They typically teach more than just what they personally have produced. Whoever the faculty members, their competence in part consists of their being able to follow the developments in their field and to choose the best material available for presentation to their students. As teachers, their responsibility to their students, to the institution, and to society is to choose such material. Since this is a function of their knowledge, part of their academic freedom is their freedom to choose the materials for their courses, to organize them, and to use the best techniques they have to present them. In advanced courses, their lectures, if they lecture, may be the contents of the book they are writing, and not infrequently books that appear are reworked class lectures. This is part of what it means to expose students to cutting-edge material—material that is sometimes not even published or that has just recently been published.

Of course not all teaching is at this level. Some courses are fairly straightforward and comparable to material taught in high school. Students who learn a foreign language in college must learn that language's grammar, its vocabulary, and how the language is spoken and written. There is no choice about whether or not to accept it. The same is true when a student learns algebra or geometry or calculus. There are better and poorer texts, less effective and more effective methods of teaching. But the content is standard. French is French, wherever it is taught, as are algebra and calculus. Yet even in these areas, someone writes the textbooks, and whether this one is better than that one for the course is a professional decision properly taken by the faculty member in charge.

Nonetheless, there are many more appropriate restraints on the academic freedom of faculty as teachers than there are on faculty as researchers. Typically faculty members pursue research of their choice. That is part of what they are free to do. No one commands them to pursue this rather than that, even though they may suggest it and even though funding may be available for this rather than that. Faculty members do not always have the choice of the courses they teach because there may be certain courses—such as those required by students in order to graduate—that have to be taught and that a faculty member might be assigned to teach. It would be counterproductive for the students, the department, and the institution to assign a faculty member to teach a course that he or she strongly objected to teaching, since it would probably not be well taught. And faculty should not be assigned to teach courses that they do not have the competence to teach. Academic freedom implies some freedom in what one teaches, but that is compatible with a faculty member's being hired to teach in a certain area and being expected to do so, as well as with the faculty member's being expected to share in teaching required general survey courses in the department, and other required courses and courses that the department deems it important to teach.

A faculty member's freedom may also be legitimately restricted in the content of a course. Courses are usually described in a college or university catalog. This is a kind of contract with the students that if they choose that course the material indicated will be addressed or covered. To advertise a course in this way and then change the contents as one pleases is to break the contract and to be guilty of false advertising.

The course description also limits what a faculty member may appropriately do in the classroom. If a course is English literature, then the teacher should not spend long periods recounting fishing techniques to the exclusion of English literature. Academic freedom does not mean that a teacher has the right to teach anything under any course title and description. The aim of academic freedom is to promote knowledge, its development in research, and its preservation and critical transmission in teaching. This is not license and does not provide the teacher with any right to do or say anything he or she pleases in the classroom. The restriction of subject matter is real, but it should not be taken too narrowly and what is appropriate in a class is determined by the subject matter in question.

While there are no restrictions in what a faculty member writes for publication, if an author digresses at length to trout fishing in an article on English literature, the article will not pass critical review and will not be published. There is no such barrier in the classroom. A teacher has a captive audience, forced to attend class if they wish to get enough material to pass the course, and perhaps forced to take the course because it is a requirement. The teacher holds power in the class. The teacher should be the epistemic authority in the class, with subject knowledge the student does not have. In this way the student is in a subservient and dependent role. The teacher also has operative authority in the class, setting the requirements and assigning the grades. This puts the teacher in a very different relation vis-à-vis the students than vis-à-vis peers in one's academic field. This difference imposes obligations and restraints on the faculty member. These obligations and restraints are limits on their freedom. They are not an attack on academic freedom but an integral part of it.

Academic freedom—which includes the freedom to teach and the freedom to learn—balances the freedom of teacher and student and the respect due each. Since what is protected is the freedom to teach one's courses as one sees fit, and to teach what one believes within the context of the course, those criteria must be used to determine what is or is not appropriate. For a teacher in a calculus course to argue his or her view of abortion seems clearly inappropriate and not part of what academic freedom is supposed to protect. For a faculty member teaching a course in sexual ethics to argue his or her view on abortion might be appropriate. Yet even here, since the students are a captive audience, it is appropriate that they be told there are arguments on the other side and that they are not required to agree with the teacher's views. What they can be held responsible for is knowing the arguments presented.

Academic freedom in teaching, however, is compatible with faculty accountability. Since the quality of faculty teaching is appropriately evaluated both prior to and after the awarding of tenure, it must be possible for those responsible for the evaluation of a faculty member's performance to gain appropriate information about that performance. The faculty member is accountable to the students for what and how he or she teaches, and hence they can appropriately give their assessment of that teaching. Their assessment should certainly count, even though it need not and should not be the only assessment, since they are still learners and not yet masters of the material to which they are exposed. Peer review is also appropriate, since it is one's colleagues who know the field and are best placed to judge the quality of the material presented. Some faculty members claim that their academic freedom is violated if their colleagues or faculty members from other departments sit in to observe their teaching. The presence of other faculty members may make some teachers anxious and nervous. And every teacher may have an off day. But teachers are supposed to profess, and secrecy is not part of what academic freedom provides. It is usually considered polite to let a faculty member know when one will be visiting his or her class. But if there were a general understanding that peers may sit in on their colleagues' classes for purposes of periodic evaluation, that would in no way violate academic freedom. For faculty are accountable not only to students but also to their colleagues for what and how they teach, even though they are rarely called to account.

Exactly what is allowed in the classroom by academic freedom and what is not allowed is a matter of some controversy. In terms of academic freedom, the evaluation and argument should be based on what academic freedom is perceived to be and the end it is to preserve or achieve.

I have not discussed freedom of speech in the classroom. As a citizen in a free country, a faculty member may say whatever he or she pleases, just as any other citizen may. Knowledge and position are not relevant. But freedom of speech does not mean one may express one's opinions anywhere and any time one chooses. In the context of a college or university, faculty members are paid not to express their opinions on any topic any time they wish but to teach and pursue research within the context of the institution. They are paid to teach courses with academic content.

Does freedom of speech have no place on a campus and does it have no connection with academic freedom? Faculty and students do not give up their civil liberties when they walk on campus, and they do not lose their freedom of speech. But that freedom is limited, and in the classroom it is limited by the purpose of the class and the administrative rules that appropriately govern its conduct. Faculty members and students outside of class and in their capacity as private individuals may express their views, no matter how outrageous, on any topic they wish within the limits set by the laws on free speech. Faculty should not be penalized in their professional role for what they say in their private lives as citizens. This is not peculiar to faculty members. It is inappropriate to fire people in any area for voicing their positions off the job in ways that do not adversely affect the entity employing them. Moreover, because faculty members appropriately share in the governance of their institutions they should not be penalized for criticism of the institution. That is part of their professional and academic role, and academic freedom includes their freedom to do so. The danger is that faculty members who profess unpopular scholarly views and who cannot be removed or penalized for doing so may be put in jeopardy for things they say in their nonprofessional lives. That would be a violation of their academic freedom, because the real reason for their jeopardy is their professional views, the other being only a pretext.

Freedom to Participate in Governance

Since the university's autonomy extends to setting curricula, fixing course requirements for graduation and major concentrations, and hiring and firing faculty, the question arises as to who rightly performs these functions. The appropriate answer is that since the university claims autonomy in these areas because of academic expertise, those with the expertise should perform the functions. But those with the expertise are the faculty. Since graduation requirements are set for all students and involve all departments, it is appropriate that all faculty members have a voice in the final determination and decision. With respect to departmental major requirements, it is appropriate that the faculty of the department make that decision. There is no reason to think that the chair of the department has more knowledge in this respect than other members of the department. The chair has executive authority in certain areas, but setting requirements is an area in which epistemic and not executive authority should carry most weight.

With respect to hiring, promoting, awarding tenure, and letting faculty go, these again are primarily faculty matters where the evaluation of people with knowledge of the field is essential. Members of a department should have a say in who is hired, and they should evaluate a faculty member's publication, teaching, and service in making recommendations for tenure and promotion. Since a faculty member is not tenured in a department but in the university, it is also appropriate that the decision on tenure be made not only by the department but by the larger university community. Thus, usually a college and/or university committee makes a recommendation to the officers of the institution, who typically have the legal authority to bind the institution to permanent tenure. Any decision to overrule the recommendation made by the faculty or its elected representatives should be justified to the faculty body.

For like reasons, in cases of financial exigency, the faculty should have a voice in how the institution is restructured, since this importantly affects the academic mission and structure over which the faculty, in virtue of its academic authority, rightly holds sway.

Which faculty should have a voice in these decisions, and how great a voice? The principle of faculty participation in these decisions is essential. But that principle can be implemented in a great many ways. In some institutions all full-time faculty have an equal voice and vote on all matters. In others, with respect to promotion and tenure, only those in a department who are in the rank or ranks above the person being considered have a vote. In some large institutions the faculty has turned over many curricula and other matters to representative elected committees. The principle is maintained in all these cases, and the principle by itself does not determine one structure rather than another. Committees can and should be held accountable by and responsible to the whole faculty for what they do.

Funding for programs and faculty, including raises and research grants, and the use of funds for staff support all impact on the faculty and on the academic functioning of the institution. Yet often the faculty has no voice in budgetary allocations, which are seen as falling under the administrative and not the academic side of the institution, under executive and not under epistemic authority. The administration is responsible for helping the faculty members achieve the ends for which they are hired and for helping the institution as a whole achieve its ends, and can be held accountable for so doing. The institution as whole is accountable to the board and/or legislature for its use of funds.

If the faculty has no voice in any budgetary allocation, then it may be restricted in its ability to exercise its academic freedom in setting the academic agenda of the university. It should have some role, but the principle of faculty participation once again does not specify any particular role the faculty must have and there are many ways to satisfy the participation requirement. Salary increases are sometimes made administratively at the college level, sometimes at the departmental level with or without faculty consultation. What is important is that however the decision is made the increases or lack thereof are justified together with an evaluation of performance and with some method of grievance resolution in which faculty members have a role. Otherwise the danger exists that a faculty member who teaches or holds or publishes unpopular views may be continued in his or her position but given no raises and so eventually forced out in this way. The danger of such faculty members also being given inappropriate courses and the worst times of day in order to make their lives as unpleasant as possible in the hope they will resign is a danger against which there should be some grievance procedure involving faculty.

These are the minimal areas in which faculty should have a say in the institution's governance. Because the faculty members are the epistemic authorities, their advice is appropriate as well in institutional planning, budgetary planning, the institution's organizational structure, and a large number of other areas in which the administration properly has the final word. In speaking that word, however, the administration remains accountable to all those who will be affected by the decisions in the sense that the administrators can and do give the justifications and rationale for their actions when asked.

Teaching Assistants and Part-Time Faculty

Do the general justifications of academic freedom applicable to full-time faculty apply equally to teaching assistants and part-time faculty? Since academic freedom applies to students as well as to full-time faculty, it surely applies to these other two groups as well. But how it applies depends on their relation to the development and transmission of knowledge.

Teaching assistants are usually graduate students. Their research capacity has yet to be proven. But to the extent that they do original research at the university they, just as a faculty member, should be allowed to pursue their research where it leads. Usually they work with or under the supervision of a faculty member. The constraint on their research, if it is for a degree, is that it satisfy the requirements set for the research as part of a degree program. Typically, however, they do not teach their research but teach introductory courses, most frequently as assistants to a full-time faculty member. As assistants, they assist, which means they do not on their own choose the course text or draw up the curriculum. Even if they do, they are subject to the approval of the supervising faculty member for what they do. If they lead discussion sections or lab sections, they are usually told what to do and what to cover and how to conduct the section work. This is appropriate since they are assistants and still in training.

If student assistants are given their own courses to teach, once again it is not inappropriate for them to be supervised by a faculty member, to have their texts and syllabi approved. As any teacher they have the obligation as well as the freedom to teach the course as best they can, which means following the arguments where they lead and teaching the truth with respect to the subject matter of the course as they see it. The constraints on the academic freedom of faculty members apply as well to teaching assistants.

Part-time teachers who have their doctorates fall between full-time faculty and teaching assistants. By earning their doctorates they have proven their research ability, and they legitimately exercise the freedom of faculty members in their research. But their research is rarely university-funded. In their teaching they deserve the same status as full-time faculty, even though, like teaching assistants, they often teach only introductory courses.

Part-time faculty usually have very little power in the university structure. With good reason they may feel that if their academic freedom is violated they cannot complain without endangering their academic appointments, which are usually from year to year, if not semester to semester. It is the responsibility of the faculty, especially the tenured faculty, to help guarantee the academic freedom of part-time faculty. Unfortunately, the full-time faculty is seldom informed and often not very interested in the status and freedom of part-timers.

Just as the price of freedom is eternal vigilance, that too is the price of academic freedom. Such vigilance requires that the faculty and the university not only think about academic freedom when it is threatened either by a particular incident or in a particular tenure case or case of threatened dismissal, but that they exercise it, hold themselves accountable, articulate the principles of academic freedom they believe are integral to the university and its faculty members, and accept both the limits on freedom and the responsibilities that academic freedom at its best requires.

In the end academic freedom is not static but dynamic. It is not attained but exercised. Only if exercised does it make sense. And only if those who exercise it do so in such a way as to fulfill the responsibilities that accompany it is it justified.

Notes

1. For instance Robert F. Ladenson, "Is Academic Freedom Necessary?" *Law and Philosophy* 5 (1986), 59–87, argues "that if a reasonable conception of rights in the workplace for all employees came into practice then the idea of academic freedom would become obselete."

2. For an analysis of different kinds of authority, their justification, and limits, see Richard T. De George, *The Nature and Limits of Authority* (Lawrence: University Press of Kansas, 1985).

3. For a fuller discussion of this complicated issue, see Norman E. Bowie, *University-Business Partnerships* (Lanham, Md.: Rowman & Littlefield, 1994).

4. For a discussion of some of the differences, see Howard Mumford Jones, "The American Concept of Academic Freedom," *Academic Freedom and Tenure,* Louis Joughin, ed. (Madison: University of Wisconsin Press, 1967), 224–41; and Ralph F. Fuchs, "Academic Freedom—Its Basic Philosophy, Function, and History," *Academic Freedom,* Hans W. Baade, ed. (Dobbs Ferry, N.Y.: Oceana Publications, 1964), 1–15 (reprinted in this volume).

5. See Richard T. De George and Fred Woodward, "Ethics and Manuscript Reviewing," *Journal of Scholarly Publishing* 25, 3 (April 1994), 133–145.

Chapter Four

Ethical Issues in Academic Freedom

In the previous chapter I developed and defended what is sometimes called the narrow version of academic freedom.[1] This is the version that stems directly from the academic nature of the claim. It is conditional on a number of different factors, as we have seen. There have been universities without it. I have argued for its importance in a certain kind of society, namely an open and democratic one that believes in the possibility of attaining knowledge and that charges its universities to do so. A closed society, such as the former Soviet Union or China, would not sanction academic freedom of the kind I have defended, for the purpose of universities in such societies is not to advance knowledge, but rather to teach the kind of knowledge the leaders want, and otherwise to inculcate the government's political views and values in its students.

Not every college or university in the United States may have as its aim the advancement of knowledge, although few would admit this openly. Some private religious or proprietary institutions may in fact have as their aim the promulgation and inculcation of the institution's views or the narrow training of people in certain fields or professions. The faculty may or may not be expected to do research. Such institutions do not and would not grant their faculties academic freedom. There is no way to force them to do so. But they can be openly labeled as being such institutions, if they do not do so themselves. They should not be allowed to mask as something they are not.

The situation is somewhat different in state-run institutions because they are bound by the obligation to respect the civil right of all their members—students as well as faculty—to freedom of speech. The civil right of freedom of speech guarantees the right of citizens to say whatever they wish (within certain limitations, such as not yelling "Fire!" in a theater) without interference or punishment from the government. Private institutions are not so bound, and they can set whatever rules they wish about what is and is not allowed within their precincts. Nonetheless most American colleges and universities recognize the same right to freedom of speech as the state-run institutions do. This has led to a conflation of academic freedom and freedom of speech, and some people construe academic freedom in its broader version to be equivalent to freedom of speech. The narrow version includes freedom of speech only to the extent that it protects the faculty members and students from any sort of punishment or retribution in their academic status for statements that they make as citizens, whether on or off campus.

The reason for distinguishing the two is that the civil right of free speech does not yield autonomy for the university any more than it does for any other business or institution, nor does it acknowledge any special consideration for the pursuit of knowledge. Some claim that this is appropriate, and if everyone were granted the right of free speech in any position they held, then academic freedom would be superfluous. But there is a difference between faculty at a university and people in other positions. Although in neither situation should one be penalized for what one says off the job, providing it comes within the protection of free speech, the faculty are paid precisely to profess or teach and advance knowledge. They are not free to say anything they want in their professional positions, for example in the classroom, as I have argued. Therefore what they are or are not allowed to profess and pursue is not the same as what is covered by the civil right of free speech. People working for a corporation cannot claim that because they have the right to free speech they can say anything they want in their official positions. They are paid to do certain things and what they say on the job is appropriately evaluated by its effect on the corporation. Criticizing the corporation or professing ideas unpopular with their superiors is in no way protected, nor is it clear that it should be.

Similarly the aspect of freedom of speech that secures participation in governance at least insofar as that concerns the academic sphere is not secured under the right of free speech. Nor is this something that any worker can claim at work, even though some firms allow worker participation in some aspects of the organization of work. None are required to do so. The empowerment of workers and managers that some companies have begun to talk about is not a necessary part of a business; it is, however, an essential part of the appropriate structure of a university.

I. Internal Threats to Academic Freedom

The external threat to academic freedom, as we have seen, comes from legislatures, boards, alumni, and the general public. During the past century we have seen many instances of this threat. During the McCarthy era in the early 1950s a witch hunt took place for Communists and Communist sympathizers. Teachers were not the only targets. Actors, playwrights, screen writers, and many in the media were also the focus of attacks.

Internal threats come from the administration, students, and the faculty. We have already noted the threat from the administration. But it is the threat from the faculty, and to a lesser extent from students, that has recently come to the fore.

The threat from the faculty has during the past few years taken a new turn. There has always been the threat of those in positions of power, whom some identify with the tenured faculty, imposing or attempting to impose their view of what is academically acceptable on junior or untenured faculty. It is the fear of not pleasing one's academic seniors, and so being denied tenure, that leads some critics to argue that tenure tends to keep junior faculty meek and subservient rather than protecting their academic freedom. Instead of the senior faculty members accepting their secure positions to defend the academic freedom of nontenured faculty, they use their positions to enforce views that they see as orthodox or correct, and as alone worthy of tenure. The charges undoubtedly have validity in some cases and departments. Sometimes those who act in this way do so in good faith and in the belief that they are upholding quality. Other times they are morally at fault. Because power is at issue and not necessarily or only academic competence or knowledge, some critics argue against tenure. But it is not clear that eliminating tenure would do anything to help academic freedom in this regard.

The attack has been taken one step farther by those who argue that power is always at issue because in many—perhaps all—academic disciplines there is no true knowledge, no right or wrong view, just a wide range of competing views. The search for truth is a cover for the imposition of one's beliefs. The argument is mounted most clearly against the humanities and social sciences, but also to some extent against the hard sciences. The view that faculty are engaged in the pursuit of truth, they say, is an Enlightenment myth, in which reason was thought capable of reaching truth in all realms—science, history, politics, ethics, religion. That myth, the argument goes, has now been exposed as untenable.

Suppose someone holds this very strong view. Then the conclusion to which they are led seems to be that since there is no truth or real knowledge to be found, the university is not a place where it is sought but a place where the academic battles of which view is to prevail are fought. Tenure yields power in this battle, and therefore is a target for those without it. But what then of academic freedom? If the basis is not the search for truth, the discovery of which benefits society, what justifies society's funding academics in their battles, and what is the payoff for society? If there is no payoff for society in the way of increased knowledge, then society has no incentive to grant an institution academic freedom and all that it entails—autonomy, freedom in research and teaching, a voice in governance, and freedom to learn. If what is at stake is really power, then those who fund the institution have power, and they can insist that the institution be run as they wish. This reaction is clear in the debates about the contents of Western Civilization courses. If there are no books that are better than any others for students to read, why leave the decision of what is to be read up to the faculty? If they have no knowledge, and if informed opinion is simply one prejudice rather than another, why allow any of them the freedom to set readings or curricula?

The reaction is understandable, and if nourished will go even further. If the faculty members have no knowledge, and they are simply teaching students their prejudices, why support them to do that? Why not rather hire faculty who will teach prescribed material that is necessary for practical jobs after students graduate? Whatever the faculty members think about truth and knowledge, engineers know that they must master certain areas in order to build buildings that do not collapse, airplanes that fly, space shuttles that can escape gravity and orbit the moon. Businesses know that they need people who can balance their books. People know they need doctors who can help them when they are sick or injured. Therefore faculty can prescribe curricula in those areas. Those outside the university are no more secure in knowing what students need in the humanities and social sciences than the faculty. But if the faculty doesn't know better, why leave curricula decisions up to them? If the faculty does not have any more knowledge than those outside the university, the answer seems to be that there is no good reason to grant the university academic freedom, at least in those areas.

The argument would be persuasive if the premises from which it proceeds are true. But those outside the university interested in controlling it have taken attacks made from inside the university on curricular and other matters as if they were true, accurate, and correct, whereas they are attacks and as such can be seen as part of the ongoing process of debate and discussion within the university.

The question of whether faculty members in the humanities and social sciences have knowledge, and what exactly that means, is part of the debate, which is far from being resolved. But even when resolved, it is unlikely the conclusion will be the simplistic one that no interpretation is better than any other, that no work of literature is better than any other, that no facts of history can be ascertained, and that no economic or social system can be described or evaluated. The presumption since the start of the university in the Middle Ages has been that faculty members do have knowledge. The fact that some faculty members now question that presumption does not mean that they are correct. In fact, the best place to determine the validity of that claim is in the university, not outside of it, since it is a question about knowledge and about the content of the academic disciplines. What is really at stake is what knowledge is, and the extent to which what poses as knowledge is in fact ideologically, culturally, and historically tainted. The question is not new, even if some of the presentations and attacks have been couched in a new way and use a new terminology.

The nature of that debate is still in the process of formation. Suppose that those are correct who claim that there is no knowledge in any strong sense, just opinion and power, at least in some areas. The question still remains whether some opinions are better than others for certain purposes. If no opinions are better than any other for any purpose, then it seems it makes no difference which opinions one holds. If this is the case, then those who have power have no reason to consider the claims of those who do not have power. The latter are not making any claim about truth or knowledge; they are simply voicing their preferences and prejudices. In the process they wish to seize some of the power they presently lack. But if this is what is at issue, those with the power would have no reason to yield any, and it would be in their self-interest to keep as much as they can.

A reply might be that those who have no power, who have always been powerless, deserve a voice in the academy. Yet that claim itself, according to those who espouse it, is simply a statement of their belief, which is no more true than the claim that those without a voice don't deserve one. Desert implies some basis upon which it is made. But there is no basis if there is no better or worse, no true or false. There is only the observation that might makes right and true and whatever else it wishes.

So the claim that the accepted canon of great works is arbitrary and political and expresses a point of view that should be corrected requires not that one argue that any list is as good as any other. For if that is the case, then the accepted canon imposed by those in power is as good as any alternative and need not be changed. The point of changing it or enlarging it or of introducing different points of view and different voices is that the change will be better than the traditional canon for some reason that can be articulated. That articulation is then part of the ongoing attempt to find the best and most valid reasons for what is taught.

In the process the question arises about the rules of debate and the procedures of discussion. If the debate must be carried on within the framework set by those in power, then the odds are against those who would attempt to challenge that framework. That seems neither fair nor likely to yield whatever insight the attackers have. The solution is not to impose any specific approach, framework, or set of rules, but to allow the free dialogue among the parties. In a rather messy and unclear way this is in fact what is going on in the colleges and universities. The voices of those who claim they have not been heard—the voices of feminists and of minorities in particular—are being heard. Many colleges and universities have programs and concentrations and faculty in feminist studies or black studies, for instance. Is there knowledge in those areas that qualifies for college courses and for academic research? Those who claim yes have made their case, have achieved some recognition, and have produced some changes in colleges and universities around the country.

The resolution of disputes about knowledge, objectivity, prejudice in points of view, and power are all areas of legitimate debate that appropriately take place on campuses. To the extent that they have to do with knowledge the debates come within the compass of academic freedom. But even if the conclusion is that there is no knowledge in any strong sense of being objective, disinterested, ahistorical, and eternal, academic freedom would still make sense. Academic freedom continues to make sense because even those who attack traditional meanings of knowledge and specific beliefs and evaluations do so in the name of other meanings and beliefs and evaluations. Which of these are best for society to follow, adopt, and build upon, is still of interest to society and best resolved by letting the debate work itself out to a resolution, which in turn will be challenged. That is not to be avoided but that is the point of having universities and of guaranteeing academic freedom.

A by-product of the debate about knowledge and what constitutes the canon of material important to teach students, however, has been internal attacks on academic freedom in the name of what is sometimes called "political correctness." Exactly what political correctness is, is itself problematic and is in fact claimed by very few, if anyone.[2] If it is defined simply as an enunciation of the demand that people in the university treat each other—students as well as faculty—with respect, that they not sexually harass each other, that they not use racial epithets, and that they not demean each other, then the demand is a demand for basic morality and civility. If civility and the basic respect for people that morality demands are the issue, then there should be little objection and widespread support of such demands. All members of the academic community, indeed all people, deserve respect. There is nothing particularly academic at issue. And if society in general has lost some of its sense of civility and basic respect for people, the university might well be a place where society can start to recover these. They go along with the tolerance of ideas that the university and academic freedom seek to foster.

The difficulty comes in interpreting civility and basic respect, and in some instances the interpretation comes into direct conflict with academic freedom.

Academic freedom does not give any faculty member or any student the right to sexually or racially harass anyone. The courts have distinguished two types of sexual harassment: quid pro quo sexual harassment and hostile environment sexual harassment. The first involves a request or demand for some sexual favor by a person in a superior position of authority or power in return for some special treatment or for refraining from imposing damage on a subordinate, for instance by firing or giving a failing grade in class. Hostile environment sexual harassment consists in an environment in which workers or students are made to feel uncomfortable and unable to carry on their tasks because of sexually oriented jokes or posters or conversations that make them feel threatened or uncomfortable.

Academic freedom does not give a teacher the right to sexually harass students, nor to harass them because of their race or religion or national origin, or for any other reason. Any teacher who is prejudiced against any member of his or her class acts unethically if he or she lets that prejudice influence the way the student is treated in class or the grades the student gets. The difficulty comes not in interpreting what quid pro quo harassment consists of, but in interpreting what constitutes a hostile environment, if hostile environment is to be decided, for instance, by the students in a class.

Education is sometimes unsettling to one's beliefs and values, which are challenged. This is often uncomfortable. But it does not constitute a valid reason for restricting academic freedom. If in a philosophy class a teacher raises the question of the validity of proofs for the existence of God, some religious believers may feel uncomfortable. But that discomfort is not a reason to prevent discussion of the validity or invalidity of philosophical arguments. It would be improper for a teacher to ridicule believers, and ridicule is not protected by academic freedom. The same line of reasoning applies to a great many areas. The American South tolerated and some in it defended the institution of slavery. To look at the defenses that were given and the justifications may make some black students today feel uncomfortable. But that is no reason to prevent discussion of those arguments. Some women at various periods in history defended what were considered traditional women's roles. That they did and their arguments are appropriate in some courses, even if some women would prefer that they not be raised.

Raising issues in their appropriate contexts for discussion and analysis does not constitute creating a hostile environment, even if some issues, especially controversial ones, make some students uncomfortable. Discomfort is not the major criterion. The notion of a hostile environment that inhibits one from carrying on one's work can and should be distinguished from raising issues in an academic context and allowing free discussion of them, even if they make some people uncomfortable. It may not be possible to spell out exactly how to draw the line in borderline cases. Ridicule is clearly inappropriate. But since offense is in the eye of the beholder, no general rule can be made about discomfort, except that any claimed right not to feel uncomfortable comes up against the right to raise controversial issues.

Whether some arguments for the existence of God are valid or sound is a debated issue and a central one in the history of philosophy. A teacher examining the question will probably have a view about whether or not individual arguments are sound, and in explaining and analyzing the arguments will give the reasons for accepting or rejecting them. Expressing that view and giving the reasons for so doing are part of the way philosophy is typically taught. Unless the teacher draws the conclusion to which he or she is lead and gives the reason why, students do not learn how to analyze arguments. The teacher may say why some philosophers disagree with the analysis presented or the disputed issue at stake. The teacher cannot appropriately demand that the students agree with the analysis he or she presents, but the teacher can expect students to understand the argument and analysis. Unless they do, they cannot argue against it, if they feel it is mistaken. Academic freedom protects philosophy teachers whichever side of the controversy they come out on.

By like reasoning, academic freedom should protect teachers who raise other controversial questions pertinent to their subject matters. Is there any valid evidence that shows that some races differ genetically in some areas when compared to other races? The question is sometimes controversial. Although concluding that one race is more susceptible to a certain disease than another is not controversial, concluding that one race is more intelligent than another—however intelligence is defined—is controversial. It would be similarly controversial to say that women differ from men genetically with respect to certain intellectual or affective aptitudes. These are controversial issues that some people would rather not have pursued. But that is not sufficient reason to prevent their pursuit. If there is no validity to the claims that races or genders differ in their genetic intellectual, affective, or other abilities, then that should be shown and the contrary views be shown to be incorrect. If there are differences, then the question is what difference that should make in social structures. Any discovered differences that might be found would not show in any way that people should not be shown equal respect as people, nor would they undermine anyone's moral worth.

The pressure put on those investigating controversial issues to refrain from researching, publishing, or teaching those issues because their conclusions may be unpopular or make some people feel uncomfortable is inappropriate and a violation of academic freedom. Those who feel the pressure sometimes claim that they are being silenced in the name of political correctness, because their conclusions may not be or are not acceptable to some group. Those who have found a voice on campus that was previously little heard include feminists, blacks and other minorities, and gay and lesbian groups, among others. That there was and still is racism, sexism, and intolerance on campuses is true, just as all these exist in society in general. That racism, sexism, and intolerance should be overcome is clear. However, not everything said and done in the name of overcoming them is justified. Being on the side of the oppressed does not mean that all their claims are valid and justifiable. Nor does it mean that oppressing others is in turn justified.

The claims that members of the majority cannot be oppressed or that attempts at silencing them is justified because their message is necessarily biased cannot be adequately defended. Academic freedom should defend all researchers and teachers in their pursuit of knowledge. Silencing any academically defensible position on nonacademic grounds undermines the ability of any individual faculty member, faculty members in general, and colleges and universities to fulfill their mission. Majority views should not be silenced any more than minority views. Being either a majority or minority view is no guarantee that it is a correct view. That is the reason behind academic freedom. Any action that fosters fear in pursuing one's research and teaching is a betrayal of the institution and its reason for existence.

One difficulty is that the line between academic freedom and the legal enforcement of certain basic rights—such as the right to be free from sexual harassment—is becoming blurred. There are isolated horror stories of faculty members being sued for comments made in class or for raising uncomfortable issues. There is little evidence of the success of such suits or data on their numbers, although there is anecdotal evidence of some chilling effect on teaching. It is difficult to gauge how extensive or how serious this is. If the effect is that teachers now make fewer off-the-cuff remarks that are sexist or racist, that is surely a gain and not a loss. If the effect is that faculty members avoid controversial topics in teaching or research, that is surely a loss for faculty, students, and society in general.

Academic freedom is not a tenable doctrine if it applies only either to those holding orthodox views or to those whose views are politically correct (however either of those is defined) or only to any other group. For any attempt to so limit the notion presupposes that someone or some group can decide what is true or acceptable or correct, and that is precisely what academic freedom aims to preclude. Yet not every view must be allowed a full hearing at a college or university. Someone who claims that the earth is flat deserves a hearing only if there are good arguments that the person can mount in its defense and some plausible interpretation of all the facts and data that should be accounted for. A simplistic statement that all the data are inventions of charlatans, that pictures from space satellites are fabrications, that round-the-world air trips are a hoax, and so on, will not bear the weight of evidence that is required. And a claim that requiring evidence is oppressive and a power play will again not bear the weight that a reasonable argument demands. It is appropriate that people in the various disciplines consider for positions only those who have shown they have mastered the basics of that area, and if they attack the foundations of a discipline or area, that they do so from a position of knowledge of that discipline and not from ignorance of it.

The claims of attempted indoctrination of students by faculty is a different issue if made by the student and not by another faculty member. Indoctrination is not protected by academic freedom because it violates the freedom of the student to learn. But teaching what one believes about the subject matter of a course is not in itself indoctrination. Faculty cannot and should not try to force the belief of students. The claim that if they are bombarded on all sides and in all their classes with a certain ideological point of view, they are in fact being indoctrinated, is a broadside claim that needs defense. It is not indoctrination if the appeal is to argument, evidence, and reasons for a position and if the right to question and challenge is preserved and encouraged.

The claims of intellectual oppression, of silencing free inquiry, of rejecting views because of the person who propounds them rather than because of their intrinsic merits or defects—all are claims that require proof, arguments, evidence. Not every claim of injustice is defensible. Not every rejection of an idea is automatically a result of prejudice or a power play. To claim otherwise is itself to make a statement that does not carry its validity on its face and that requires justification. The chance to make the case is included in the conception of academic freedom. Just as academic freedom itself requires a defense, so those who would attack it require reasons and arguments. Those who attack it from within, however, cannot expect to enjoy its protection for themselves if they are successful in depriving others of it.

II. Hate Speech

Related to so-called political correctness is the issue of hate speech on campus and the various regulations and codes that some colleges and universities have adopted in an attempt to control it.[3] I am concerned here not with the wisdom or lack thereof of such codes in general or of any particular code. Nor am I concerned with the issue of free speech. There are limits on the right of freedom of speech, but these do not protect people from insult. Threats of harm are another matter, because people have a right to be free from harm. They have a moral right to be free from insult because they have a right to respect. Legally that right gives way to freedom of speech, which is considered a more important right. Freedom of speech encompasses the right within limits to act unethically toward another in speech.

The argument against hate speech is both that it offends those against whom it is addressed and that it creates a hostile atmosphere that is not conducive to learning and so violates a student's freedom to learn. The latter is surely the case if people are subjected to racial epithets directed at them or painted on their dorm room doors (which is vandalism as well as a not-so-veiled threat of harm). Such action is not protected by academic freedom. Whether rules against epithets violate freedom of speech is a legal matter. Private universities may make their own rules, since freedom of speech laws prevent government interference and so apply to state but not to private institutions. [4] Whether speech codes are desirable is another matter. As a moral matter, hate speech should not be countenanced on a campus, and should be morally condemned. But how broadly or narrowly hate speech is to be construed is a difficult issue. Some questions of race and the extent to which there should or should not be public policies of one kind or another are political and are appropriately matters for public debate. Not all discussions of race are hate speech, even if some people find some of the things said in such discussions to be offensive or insulting.

We can distinguish the arenas of speech on campus. In the classroom academic freedom does not protect personal insults or abusive or profane speech by the teacher or by students. It is within the competence of the institution and of the faculty member in charge of a class to insist on basic common courtesy, civility, and mutual respect. This in no way violates either academic freedom or freedom of speech, for in the latter case such speech is disruptive and creates an atmosphere ill suited to the freedom to learn. But academic freedom protects the right of teachers and of students to defend or argue for certain public policy positions or for the ethical justifiability of certain controversial practices in appropriate classes at appropriate times. In a class discussion on abortion neither pro-lifers nor pro-choicers should be kept from presenting a view. Neither those in favor of gay rights nor those who oppose them should have a privileged position. Neither those who attack Marxist economics nor those who defend it should be silenced. Neither those who argue for special privileges for the previously and still oppressed minorities nor those who argue against them should be given preference. What a teacher can insist on and what students can expect is that arguments be presented in a proper context and that appropriate rules of evidence and levels of argument be adhered to and imposed.

Yet these restrictions within the classroom do not apply automatically on the campus as a whole. Freedom of speech allows people to make judgments and express opinions without being able to defend them. Students can be held to a higher level of discourse in the classroom than outside of it. Nonetheless, even outside of class it is appropriate to expect all members of the academic community to treat each other as worthy of basic respect and to avoid speech that creates an atmosphere inimical to learning. Sexual and racial harassment may be properly prohibited not only to the extent that they are illegal but to the extent that they interfere with the academic enterprise and the institution's academic mission.

May a university group invite anyone it pleases to give a public lecture on campus? Restrictions on hate speech apply to invited speakers as well as to members of the academic community itself. A known rabble-rouser or hate monger has no claim on academic freedom, nor does the group that invites such a person. On the other hand, controversial speakers with academic credentials or political speakers, while having no right to being invited, have a right to present their views once invited. Preventing their speaking is a violation of the academic freedom to learn, even if their views are repugnant to some on campus. The appropriate response is to boycott the lecture or to reply in some proper form—letters to the newspaper, a counter lecture, or something similar.

Some speech codes have been tested in court. Some have been found wanting; others have been upheld. The legal status of such codes does not coincide with judgments about them made from the point of view of academic freedom, since freedom of speech, as we have seen, is a broader concept. Whether codes are ethically defensible and whether they are practically implementable depends of course on their specific content. No matter what that content, the penalty for violation need not be dismissal of either faculty or student, and rarely is. A faculty member guilty of using racial epithets in class, of subjecting his or her students to verbal abuse, or of otherwise mistreating members of the class can be called to account for unprofessional behavior with or without speech codes. Both faculty and students may be reprimanded for improper conduct or behavior, verbal or otherwise. There usually is a wide range of penalties available short of dismissal. The penalty appropriately suits the gravity of the offense, and may include dismissal even of tenured professors.

The greatest difficulty with speech codes is that they sanction some type of prior censorship and so set a precedent for restricting speech of other kinds. What any institution must weigh is the harm that can be prevented by instituting such codes and the harm that they may allow down the line. Censuring hate speech is always appropriate. Speaking out against it and refusing to associate with those who practice it are appropriate moral responses. Not all unethical activity must be made illegal or be restricted by rules. Even protecting such speech does not mean that anyone must listen to it. The rules of civility can be fostered and encouraged and hate speech discouraged without speech codes. Whether they produce more harm than good is a function of what they say, how much harm they actually prevent, and how much danger to free speech and to academic freedom they potentially or actually involve.

III. Two Legal Cases

Two fairly recent cases, both from City College of the City University of New York, illustrate some of the issues in academic freedom, as well as its relation to the law. The first is the case of *Levin v. Harleston,* and the second is *Jeffries v. Harleston.*

Levin v. Harleston[5]

Michael Levin was a tenured professor of philosophy at City College of the City University of New York. The case stems from three of his published writings. The first is a letter to the editor of the *New York Times* (January 11, 1987) in which he corrects the use in an editorial ("Fear of Blacks, Fear of Crime") of a principle of justice enunciated by Harvard Professor John Rawls. Levin concludes the letter by asking: "Is discrimination against innocent whites a tolerable price for insuring jobs for blacks while discriminatory inconvenience for innocent blacks is too high a price for reducing the risk of murder for white store owners?" [6] The second publication is a book review that appeared in the 1988 issue of the Australian journal *Quadrant.* In it Levin argues against a position taken by E. D. Hirsch in *Cultural Literacy.* In making his argument Levin states that ". . . there is now quite solid evidence that . . . the average black is significantly less intelligent than the average white" and uses that to argue against one of Hirsch's proposals.[7] The third publication is a letter published in the *Proceedings of the American Philosophical Association* (January 1990) concerning the Association's survey of blacks and minority members in philosophy. Levin states that "It has been amply confirmed over the last several decades that, on average, blacks are significantly less intelligent than whites."[8] He concludes that it is not surprising that only 2 percent of philosophers are black, even though blacks constitute 12 percent of the population.

On the basis of these publications the president and the dean of City College and a number of faculty members and students there accused Professor Levin of being a racist. Groups of students on several occasions disrupted his class, documents attached to his door were burned, and he received two death threats. The president of the college, Barnard W. Harleston, authorized a "shadow section" of Professor Levin's required Philosophy 101 course, and Dean Paul Sherwin sent students enrolled in the class a letter stating that

"Professor Levin has expressed controversial views on such issues as race, feminism and homosexuality. . . . Taking into consideration the rights and sensitivities of all concerned, and wishing to permit informed freedom of choice for students . . . I have in this instance decided to open a second [section]. . . ."[9] President Harleston requested that the college's Faculty Senate appoint a committee to investigate allegations of racism with respect to Professor Levin. After the Senate chair refused to do so, the president appointed an ad hoc committee "to review the question of when speech both in and outside the classroom may go beyond the protection of academic freedom or become conduct unbecoming a member of the faculty or some other form of misconduct" and "to specifically review information concerning Professor Levin . . . and what the College response should be."[10] "Conduct unbecoming a member of the faculty" is grounds for dismissal of tenured faculty members.

Professor Levin claimed that the actions of the president and dean violated his academic freedom and had a "chilling effect" on his ability to pursue his research, publication, and lecturing for fear of what the administration may do to him. He turned to the courts. They supported his position and after appeal ruled that "the commencement, or threat thereof, of disciplinary proceedings against Professor Levin predicated solely upon his protected speech outside the classroom violates his First Amendment rights"[11] and that the college was enjoined from creating or maintaining "shadow" or "parallel" sections of his classes.

The case clearly demonstrates the danger to academic freedom from within by the administration, faculty, and students. No one challenged the accuracy of any of the statements Professor Levin made. No one attempted to refute the claims he made about studies of the IQ of whites or blacks, and no one challenged the arguments he put forth. Rather they denounced his conclusions as racist. Moreover, none of Professor Levin's own students complained about his class. There were no complaints that he expressed racist views in class, that he was unfair to any student, or that because of his beliefs he treated black students differently from white students.

The president, the dean, and some students not in his class simply took the position expressed in these three publications as proof that he was racist, and then extrapolated to the conclusion that being racist he must act in a prejudiced way toward his students, and was therefore unfit to teach. There was no attempt to present the missing pieces of this argument.

The actions of the president, dean, and some students violated the academic freedom of Professor Levin. But there is more to learn from the case.

A number of faculty showed that they understood their responsibility with respect to academic freedom and took what action they could to defend it. The chair of the Philosophy Department resisted establishing a shadow section of

Professor Levin's class, forcing the dean to do so. The Faculty Senate refused to establish the committee to investigate Professor Levin that the president requested because of the "chilling effect" it would have. Forty-three academics from a variety of institutions wrote to Dean Sherwin protesting the "increasing encroachments on the academic freedom of Professor Michael Levin."[12] Their efforts, unfortunately, were not enough.

The defense given for their actions by the president and dean is also instructive, since they argued against Professor Levin in the name of the academic freedom of students. In defense of the students who disrupted Professor Levin's course the president said, "The students have academic freedom as well, and their academic freedom is protected."[13] Yet in no way does student academic freedom give them a right to shout and chant so as to prevent a teacher in a class in which they are not enrolled from teaching. Nor did the students consider what their actions implied. If they were permitted in the name of academic freedom to disrupt whatever course taught by a teacher they did not like, so would all other groups. Those who oppose abortion would have the right to disrupt the classes of those teachers who support it, and those students who support abortion could disrupt the classes of those who oppose it, regardless of what course the respective teacher was teaching. Any other group for whatever reason could do likewise to any other teacher. The result clearly would be anarchy, and teaching and learning would come to a halt.

The dean claimed that his principal concern was that students be permitted "freedom of choice" and that their sensitivities be protected. But he did not bother to find out whether the students who took the course felt that their freedom had been restricted or their sensitivities violated. There is no evidence of either. The claim of the defense of the academic freedom of students was an excuse for, not a defense of, the actions he took. The use of nice-sounding principles to defend unethical actions is a misuse of those principles, and in this case was a misuse of the principle of academic freedom.

It is noteworthy that Professor Levin sought and obtained the protection of the law to prevent his being fired. But his academic freedom was clearly abridged without his being fired, and the case shows that firing is not the only threat to a faculty member's academic freedom, although it is the most drastic.

The protection Professor Levin received from the law was based on the First and Fourteenth Amendments, and so his case illustrates the legal connection between academic freedom and tenure on the one hand and these amendments on the other. Neither amendment, of course, mentions academic freedom or tenure. In his opinion Judge J. Conboy cites U.S.C.A. Const. Amends. 5, 14: "A long standing, historic 'understanding' officially promulgated and fostered by state college, that all tenured and nontenured teachers would be free of thought control by university or college officials and administrators both inside and outside the classroom, had been guaranteed and made an inherent part of tenure at the college and thus was a protected property right," and U.S.C.A. Const. Amends. 1, 14: "Academic tenure is more than the right to receive a paycheck, and must encompass the right to pursue scholarship wherever it may lead, the freedom to inquire, to study, and to evaluate without deadening limits of orthodoxy or the corrosive atmosphere of suspicion and distrust." The courts have come to assimilate academic freedom under freedom of speech and tenure under property rights. From a legal perspective these are ways by which the courts have been able to protect both academic freedom and tenure. But for ethical and other purposes it is possible and often useful to keep freedom of speech distinct from academic freedom and tenure distinct from simply a property right.

Professor Levin was forced to seek protection from the law because the mechanisms in place at City College failed to protect his academic freedom. The ad hoc committee that investigated him did not afford him any due process, did not inform him of the charges against him, and gave him no opportunity to rebut or refute them. Although some members of the faculty and the Faculty Senate did not simply follow the lead of the administration, there was no internal process available to him to get a fair hearing or protect him against the administration and student disruptions. That failure is an institutional one, and underlines the importance of faculty governance mechanisms in the protection of academic freedom.

Jeffries v. Harleston[14]

The second case also took place at City College under the administration of President Harleston. But the issue is almost the mirror image of the Levin case.

Leonard Jeffries was a tenured professor and chair of the Black Studies Department at City College, a position he had held since 1972.[15] On July 20, 1991 he made a keynote speech off-campus at the Empire Black Arts Cultural Festival in Albany. His talk was primarily about bias in the public school curriculum and the reforms needed. During the speech, he attacked individuals and made derogatory statements about Jews. He claimed Jews had a history of oppressing blacks, blamed "rich Jews" for financing the slave trade, and claimed that "Jews and Mafia figures in Hollywood had conspired to 'put together a system of destruction of black people' by portraying them negatively in films."[16] The speech, which had been carried on TV, was reported in New York newspapers and provoked a strong reaction among the general public, City College alumni, and some of the trustees of City University. On August 8, 1991 President Harleston wrote a letter to the faculty saying that Jeffries's speech contained "clear statements of bigotry and anti-semitism."[17]

On September 12, 1991, the president requested the provost to review whether Professor Jeffries could, after his speech and the reactions it provoked, continue to act effectively as chair of the department. The review was completed in early October and concluded that he was performing "at least as efficiently as over the last ten years."[18] Nonetheless, on October 28 the president recommended to the Board of Trustees that they reappoint Professor Jeffries as chair for only one year, rather than the customary three-year period. On March 23, 1992 the board appointed a new chair to take over as of July 1, when Professor Jeffries's one-year term expired. In June Professor Jeffries sued, claiming that by denying him his remaining two years as chair, the university had violated his rights under the First and Fourteenth Amendments. As a result of a trial, a jury found on May 18, 1993, that the university had indeed denied him his additional two-year term primarily because of his speech, and that he should be reinstated for the full two years. The finding was upheld upon appeal.

The case is interesting for a number of reasons. Academic tenure was not at issue. Academic tenure does not cover administrative positions, and the college administrators did not threaten to dismiss Professor Jeffries from his teaching position. They might have, as we shall see, but they did not. Academic freedom was pertinent, but the courts decided on the basis of freedom of speech, not on the basis of academic freedom. The court noted that "retaliation against a faculty member for exercise of his free speech rights, in the absence of any actual interference in the functioning of the University, is prohibited by law."[19] The jury as well as the appellate court concluded on the basis of the evidence presented that Jeffries was appointed as chair for only one year rather than three because of the speech he made. That was inappropriate, even though a number of his remarks were "vulgar, repugnant and reprehensible."[20]

Nonetheless, Judge Conboy in his opinion notes, "This need not have been the case if the University had offered convincing, firsthand proof at trial that either the consequences of the speech disrupted the campus, classes, administration, fund-raising or faculty relations, or that the professor had turned his classroom into a forum for bizarre, shallow, racist and incompetent pseudo-thinking and pseudo-teaching."[21] Later he adds, "had the University adequately established that the professor, whose teaching has after all been tolerated for twenty years, conducts his classes or his Chairmanship in a racist, anti-semitic or incompetent manner, we would not order him to be reinstated. . . . [T]he University is in no way restricted from monitoring the Professor's classes and his on-campus stewardship of the Chairmanship, and . . . he may be removed from either if a good cause basis for finding abusive or indecent behavior is adequately established."[22] Professor Jeffries is reported on

October 18, 1991 to have threatened to "kill" a reporter sent from the *Harvard Crimson,* Elliot Morgan, if the reporter revealed the content of the interview in which Jeffries made disparaging remarks about other faculty and homosexuals. Later in October he sent a memo to the dean "declaring 'war' on the faculty."[23] A student described theories espoused by Professor Jeffries in his classes, including a theory that "white people are genetically inferior 'ice' people, and black people are 'sun' people."[24] The court indicates that the university should take "disciplinary action against a professor who engages in a systematic pattern of racist, anti-semitic, sexist, and homophobic remarks during class" or who teaches "patently absurd and wholly fallacious theories in class."[25] Clearly, not all speech is protected in the classroom by the First Amendment, any more than it is by the doctrine of academic freedom.

The court appropriately did not "enter debate on relative qualifications of professor and his replacement"[26] but it notes that "the University inexplicably and perhaps cowardly, chose to ignore these improprieties" adding, "We observe, regrettably but necessarily, that the students of CUNY and the people of New York State are entitled to a higher standard of decision-making on the part of its public officials."[27] In effect the administration had an ethical responsibility to take action against faculty members who use their classrooms to make racist remarks, teach unfounded theories, and otherwise abuse their authority in the classroom. The tragedy is that, as the court notes, some administrations are cowardly and take no action. At fault is not academic freedom or tenure or freedom of speech, but administrations that tolerate such teachers and the faculties that often ignore the actions of their colleagues.

Implications of *Levin* and *Jeffries*

The difference in President Harleston's reaction to the two cases is significant. Professor Levin cites some studies according to which, on average, blacks have lower IQs than whites. President Harleston considers this evidence of racism of which students should be informed and from which students should be protected, and is concerned enough to wish to have Professor Levin dismissed from his position. Professor Jeffries says that blacks are superior to whites (ice people) and cites no studies. He also makes anti-Semitic remarks. President Harleston's reaction is not to warn students (even though there is some evidence Professor Jeffries makes such remarks in as well as out of class) nor to seek to dismiss him, but to reduce his term as departmental chair from three years to one. There seems to be a double standard operating. Remarks against blacks are racist, even when based on some evidence or studies. Remarks against whites are not, even when no evidence is cited. Students must be warned and protected from remarks that they may not like if the students are black (or women or homosexual). They need no warning or protection from remarks they may not like if they are white (or male or straight).

This is part of a syndrome found in many colleges and universities and associated with the label "political correctness." White males and their views are dominant in the culture and therefore need no protection. Minority views are marginalized and so need protection. The latter can only flower if protected. The former will thrive no matter what. The double standard, it is claimed, simply helps rectify the imbalance that in fact exists. The extension would be to add that truth in advertising requires that students be warned of racist or sexist attitudes of white males and their classes, but not of the racist or sexist attitudes of classes in Afro-American studies or feminism, because in the latter the bias is clear from its presence in the program or department, while in the former it is not.

This seems to have been President Harleston's implicit position, even though the court mused about whether his failure to seriously investigate Professor Jeffries's conduct of his classes was a failure of nerve, which the judge termed cowardice.

Truth in advertising is surely appropriate in courses, but racism, sexism, and other kinds of unjust discrimination are not, whether the target be women or men, blacks or whites. The sensitivities of students deserve consideration when they are individually addressed. On the other hand, their sensitivities are not the dominant consideration in the presentation of course material based on evidence. Some students may not wish to know there were corrupt church officials; others may not wish to learn about slavery; others may prefer not to hear about evolution. Teachers have no obligation to avoid these topics because some students may be offended by their discussion. In fact, if students are never exposed to new ideas, some of which may challenge their biases or prejudices or preconceived ideas, one can wonder about the quality of the education they are receiving. Enabling the faculty to pursue, publish, and teach the results of research, even when the results are unpopular or contrary to commonly held opinion, is the purpose of academic freedom.

Feminism, black studies, critical legal theory, and other views have gradually found a place in the curricula of many colleges and universities because they add a new perspective and challenge orthodox thinking. A liberal university does not impose orthodoxy in thought. But it does have one criterion to which it must adhere: respect for standards of truth, adequacy, facts, reason, and theory. Not everything and not every voice deserves to be in a university. Alchemy is not present; nor is astrology; nor are voodooism, flat earth theorists, and others whose views have been shown to be sufficiently poorly supported by evidence, facts, reasoning, and theory so as to deserve no place at a university. If a university in fact adopts the view, implicitly or explicitly, that there is no reason for including or excluding any view, then society will rightly be suspicious and conclude that the university deserves no special autonomous status or that its teachers deserve no special protection such as academic freedom.

The responsibility of a university that wishes to protect academic freedom is to allow all within it to pursue their research on equal grounds. Critical legal theorists seek to expose the injustice of the existing legal structure. They pursue their research where it takes them and their conclusions stand or fall on the evidence and arguments they produce. Postmodernist critics attack Enlightenment ideals and pursue their research where it takes them. Feminists and faculty in Afro-American thought do likewise. All of this is part of what academic freedom allows and encourages. Academic freedom does not render any discipline or position immune from criticism, including the new disciplines and views that are critical of entrenched ones. To claim special privilege for any view or discipline is implicitly to give up the notion of academic freedom.

President Harleston seems to have reacted to pressure—public pressure and student pressure. His actions do not reveal any firm sense of what academic freedom is. Part of the present problem in colleges and universities is that what is true of President Harleston is true as well of many other administrators, faculty, and students. Academic freedom is rarely discussed except in the context of a threatened or actual firing of a tenured faculty member. It is not too much to say that colleges and universities have an obligation to promote such discussion and to work out what it means in the contemporary context. If it is no longer justified because there is no knowledge, pretending that there is would be deceitful and hypocritical. The general public as well as legislators hear enough about the internal disputes concerning the status of knowledge that they are rightly concerned. The responsibility of the university is to explain and justify its claims to academic freedom in this context.

IV. Academic Freedom in a Technological Age

The defense of academic freedom that I have presented so far, it might be objected, is a defense of a university in an era that is passing. Universities may once have been institutions that valued research, teaching, and service. But in the contemporary period, with the cost of education so dramatically high, students, their parents, legislators, and taxpayers are using a different measuring rod to evaluate colleges and universities. That rod is whether the students are getting their money's worth. College education has been seen as a way to achieve a better life. If that meant greater enjoyment of culture as well as higher pay, that was fine. But if higher education does not produce graduates who can find and keep good jobs, then the value of such education becomes suspect, and it does not seem worth the high cost it involves.

The present mood of many of the university's constituencies, including many members of the faculty, is to question the traditional aim, mission, and point of the university. The emphasis on teaching is a direct correlate of the concern about jobs for graduates. Research and the development of knowledge, just as liberal education for the personal development of students, may be acceptable, but both are seen as secondary to training students for positions. Teachers should teach first, and what they should teach should have practical application. Debates about postmodernism and questions about the possibility of attaining knowledge are only additional reasons to question the value of a college education and of whether and what students actually learn.

To this is added the recent emphasis on technology as a means of education and of the university in cyberspace, in which the traditional campus may no longer be necessary and a cadre of superstar teachers may produce their classes in multimedia format for transmission to as many students as sign up to receive it via electronic means.

Is the notion of academic freedom, tied as it is to a certain conception of the university and society, really obsolete and a leftover from a bygone age?

The view of the university as simply an extension of the teaching that takes place in high school is a common one, as is the view that the primary aim of the university is to prepare students for jobs that pay well. The absence of adequate jobs for all college graduates is not the fault of the colleges and universities, and is ironically an argument for the kind of education that colleges and universities can give and especially for what is generally referred to as a liberal education.

A liberal education in one sense is an education that frees the student. It frees students *from* dogmatic chains of thought and preconceptions by forcing them to confront their preconceptions and values, to question them, and to test them. But education is also liberal in that it frees students *to* do what they were not able to do previously. Learning to read opens up a whole area of life that is closed to the illiterate. Learning mathematics makes accessible the world of science, among other things. Learning a foreign language opens up a culture closed to those without that language. Studying literature opens up the world of human experience and emotions and beauty in a new way. Studying history opens up the human past for insight into human tragedy and triumph. Studying philosophy gives students tools to analyze their beliefs in every area, especially those fundamental to reasoning in general, and to questions of truth and of values. Knowledge of computers and technology opens up a whole new host of possibilities.

The point of a college education should not be simply to prepare students for immediate jobs, for that is too short term a goal. The technology that engineers are taught in engineering school, for instance, can be expected to be obsolete in seven years. An education today more than ever must prepare students to learn on their own, to think critically, to use their imaginations, and to adapt quickly to new situations and new environments. Knowledge is increasing so quickly that no one can master it all, or even all that one needs in a particular discipline or area for the indefinite future. As the pace of change increases, the need is to teach students to keep up with advances on their own. Producing students of this type requires teachers of this type. And since a key ingredient is an inquiring mind that is not bound by orthodox beliefs, academic freedom for both teacher-researcher and student is more important than ever. If the general population or legislators or even some faculty members fail to see this, then the colleges and universities need to educate them to the true purpose of these institutions and their important role in the contemporary world. What is surprising is the general failure of these institutions even to try such an educational process, indicating a lack of clear vision on their part or a failure of nerve or both.

The vision of the future university as perhaps very different from the present university is not far-fetched, and in some ways we can already see it taking shape. But as it develops, academic freedom becomes more important, not less so. The autonomy of the university is crucial in the process. For just as the autonomy of the university, based on the authority of the knowledge of those within it, has appropriately determined what the university is today, so those with knowledge are the best placed and the best source for determining what the institution should be like in the future. Those outside the university— the general public, legislators, boards of trustees—may have ideas of what they would like to see universities become, and their views, ideas, and visions should be considered. But in each case they are driven not by knowledge of the university from the inside or from within any discipline, and hence they do not have the epistemic authority that should be central in designing the university.

There are three temptations of which those both in and out of the university ought to be aware, and which they should resist. One temptation is to pursue only or primarily that work and those problems that it is possible to pursue by computers or technology and to ignore or downplay those that are not amenable to such pursuit. This is to let technology dominate the investigator, rather than the other way around. I am not sure that Copernicus and others would have given up the geocentric view of the universe if powerful computers were available in those days. For with good computers one could figure out all the epicycles needed to account for any observation and it would have made the heliocentric theory unnecessary. The latter gives us ease of calculation and simplicity. But the computer would have provided sufficient power to do the calculations such that simplicity might not have had much appeal. The temptation to pursue what can be done by technological means sometimes replaces the need to think imaginatively and creatively in certain directions. Soviet scientists became much better at conceptual problems in some areas than their counterparts in the West who had access to computers and who chose problems that the computers could solve.

Furthermore, there are many problems that the computer cannot solve. These include many philosophical problems, which must be solved before we use the computer, because they are presupposed by its use. The notion of instrumental reason and the primacy of analytical reason, for instance, are just two examples. Yet knowledge is not just data and not just processed data. It is information that is critically assimilated and unified into a whole. The danger of information overload is fragmentation of knowledge, loss of critical assessment, and the inability to synthesize and form coherent wholes. The result is a fragmentation of culture, of society, and of one's personality. Despite the rise of the multiversity, the ideal of a university as providing a coherent approach to knowledge is and will still be a viable ideal. Academic freedom is crucial to making possible challenges to an imposed use and possible abuse of technology in education as a substitute for other approaches to knowledge.

Technology may help us achieve our purposes but technology cannot supply our purposes for us. Technology or technologists or those mesmerized by it may seek to do just that, but we should see this as a temptation to be resisted. The end of the university is properly determined by those within it, and the autonomy of the university is necessary to allow them to do so based on the critical knowledge they possess.

The second temptation to be resisted is to do whatever is technologically possible. That is a technological imperative. We see this already in the fields of biology and medicine. There is a temptation to go that way in research in many areas, and it is a temptation that I believe must be resisted. When Joseph Weizenbaum suggested in *Computer Power and Human Reason*[28] that there were things that computers should not be made to do, he was considered by many of his computer science colleagues to have passed his peak and to have gone over the hill. But I believe he was right. Not everything that can be done should be done. The temptation takes many forms.

One form is what I shall call the myth of amoral technology. It says: technology is neither good nor bad. If it is possible, then someone will pursue it. It is hence both foolish and idle to attempt to place limits on where research in technology and technological development will go. Technology is not moral or immoral in itself, and hence it is a mistake to use that language with respect to it. It has a life of its own and will develop on its own. It will in turn affect what values people hold, and it will be the generator of values or provide the ambiance for the development of values. But in itself it is value free.

Like most myths this is only partly correct; it hides a portion of the truth, which should be brought to light. Technology is certainly not value free, and it certainly can be subjected to moral scrutiny—not only the uses to which it is put, but the development of certain technologies themselves.

There is a temptation to turn over to the computer responsibility for what is done or for what happens as a result of its use. "Blame the computer" is not an unheard phrase. Yet it is always human beings who are responsible for harm done by computers and for the uses to which computers and technology are put. The university must remain a place where the purposes and the direction of society are articulated and challenged, criticized when necessary, and championed when appropriate. The autonomy of the university and the academic freedom of those within it is essential if the technological imperative is to be assessed, evaluated, and when appropriate, resisted.

The university is and will be caught between two competing imperatives and two competing pushes and pulls. One is to prepare students for the technological world in which they will live. Unless we do so, we do them a disservice. The rise of technology may well produce two classes of people, two classes of society, two classes of nations—those that are technologically literate and advanced and can keep up with the growing changes and compete using them, and those that cannot. One job of the university is to produce those who can compete. The push will be toward keeping up, and toward developing and using technology. The cutting edge of knowledge will be to a large extent technologically linked and technologically driven. At the same time the division in society resulting from the rise of a technocratic elite is a danger that the university must articulate and help society work through and prevent. Universities are going to be part of the problem and they should also be part of the solution.

The other pull will be to fight the two temptations that I outlined. And fighting them will seem retrograde or Luddite. But it is not. The university should be a place where human purposes are examined, where human experience is remembered and utilized. I do not know how philosophy will be taught in the future, for instance. But I know of no central issue in philosophy that we yet know how to solve with computers or technologies, even though these are useful in a variety of ways in research and teaching. Philosophical problems are not amenable to being put into a computer and having it churn away and produce a solution. The human use of human beings should lead us to see that those problems that computers can solve should be so solved. But rather than using all one's time working on and with technology, one aim might be to free scholars, teachers, and students from those tasks so they can think and work on those problems not amenable to technological solution. The question of values is a central issue that is not solvable by computers or technology. The university of the future should continue to be the place where such issues are pursued because they cannot be solved technologically. Even more than that, the university might be the only haven for the consideration and pursuit of those problems, and they may not be pursued unless the university takes upon itself the task of bringing their consideration to the larger community and society, utilizing the mass communication media and the possibilities that computers and technology make possible.

Demagogues will certainly use technology. Those who dedicate their lives to the pursuit of truth and knowledge will have to learn to use the available tools effectively to offset the demagogues on a computer screen. In a technological age a sanctuary for the pursuit of knowledge independent of the control of the state is more important than ever.

What is the human use of human beings? That is not a question to ask computers or technology or technologists. That is a human problem par excellence. And that may well be the central problem for universities to pursue and ponder. It has traditionally been the question asked in the humanities. Seeking answers to it is necessary to make technology liberal and to keep society human.

The question of the use and development of technology has to be raised on campuses as well as in society, and serious thought and dialogue about values and the human use of human beings should be a component of any university-based initiative in the use and development of computers and technology. Although the technologized university will be different from the one we know, the perennial questions will remain. A proper complement to technology across the curriculum will be values across the curriculum. In the university of the future values without technology may well be impotent, but technology without values will be blind.

The cyber-university of the future is already available—we call it "distance learning." Will master teachers of the future be available to students at all universities, and will the universities be dispersed into the living rooms of whoever wishes to tap into their TV sets or computers or combination thereof? Under such conditions what is the role of academic freedom, and won't tenure simply be a commitment to teachers who may no longer be needed some years after they have been given tenure?

This is the third temptation: to think that a small group of electronically projected master teachers, plus lesser paid part-time and/or full-time teachers will make it possible to maintain the level of education presently offered at greatly reduced cost. The kind of thinking reflected in this view, which is already being pushed in some states, is a view of knowledge as building blocks that once formed are ready to hand. The master teacher knows how to put them together to make them accessible to students. Ordinary teachers will be available to give further explanation and to grade papers and examinations. This is to misconceive both knowledge and the university.

Computers and interactive technology—joined with TV and mass entertainment and culture—are changing the culture of the university and approaches to education that we cannot and should not ignore. With the advent of computers and the interconnectivity that is on the horizon, books may in the not too distant future no longer be the prime instrument for learning or teaching. Those brought up on books may be saddened to see them go, but the new age may be bookless, or essentially so. Libraries may well no longer be necessary, if we mean by that a place for the storage of paper products. Nor may textbooks be used. It will not be surprising to find courses that are interactive and multimedia, rather than based on a written text. And lectures in the traditional style may soon be a thing of the past. Already many teachers know they must do more than simply talk. Overheads are now widely used and overused. But multimedia presentations may not only be the way to get and keep a student's attention, they may also be better ways to teach. Many courses that are now taught by instructors will be replaced by computer-taught courses, in which the student works through modules on a computer as he or she masters various skills—whether they be mathematics, logic, biology, or any number of other subjects. Research in the humanities may change significantly, and dissertations will no longer be bound volumes, but may well be themselves multimedia presentations stored on a disk.

Teachers will not become obsolete, but funding for technology will compete seriously and often successfully with funding for professors or teaching assistants.

These trends and projections will change the university. But they will not change the need for faculty who pursue research or for teachers who will critically transfer knowledge to students and teach them by example as well as by interaction. Master teachers on TV or cyberspace may make some sense in introductory courses or in very specialized courses. They make less sense as a means of general education. And administrators or legislators or boards of trustees or governors should not force these approaches upon colleges and universities as money-saving panaceas. As part of the academic program, the extent to which such approaches should be instituted is for the most part an academic decision. As an academic decision, it belongs to the institution and ultimately to the faculty to make. The autonomy of the university and the academic freedom of the faculty are crucially at stake here. In making this decision there is some inherent conflict of interest that those outside are aware of, and their fears that the faculty may be tempted to defend their jobs at the expense of the good of the institution or of the students must certainly be allayed. That is where accountability comes in once again. But the decision on what the university is to become, just as the decision on what knowledge is, is clearly an academic decision. It is a decision that the university and its faculty must be allowed to make and that they must be able to explain and defend to outside constituencies. To pretend otherwise is to fail to understand what the university is and its real contribution to society.

The changes that are taking place do not show that either academic freedom or tenure is obsolete, even though their rationale should be stated so as to fit the changing conditions.

V. Critiques of Academic Freedom

Academic freedom, some claim, is really not necessary. The attacks resemble to some extent attacks on academic tenure. But three are worth considering briefly nonetheless.

First, the professors who are most at risk are the untenured professors, and for them in fact academic freedom is severely limited not by outside pressure but by the need to conform and please administrators and those who have tenure and who will decide whether they in turn receive it. Most of those who have it do not need it. Those who most need it do not have it.

Second, academic freedom is not necessary for most professors who do not do work or research that is in any way controversial. Their work, if not routine, is within the accepted parameters of their field. Moreover, in some fields academic freedom is not necessary because the field is sufficiently developed that there is little danger of its being successfully challenged.

Third, the theoretical justification of the good of society may sound nice in theory, but it does not actually function in practice.

The three critiques are related, as are their replies. I have already implied an answer to the first charge. Academic freedom is necessary for all faculty members. The institution and the tenured faculty should be in the forefront of defending the academic freedom of all, including the academic freedom of those without tenure. Their failure to do so threatens the academic freedom of all.

The second critique correctly notes that the research as well as the teaching of most professors is conventional, acceptable, often routine, and unlikely to offend anyone or to come to the attention of any but their fellow professional colleagues. This is the norm, and is not surprising. Disciplines are not always in turmoil, and challenges to the dominant position come only once in a while.

Nonetheless, the claim that for most professors academic freedom is not necessary ignores several realities. The first is the external threat to the autonomy of the university, which in turn threatens the independence and so the freedom of all the faculty members at an institution. If legislatures or boards of trustees or alumni or other groups enter into the internal workings of the university and preempt the faculty's authority in academic areas and in the decision-making process in which the faculty has proper sway and collegial governing authority, then the academic freedom of the faculty is significantly eroded. Without the claim to justifiable academic freedom it is not clear what will prevent such interference from taking place. The result may not threaten faculty members in certain disciplines, but it may. Courses may be prescribed or dropped, research allowed or prohibited; rules instituted governing the proportion of time to be spent in teaching, research, and service; decisions made as to which areas to strengthen and which to weaken, without faculty consultation or input. These are all threats to academic freedom that are not just theoretically possible, but threats that are being actively discussed and considered in a number of legislatures and some boardrooms.

The other consideration is that it is never clear where the next threat will come from and what it will be like. The McCarthy era, with its quest for Communists, looked in all areas—the arts, the humanities, the social sciences, the hard sciences. It did not make any difference what one's area was or what research one did. If one was identified as a Communist or Communist sympathizer, one's job could well be in jeopardy. That period is over. But there is no guarantee that some other threat to academic freedom may not emerge on the right or the left. One can imagine liberals facing the same fate as Communists, and scientists being attacked by extreme conservative religious groups. Humanists and social scientists are presently under attack from within and from without by those who have picked up on postmodern critiques of traditional disciplines.

There is no area that is immune. Nor is there any guarantee, unless there is real respect for academic freedom, that someone may not take offense at some published research or at some statement made by a faculty member.

Academic freedom is essential to a university that is to fulfill its rightful and traditional function in a free society. Tenure is an important corollary. The two go together, and it is difficult to image either one standing long without the other. Without academic freedom tenure loses its rationale. Without tenure, academic freedom loses its most important support.

The greatest danger to both academic freedom and tenure is that those within the university seem too often to forget what they are and what they are for. Those who do forget, or who never knew, are unlikely to know the responsibilities that go with them. And not knowing, they are unlikely to fulfill those responsibilities. Not knowing, they are also unable to articulate the rationale and defense of academic freedom and tenure to those outside the university, and to their friends and constituents.

The third critique is one that has some force, and the gap between theory and practice poses a potentially serious threat to academic freedom.

I have argued that there are ethical requirements that go along with academic freedom and tenure and that only if these are fulfilled are academic freedom and tenure defensible. To the extent that they are not fulfilled, academic freedom and tenure are rightfully under attack. Yet there is surprisingly little discussion of the ethical responsibilities of those within the university regarding academic freedom in general and in particular cases. There is great reluctance to criticize or call other faculty members to task. There is too little institutional self-critique. The result is increasingly vocal critique from the outside. There is a trend to look to the law rather than to ethics, civility, common sense, self-restraint, and self-governance. Law in some cases is a legitimate last resort. But it should be a *last* resort and not the norm to which one looks for guidance. Proper guidance comes from the nature of the institution and the task it is meant to fulfill. Academic tenure and academic freedom are distinctive because of the nature of the university and the role it plays in society. Colleges and universities that fail to defend and that fail to live up to the responsibilities entailed by academic tenure and academic freedom undermine them at their own peril. Without them society will suffer a great loss from which it will take at least a generation to recover.

Notes

1. See Edmund L. Pincoffs, ed., *The Concept of Academic Freedom* (Austin: University of Texas Press, 1975), especially John Searle's article, "Two Concepts of Academic Freedom."

2. See, for instance, "Debating Political Correctness," *Academe* (May–June, 1995), 8–15, which contains presentations by Elizabeth Fox-Genovese and Larry Scanlon. See also Paul Berman, ed., *Debating P.C.: The Controversy over Political Correctness on College Campuses* (New York: Dell 1992).

3. For three views on hate speech and what to do about it, see Cass R. Sunstein, "Liberalism, Speech Codes, and Related Problems," *Academe* (July–August 1993), 14–25; Patricia S. Mann, "Hate Speech, Freedom, and Discourse Ethics in the Academy," *Radical Philosophy of Law,* David S. Caudill, ed. (Atlantic Highlands, N.J.: Humanities Press, 1995); and Diana Tietjens Meyers, "Rights in Collision: A Non-Punitive, Compensatory Remedy for Abusive Speech," *Law and Philosophy,* 14, 2 (1995), 203–43.

4. For some of the legal aspects of freedom of speech see Sunstein, op. cit.

5. *Levin v. Harleston,* 752 F. Supp. 620 (S.D.N.Y. 1990), *Levin v. Harleston,* 770 F. Supp. 895 (S.D.N.Y. 1991), *affirmed in part and vacated in part,* 966 F. 2d 85 (2d Cir. 1992).

6. Cited in *Levin,* 770 F. Supp. at 901.

7. Id. at 902.

8. Id.

9. Id. at 908.

10. Id. at 911.

11. *Levin,* 966 F. 2d 85 at 90.

12. *Levin,* 770 F. Supp. at 908.

13. Id. at 904.

14. *Jeffries v. Harleston,* 828 F. Supp. 1066 (S.D.N.Y. 1993), *modified,* 21 F. 3d 1238 (2d Cir. 1994), *cert. granted and judgment vacated by* 115 S. Ct. 502 (1994).

15. *Jeffries,* 828 F. Supp. at 1072.

16. *Jeffries,* 21 F. 3d at 1242.

17. *Jeffries,* 828 F. Supp. at 1073.

18. Id. at 1074.

19. Id. at 1092.

20. Id. at 1069.

21. Id. at 1071.

22. Id. at 1072.

23. Id. at 1075–76.

24. Id. at 1097–98.

25. Id. at 1097.

26. Id. at 1070.

27. Id. at 1097.

28. Joseph Weizenbaum, *Computer Power and Human Reason: From Judgment to Calculation* (New York: Freeman, 1976).

Part II

Readings

1

1940 Statement of Principles on Academic Freedom and Tenure

With 1970 Interpretive Comments

In 1940, following a series of joint conferences begun in 1934, repre-
sentatives of the American Association of University Professors and
of the Association of American Colleges (now the Association of
American Colleges and Universities) agreed upon a restatement of
principles set forth in the 1925 Conference Statement on Academic
Freedom and Tenure. *This restatement is known to the profession as*
the 1940 Statement of Principles on Academic Freedom and Tenure.

The 1940 Statement *is printed below, followed by Interpretive Com-*
ments as developed by representatives of the American Association of
University Professors and the Association of American Colleges in
1969. The governing bodies of the two associations, meeting respec-
tively in November 1989 and January 1990, adopted several changes
in language in order to remove gender-specific references from the
original text.

The purpose of this statement is to promote public understanding and support
of academic freedom and tenure and agreement upon procedures to ensure
them in colleges and universities. Institutions of higher education are conducted for the common good and not to further the interest of either the individual teacher[1] or the institution as a whole. The common good depends upon
the free search for truth and its free exposition.

Academic freedom is essential to these purposes and applies to both teaching and research. Freedom in research is fundamental to the advancement
of truth. Academic freedom in its teaching aspect is fundamental for the

protection of the rights of the teacher in teaching and of the student to freedom in learning. It carries with it duties correlative with rights.[1][2]

Tenure is a means to certain ends; specifically: (1) freedom of teaching and research and of extramural activities, and (2) a sufficient degree of economic security to make the profession attractive to men and women of ability. Freedom and economic security, hence, tenure, are indispensable to the success of an institution in fulfilling its obligations to its students and to society.

Academic Freedom

(a) Teachers are entitled to full freedom in research and in the publication of the results, subject to the adequate performance of their other academic duties; but research for pecuniary return should be based upon an understanding with the authorities of the institution.

(b) Teachers are entitled to freedom in the classroom in discussing their subject, but they should be careful not to introduce into their teaching controversial matter which has no relation to their subject.[2] Limitations of academic freedom because of religious or other aims of the institution should be clearly stated in writing at the time of the appointment.[3]

(c) College and university teachers are citizens, members of a learned profession, and officers of an educational institution. When they speak or write as citizens, they should be free from institutional censorship or discipline, but their special position in the community imposes special obligations. As scholars and educational officers, they should remember that the public may judge their profession and their institution by their utterances. Hence they should at all times be accurate, should exercise appropriate restraint, should show respect for the opinions of others, and should make every effort to indicate that they are not speaking for the institution.[4]

Academic Tenure

After the expiration of a probationary period, teachers or investigators should have permanent or continuous tenure, and their service should be terminated only for adequate cause, except in the case of retirement for age, or under extraordinary circumstances because of financial exigencies.

In the interpretation of this principle it is understood that the following represents acceptable academic practice:

1. The precise terms and conditions of every appointment should be stated in writing and be in the possession of both institution and teacher before the appointment is consummated.

2. Beginning with appointment to the rank of full-time instructor or a higher rank,[5] the probationary period should not exceed seven years, including within this period full-time service in all institutions of higher education; but subject to the proviso that when, after a term of probationary service of more than three years in one or more institutions, a teacher is called to another institution, it may be agreed in writing that the new appointment is for a probationary period of not more than four years, even though thereby the person's total probationary period in the academic profession is extended beyond the normal maximum of seven years.[6] Notice should be given at least one year prior to the expiration of the probationary period if the teacher is not to be continued in service after the expiration of that period.[7]

3. During the probationary period a teacher should have the academic freedom that all other members of the faculty have.[8]

4. Termination for cause of a continuous appointment, or the dismissal for cause of a teacher previous to the expiration of a term appointment, should, if possible, be considered by both a faculty committee and the governing board of the institution. In all cases where the facts are in dispute, the accused teacher should be informed before the hearing in writing of the charges and should have the opportunity to be heard in his or her own defense by all bodies that pass judgment upon the case. The teacher should be permitted to be accompanied by an advisor of his or her own choosing who may act as counsel. There should be a full stenographic record of the hearing available to the parties concerned. In the hearing of charges of incompetence the testimony should include that of teachers and other scholars, either from the teacher's own or from other institutions. Teachers on continuous appointment who are dismissed for reasons not involving moral turpitude should receive their salaries for at least a year from the date of notification of dismissal whether or not they are continued in their duties at the institution.[9]

5. Termination of a continuous appointment because of financial exigency should be demonstrably *bona fide.*

1940 Interpretations

At the conference of representatives of the American Association of University Professors and of the Association of American Colleges on November

7–8, 1940, the following interpretations of the 1940 *Statement of Principles on Academic Freedom and Tenure* were agreed upon:

1. That its operation should not be retroactive.
2. That all tenure claims of teachers appointed prior to the endorsement should be determined in accordance with the principles set forth in the 1925 *Conference Statement on Academic Freedom and Tenure.*
3. If the administration of a college or university feels that a teacher has not observed the admonitions of paragraph (c) of the section on Academic Freedom and believes that the extramural utterances of the teacher have been such as to raise grave doubts concerning the teacher's fitness for his or her position, it may proceed to file charges under paragraph (a)(4) of the section on Academic Tenure. In pressing such charges the administration should remember that teachers are citizens and should be accorded the freedom of citizens. In such cases the administration must assume full responsibility, and the American Association of University Professors and the Association of American Colleges are free to make an investigation.

1970 Interpretive Comments

Following extensive discussions on the 1940 Statement of Principles on Academic Freedom and Tenure *with leading educational associations and with individual faculty members and administrators, a joint committee of the AAUP and the Association of American Colleges met during 1969 to reevaluate this key policy statement. On the basis of the comments received, and the discussions that ensued, the joint committee felt the preferable approach was to formulate interpretations of the* Statement *in terms of the experience gained in implementing and applying the* Statement *for over thirty years and of adapting it to current needs.*

The committee submitted to the two associations for their consideration the following "Interpretive Comments." These interpretations were adopted by the Council of the American Association of University Professors in April 1970 and endorsed by the Fifty-sixth Annual Meeting as Association policy.

In the thirty years since their promulgation, the principles of the 1940 *Statement of Principles on Academic Freedom and Tenure* have undergone a substantial amount of refinement. This has evolved through a variety of processes, including customary acceptance, understandings mutually arrived at between institutions and professors or their representatives, investigations and reports by the American Association of University Professors, and formulations of statements by that association either alone or in conjunction with the Association of American Colleges. These comments represent the attempt of the two associations, as the original sponsors of the 1940 *Statement,* to formulate the most important of these refinements. Their incorporation here as Interpretive Comments is based upon the premise that the 1940 *Statement* is not a static code but a fundamental document designed to set a framework of norms to guide adaptations to changing times and circumstances.

Also, there have been relevant developments in the law itself reflecting a growing insistence by the courts on due process within the academic community which parallels the essential concepts of the 1940 *Statement;* particularly relevant is the identification by the Supreme Court of academic freedom as a right protected by the First Amendment. As the Supreme Court said in *Keyishian v. Board of Regents* 385 U.S. 589 (1967), "Our Nation is deeply committed to safeguarding academic freedom, which is of transcendent value to all of us and not merely to the teachers concerned. That freedom is therefore a special concern of the First Amendment, which does not tolerate laws that cast a pall of orthodoxy over the classroom."

The numbers refer to the designated portion of the 1940 *Statement* on which interpretive comment is made.

1. The Association of American Colleges and the American Association of University Professors have long recognized that membership in the academic profession carries with it special responsibilities. Both associations either separately or jointly have consistently affirmed these responsibilities in major policy statements, providing guidance to professors in their utterances as citizens, in the exercise of their responsibilities to the institution and to students, and in their conduct when resigning from their institution or when undertaking government-sponsored research. Of particular relevance is the *Statement on Professional Ethics,* adopted in 1966 as Association policy. (A revision, adopted in 1987, was published in *Academe: Bulletin of the AAUP* 73 [July–August 1987]: 49.)

2. The intent of this statement is not to discourage what is "controversial." Controversy is at the heart of the free academic inquiry which the entire statement is designed to foster. The passage serves to underscore the need for teachers to avoid persistently intruding material which has no relation to their subject.

3. Most church-related institutions no longer need or desire the departure from the principle of academic freedom implied in the 1940 *Statement,* and we do not now endorse such a departure.

4. This paragraph is the subject of an interpretation adopted by the sponsors of the 1940 *Statement* immediately following its endorsement which reads as follows:

If the administration of a college or university feels that a teacher has not observed the admonitions of paragraph (c) of the section on Academic Freedom and believes that the extramural utterances of the teacher have been such as to raise grave doubts concerning the teacher's fitness for his or her position, it may proceed to file charges under paragraph (a)(4) of the section on Academic Tenure. In pressing such charges the administration should remember that teachers are citizens and should be accorded the freedom of citizens. In such cases the administration must assume full responsibility, and the American Association of University Professors and the Association of American Colleges are free to make an investigation.

Paragraph (c) of the section on Academic Freedom in the 1940 *Statement* should also be interpreted in keeping with the 1964 "Committee A Statement on Extramural Utterances" (*AAUP Bulletin* 51 [1965]: 29), which states *inter alia:* "The controlling principle is that a faculty member's expression of opinion as a citizen cannot constitute grounds for dismissal unless it clearly demonstrates the faculty member's unfitness for his or her position. Extramural utterances rarely bear upon the faulty member's fitness for the position. Moreover, a final decision should take into account the faculty member's entire record as a teacher and scholar."

Paragraph V of the *Statement on Professional Ethics* also deals with the nature of the "special obligations" of the teacher. The paragraph reads as follows:

As members of their community, professors have the rights and obligations of other citizens. Professors measure the urgency of other obligations in the light of their responsibilities to their subject, to their students, to their profession, and to their institution. When they speak or act as private persons they avoid creating the impression of speaking or acting for their college or university. As citizens engaged in a profession that depends upon freedom for its health and integrity, professors have a particular obligation to promote conditions of free inquiry and to further public understanding of academic freedom.

Both the protection of academic freedom and the requirements of academic responsibility apply not only to the full-time probationary and the tenured teacher, but also to all others, such as part-time faculty and teaching assistants, who exercise teaching responsibilities.

5. The concept of "rank of full-time instructor or a higher rank" is intended to include any person who teaches a full-time load regardless of the teacher's specific title.[3]

6. In calling for an agreement "in writing" on the amount of credit given for a faculty member's prior service at other institutions, the *Statement* furthers the general policy of full understanding by the professor of the terms and conditions of the appointment. It does not necessarily follow that a profes-

sor's tenure rights have been violated because of the absence of a written agreement on this matter. Nonetheless, especially because of the variation in permissible institutional practices, a written understanding concerning these matters at the time of appointment is particularly appropriate and advantageous to both the individual and the institution.[4]

7. The effect of this subparagraph is that a decision on tenure, favorable or unfavorable, must be made at least twelve months prior to the completion of the probationary period. If the decision is negative, the appointment for the following year becomes a terminal one. If the decision is affirmative, the provisions in the 1940 *Statement* with respect to the termination of service of teachers or investigators after the expiration of a probationary period should apply from the date when the favorable decision is made.

The general principles of notice contained in this paragraph is developed with greater specificity in the *Standards for Notice of Nonreappointment,* endorsed by the Fiftieth Annual Meeting of the American Association of University Professors (1964). These standards are:

Notice of nonreappointment, or of intention not to recommend reappointment to the governing board, should be given in writing in accordance with the following standards:

(1) *Not later than March 1 of the first academic year of service,* if the appointment expires at the end of that year; or, if a one-year appointment terminates during an academic year, at least three months in advance of its termination.

(2) *Not later than December 15 of the second academic year of service,* if the appointment expires at the end of that year; or, if an initial two-year appointment terminates during an academic year, at least six months in advance of its termination.

(3) At least twelve months before the expiration of an appointment after two or more years in the institution.

Other obligations, both of institutions and of individuals, are described in the *Statement on Recruitment and Resignation of Faculty Members,* as endorsed by the Association of American Colleges and the American Association of University Professors in 1961.

8. The freedom of probationary teachers is enhanced by the establishment of a regular procedure for the periodic evaluation and assessment of the teacher's academic performance during probationary status. Provision should be made for regularized procedures for the consideration of complaints by probationary teachers that their academic freedom has been violated. One suggested procedure to serve these purposes is contained in the *Recommended*

Institutional Regulations on Academic Freedom and Tenure, prepared by the American Association of University Professors.

9. A further specification of the academic due process to which the teacher is entitled under this paragraph is contained in the *Statement on Procedural Standards in Faculty Dismissal Proceedings,* jointly approved by the American Association of University Professors and the Association of American Colleges in 1958. This interpretive document deals with the issue of suspension, about which the 1940 *Statement* is silent.

The 1958 *Statement* provides: "Suspension of the faculty member during the proceedings is justified only if immediate harm to the faculty member or others is threatened by the faculty member's continuance. Unless legal considerations forbid, any such suspension should be with pay." A suspension which is not followed by either reinstatement or the opportunity for a hearing is in effect a summary dismissal in violation of academic due process.

The concept of "moral turpitude" identifies the exceptional case in which the professor may be denied a year's teaching or pay in whole or in part. The statement applies to that kind of behavior which goes beyond simply warranting discharge and is so utterly blameworthy as to make it inappropriate to require the offering of a year's teaching or pay. The standard is not that the moral sensibilities of persons in the particular community have been affronted. The standard is behavior that would evoke condemnation by the academic community generally.

Notes

1. The word "teacher" as used in this document is understood to include the investigator who is attached to an academic institution without teaching duties.

2. Bold-face numbers in brackets refer to Interpretive Comments which follow.

3. For a discussion of this question, see the "Report of the Special Committee on Academic Personnel Ineligible for Tenure," *AAUP Bulletin* 52 (1966): 280–82.

4. For a more detailed statement on this question, see "On Crediting Prior Service Elsewhere as Part of the Probationary Period," *AAUP Bulletin* 64 (1978): 274–75.

2

On Freedom of Expression and Campus Speech Codes

The statements which follows was approved by the Association's Committee A on Academic Freedom and Tenure in June 1992 and adopted by the Association's Council in November 1994.

Freedom of thought and expression is essential to any institution of higher learning. Universities and colleges exist not only to transmit knowledge. Equally, they interpret, explore, and expand that knowledge by testing the old and proposing the new.

This mission guides learning outside the classroom quite as much as in class, and often inspires vigorous debate on those social, economic, and political issues that arouse the strongest passions. In the process, views will be expressed that may seem to many wrong, distasteful, or offensive. Such is the nature of freedom to sift and winnow ideas.

On a campus that is free and open, no idea can be banned or forbidden. No viewpoint or message may be deemed so hateful or disturbing that it may not be expressed.

Universities and colleges are also communities, often of a residential character. Most campuses have recently sought to become more diverse, and more reflective of the larger community, by attracting students, faculty, and staff from groups that were historically excluded or underrepresented. Such gains as they have made are recent, modest, and tenuous. The campus climate can profoundly affect an institution's continued diversity. Hostility or intolerance to persons who differ from the majority (especially if seemingly condoned by the institution) may undermine the confidence of new members of the community. Civility is always fragile and can easily be destroyed.

In response to verbal assaults and use of hateful language some campuses have felt it necessary to forbid the expression of racist, sexist, homophobic or ethnically demeaning speech, along with conduct or behavior that harasses. Several reasons are offered in support of banning such expression. Individuals and groups that have been victims of such expression feel an understandable outrage. They claim that the academic progress of minority and majority alike may suffer if fears, tensions, and conflicts spawned by slurs and insults create an environment inimical to learning.

These arguments, grounded in the need to foster an atmosphere respectful of and welcome to all persons, strike a deeply responsive chord in the academy. But, while we can acknowledge both the weight of these concerns and the thoughtfulness of those persuaded of the need for regulation, rules that ban or punish speech based upon its content cannot be justified. An institution of higher learning fails to fulfill its mission if it asserts the power to proscribe ideas—and racial or ethnic slurs, sexist epithets, or homophobic insults almost always express ideas, however repugnant. Indeed, by proscribing any ideas, a university sets an example that profoundly disserves its academic mission.

Some may seek to defend a distinction between the regulation of the content of speech and the regulation of the manner (or style) of speech. We find this distinction untenable in practice because offensive style or opprobrious phrases may in fact have been chosen precisely for their expressive power. As the United States Supreme Court has said in the course of rejecting criminal sanctions for offensive words:

> [W]ords are often chosen as much for their emotive as their cognitive force. We cannot sanction the view that the Constitution, while solicitous of the cognitive content of individual speech, has little or no regard for that emotive function which, practically speaking, may often be the more important element of the overall message sought to be communicated.

The line between substance and style is thus too uncertain to sustain the pressure that will inevitably be brought to bear upon disciplinary rules that attempt to regulate speech.

Proponents of speech codes sometimes reply that the value of emotive language of this type is of such a low order that, on balance, suppression is justified by the harm suffered by those who are directly affected, and by the general damage done to the learning environment. Yet a college or university sets a perilous course if it seeks to differentiate between high-value and low-value speech, or to choose which groups are to be protected by curbing the speech of others. A speech code unavoidably implies an institutional competence to distinguish permissible expression of hateful thought from what is proscribed as thoughtless hate.

Institutions would also have to justify shielding some, but not other, targets of offensive language—proscribing uncomplimentary references to sexual but not to political preference, to religious but not to philosophical creed, or perhaps even to some but not to other religious affiliations. Starting down this path creates an even greater risk that groups not originally protected may later demand similar solicitude—demands the institution that began the process of banning some speech is ill equipped to resist.

Distinctions of this type are neither practicable nor principled; their very fragility underscores why institutions devoted to freedom of thought and expression ought not adopt an institutionalized coercion of silence.

Moreover, banning speech often avoids consideration of means more compatible with the mission of an academic institution by which to deal with incivility, intolerance, offensive speech, and harassing behavior:

(1) Institutions should adopt and invoke a range of measures that penalize conduct and behavior, rather than speech—such as rules against defacing property, physical intimidation or harassment, or disruption of campus activities. All members of the campus community should be made aware of such rules, and administrators should be ready to use them in preference to speech-directed sanctions.

(2) Colleges and universities should stress the means they use best—to educate—including the development of courses and other curricular and co-curricular experiences designed to increase student understanding and to deter offensive or intolerant speech or conduct. These institutions should, of course, be free (indeed encouraged) to condemn manifestations of intolerance and discrimination, whether physical or verbal.

(3) The governing board and the administration have a special duty not only to set an outstanding example of tolerance, but also to challenge boldly and condemn immediately serious breaches of civility.

(4) Members of the faculty, too, have a major role; their voices may be critical in condemning intolerance, and their actions may set examples for understanding, making clear to their students that civility and tolerance are hallmarks of educated men and women.

(5) Student personnel administrators have in some ways the most demanding role of all, for hate speech occurs most often in dormitories, locker-rooms, cafeterias, and student centers. Persons who guide this part of campus life should set high standards of their own for tolerance and should make unmistakably clear the harm that uncivil or intolerant speech inflicts.

To some persons who support speech codes, measures like these—relying as they do on suasion rather than sanctions—may seem inadequate. But freedom of expression requires toleration of "ideas we hate," as Justice Holmes put it. The underlying principle does not change because the demand is to silence a hateful speaker, or because it comes from within the academy. Free speech is not simply an aspect of the educational enterprise to be weighed against other desirable ends. It is the very precondition of the academic enterprise itself.

3

Statement on
Professional Ethics

The statement which follows, a revision of a statement originally adopted in 1966, was approved by the Association's Committee B on Professional Ethics, adopted by the Association's Council in June 1987, and endorsed by the Seventy-third Annual Meeting.

Introduction

From its inception, the American Association of University Professors has recognized that membership in the academic profession carries with it special responsibilities. The Association has consistently affirmed these responsibilities in major policy statements, providing guidance to professors in such matters as their utterances as citizens, the exercise of their responsibilities to students and colleagues, and their conduct when resigning from an institution or when undertaking sponsored research. The *Statement on Professional Ethics* that follows sets forth those general standards that serve as a reminder of the variety of responsibilities assumed by all members of the profession.

In the enforcement of ethical standards, the academic profession differs from those of law and medicine, whose associations act to ensure the integrity of members engaged in private practice. In the academic profession the individual institution of higher learning provides this assurance and so should normally handle questions concerning propriety of conduct within its own framework by reference to a faculty group. The Association supports such local action and stands ready, through the general secretary and Committee B, to counsel with members of the academic community concerning questions of professional ethics and to inquire into complaints when local consideration is impossible or inappropriate. If the alleged offense is deemed sufficiently serious to raise the possibility of adverse action, the procedures should be in

129

accordance with the 1940 *Statement of Principles on Academic Freedom and Tenure,* the 1958 *Statement on Procedural Standards in Faculty Dismissal Proceedings,* or the applicable provisions of the Association's *Recommended Institutional Regulations on Academic Freedom and Tenure.*

The Statement

I. Professors, guided by a deep conviction of the worth and dignity of the advancement of knowledge, recognize the special responsibilities placed upon them. Their primary responsibility to their subject is to seek and to state the truth as they see it. To this end professors devote their energies to developing and improving their scholarly competence. They accept the obligation to exercise critical self-discipline and judgment in using, extending, and transmitting knowledge. They practice intellectual honesty. Although professors may follow subsidiary interests, these interests must never seriously hamper or compromise their freedom of inquiry.

II. As teachers, professors encourage the free pursuit of learning in their students. They hold before them the best scholarly and ethical standards of their discipline. Professors demonstrate respect for students as individuals and adhere to their proper roles as intellectual guides and counselors. Professors make every reasonable effort to foster honest academic conduct and to ensure that their evaluations of students reflect each student's true merit. They respect the confidential nature of the relationship between professor and student. They avoid any exploitation, harassment, or discriminatory treatment of students. They acknowledge significant academic or scholarly assistance from them. They protect their academic freedom.

III. As colleagues, professors have obligations that derive from common membership in the community of scholars. Professors do not discriminate against or harass colleagues. They respect and defend the free inquiry of associates. In the exchange of criticism and ideas professors show due respect for the opinions of others. Professors acknowledge academic debt and strive to be objective in their professional judgment of colleagues. Professors accept their share of faculty responsibilities for the governance of their institution.

IV. As members of an academic institution, professors seek above all to be effective teachers and scholars. Although professors observe the stated regulations of the institution, provided the regulations do not contravene academic freedom, they maintain their right to criticize and seek revision. Professors give due regard to their paramount responsibilities within their institution in determining the amount and character of work done outside it. When considering the interruption or termination of their service, professors recognize the effect of their decision upon the program of the institution and give due notice of their intentions.

V. As members of their community, professors have the rights and obligations of other citizens. Professors measure the urgency of these obligations in the light of their responsibilities to their subject, to their students, to their profession, and to their institution. When they speak or act as private persons they avoid creating the impression of speaking or acting for their college or university. As citizens engaged in a profession that depends upon freedom for its health and integrity, professors have a particular obligation to promote conditions of free inquiry and to further public understanding of academic freedom.

4

A Statement of the Association's Council: Freedom and Responsibility

The statement which follows was adopted by the Council of the American Association of University Professors in October 1970. In April 1990, the Council adopted several changes in language that had been approved by the Association's Committee B on Professional Ethics in order to remove gender-specific references from the original text.

For more than half a century the American Association of University Professors has acted upon two principles: that colleges and universities serve the common good through learning, teaching, research, and scholarship; and that the fulfillment of this function necessarily rests upon the preservation of the intellectual freedoms of teaching, expression, research, and debate. All components of the academic community have a responsibility to exemplify and support these freedoms in the interests of reasoned inquiry.

The 1940 *Statement of Principles on Academic Freedom and Tenure* asserts the primacy of this responsibility. The *Statement on Professional Ethics* underscores its pertinency to individual faculty members and calls attention to their responsibility, by their own actions, to uphold their colleagues' and their students' freedom of inquiry and to promote public understanding of academic freedom. The *Joint Statement on Rights and Freedoms of Students* emphasizes the shared responsibility of all members of the academic community for the preservation of these freedoms.

Continuing attacks on the integrity of our universities and on the concept of academic freedom itself come from many quarters. These attacks, marked by tactics of intimidation and harassment and by political interference with the autonomy of colleges and universities, provoke harsh responses and counter-responses. Especially in a repressive atmosphere, the faculty's responsibility to defend its freedoms cannot be separated form its responsibility to uphold those freedoms by its own actions.

I

Membership in the academic community imposes on students, faculty members, administrators, and trustees an obligation to respect the dignity of others, to acknowledge their right to express differing opinions, and to foster and defend intellectual honesty; freedom of inquiry and instruction, and free expression on and off the campus. The expression of dissent and the attempt to produce change, therefore, may not be carried out in ways which injure individuals or damage institutional facilities or disrupt the classes of one's teachers or colleagues. Speakers on campus must not only be protected from violence, but also be given an opportunity to be heard. Those who seek to call attention to grievances must not do so in ways that significantly impede the functions of the institution.

Students are entitled to an atmosphere conducive to learning and to even-handed treatment in all aspects of the teacher-student relationship. Faculty members may not refuse to enroll or teach students on the grounds of their beliefs or the possible uses to which they may put the knowledge to be gained in a course. Students should not be forced by the authority inherent in the instructional role to make particular personal choices as to political action or their own social behavior. Evaluation of students and the award of credit must be based on academic performance professionally judged and not on matters irrelevant to that performance, whether personality, race, religion, degree of political activism, or personal beliefs.

It is the mastery teachers have of their subjects and their own scholarship that entitles them to their classrooms and to freedom in the presentation of their subjects. Thus, it is improper for an instructor persistently to intrude material that has no relation to the subject, or to fail to present the subject matter of the course as announced to the students and as approved by the faculty in their collective responsibility for the curriculum.

Because academic freedom has traditionally included the instructor's full freedom as a citizen, most faculty members face no insoluble conflicts between the claims of politics, social action, and conscience, on the one hand, and the claims and expectations of their students, colleagues, and institutions, on the other. If such conflicts become acute, and attention to obligations as a citizen and moral agent precludes an instructor from fulfilling substantial academic obligations, the instructor cannot escape the responsibility of that choice, but should either request a leave of absence or resign his or her academic position.

II

The Association's concern for sound principles and procedures in the imposition of discipline is reflected in the 1940 *Statement of Principles on Academic Freedom and Tenure,* the 1958 *Statement on Procedural Standards in Faculty Dismissal Proceedings,* the *Recommended Institutional Regulations on Academic Freedom and Tenure,* and the many investigations conducted by the Association into disciplinary actions by colleges and universities.

The question arises whether these customary procedures are sufficient in the current context. We believe that by and large they serve their purposes well, but that consideration should be given to supplementing them in several respects.

First, plans for ensuring compliance with academic norms should be enlarged to emphasize preventive as well as disciplinary action. Toward this end the faculty should take the initiative, working with the administration and other components of the institution, to develop and maintain an atmosphere of freedom, commitment to academic inquiry, and respect for the academic rights of others. The faculty should also join with other members of the academic community in the development of procedures to be used in the event of serious disruption, or the threat of disruption, and should ensure its consultation in major decisions, particularly those related to the calling of external security forces to the campus.

Second, systematic attention should be given to questions related to sanctions other than dismissal, such as warnings and reprimands, in order to provide a more versatile body of academic sanctions.

Third, there is need for the faculty to assume a more positive role as guardian of academic values against unjustified assaults from its own members. The traditional faculty function in disciplinary proceedings has been to ensure academic due process and meaningful faculty participation in the imposition of discipline by the administration. While this function should be maintained, faculties should recognize their stake in promoting adherence to norms essential to the academic enterprise.

Rules designed to meet these needs for faculty self-regulation and flexibility of sanctions should be adopted on each campus in response to local circumstances and to continued experimentation. In all sanctioning efforts, however, it is vital that proceedings be conducted with fairness to the individual, that faculty judgments play a crucial role, and that adverse judgments be founded on demonstrated violations of appropriate norms. The Association will encourage and assist local faculty groups seeking to articulate the substantive principles here outlined or to make improvements in their disciplinary machinery to meet the needs here described. The Association will also consult and work with any responsible group, within or outside the academic community, that seeks to promote understanding of and adherence to basic norms of professional responsibility so long as such efforts are consistent with principles of academic freedom.

5

Academic Freedom—Its Basic Philosophy, Function, and History

*Ralph F. Fuchs**

I. The Scope of Academic Freedom

Academic freedom is that freedom of members of the academic community, assembled in colleges and universities, which underlies the effective performance of their functions of teaching, learning, practice of the arts, and research. The right to academic freedom is recognized in order to enable faculty members and students to carry on their roles. It is not sought as a personal privilege, although scholars enjoy the activities it permits,[1] and the tenure rights of faculty members, which are conferred after a period of probation, bestow economic security as well as forestall restrictions on freedom that might stem from the power to dismiss. In relation to tenure the position of the faculty member resembles that of the judge who holds office during good behavior to safeguard his fearlessness and objectivity in the performance of his duties.[2]

The conception of academic freedom which is dominant in colleges and universities in the United States today rests mainly on three foundations:

(1) the philosophy of intellectual freedom, which originated in Greece, arose again in Europe, especially under the impact of the Renaissance, and came to maturity in the Age of Reason;

(2) the idea of autonomy for communities of scholars, which arose in the universities of Europe; and

136

(3) the freedoms guaranteed by the Bill of Rights of the federal constitution as elaborated by the courts.

Academic tenure is protected by procedural safeguards in proceedings to dismiss faculty members for cause, which are academically maintained and modelled to a significant extent on procedural due process of law.[3] Academic freedom, in addition, has its correlative in academic responsibility in the use of freedom, which there may or may not be recognized means of enforcing against faculty members.[4]

Student freedom is a traditional accompaniment to faculty freedom as an element of academic freedom in the larger sense; but in the United States it has on the whole received secondary consideration until recently.[5] Now students are organized to some extent to assert their right to it,[6] and recent court decisions have enforced procedural protections, based on due process of law, against dismissals by state institutions on account of student exercise of off-campus rights of free speech and assembly.[7]

Exclusion from the academic community because of race has, also, been stated of late to be a violation of academic freedom;[8] and exclusion of students or teachers from public institutions on this ground or discrimination against them for this reason, is, of course, a violation of federal constitutional right.[9] Choice of those who shall participate in higher education (which must be an institutional choice) is, along with determination of curricula and of areas of research, among the elements of that academic autonomy which is one of the bases of academic freedom and may be looked upon as its essence.[10] It is, however, itself subject to constitutional requirements, which may on occasion protect the individual student or faculty member from action by his institution as well as by outsiders.[11]

Inroads upon autonomy in respect to research are a leading cause of concern in American colleges and universities at present, because grants from government and industry for designated projects may influence the directions of inquiry. Here institutional integrity and individual self-direction both stand in need of protection—not from hostile action but from temptation.[12]

Notwithstanding the increasingly broad reach of academic freedom and the current emphasis on the essentiality of autonomy for academic institutions, the freedom of individual faculty members against control of thought or utterance from either within or without the employing institutions remains the core of the matter. If this freedom exists and reasonably adequate academic administration and methods of faculty selection prevail, intellectual interchange and pursuit of knowledge are secured. A substantial degree of institutional autonomy is both a usual prerequisite and a normal consequence of such a state of affairs. Student freedom will follow—unless, indeed, individual faculty members or departmental groups are permitted to tyrannize over particular students, as occasionally happens. Hence the main concern over developing and maintaining academic freedom in this country has focused upon encouragement and protection of the freedom of the faculty member. Institutional autonomy, constitutional freedoms, and the basic ideology of intellectual freedom have been invoked mainly to this end.

II. Development of Academic Freedom

European universities began during the Middle Ages as self-constituted communities of scholars, whether teachers or learners. The institutions they founded came under the sponsorship of the medieval church and to some degree under its authority; and the faculties, of course, were composed largely of clerics. Before the eighteenth century the Roman church and in some areas its protestant successors exerted sporadic controls against which the universities or members of their faculties found it necessary at times to contend. Scholars outside of the universities, including early scientists, engaged in the same struggles, however, and the total story is one of the effort of the human intellect to escape from bondage, rather than simply of university faculties and students to be free of external control. Within the universities a considerable censorship by dominant groups, giving rise to internal controversies, prevailed for a long time. The boundaries to learning maintained by this censorship receded on the whole, even though vestiges remained for long.[13] At Oxford and Cambridge religious tests and restrictions for students were not removed until the latter half of the nineteenth century.[14]

In the eighteenth and nineteenth centuries the political state became the sponsoring authority for most universities throughout the world—although some under religious auspices remained and in the United States particularly independent private colleges and universities have continued to exist alongside the public ones. Instances of actual or attempted political interference with public institutions have continued to arise in various countries down to the present time.[15] In the United States political control by state governments remains a danger which assumes reality under demagogic governors from time to time,[16] despite the generally good record of the states in relation to the colleges and universities they maintain. In Europe dictatorships of several varieties have supplied object-lessons of the extent to which political control can regiment and distort intellectual endeavor even while stimulating the development of learning along selected lines.[17] In some other countries, political influence may play a significant although unmeasurable role in the appointment of staff members. There is a genuine interaction between academic freedom and healthy political democracy, causing each to strengthen the other. It would be too much to say, however, that the former is wholly dependent upon the latter; for given enlightenment on the part of an autocratic government, academic freedom in a genuine sense may coexist with it, as it did in nineteenth century Germany.[18]

It was, indeed, in nineteenth century Germany that the modern conception of academic freedom came to be formulated. The idea of the university as a place where scholars are to pursue truth, as well as to formulate and transmit it to students, who at the same time learn to pursue truth for themselves, came to be dominant there. Especially in an age of science, knowledge grows as individuals ferret it out; and the free interplay of ideas is the means of purifying it. Intellectual discipline over the members of the university community is excluded, lest it distort their search. Attracted by this conception and its results, distinguished young scholars from abroad, especially from the United States, went to the German universities in numbers.[19] There they were imbued with the conception, an enlargement of which has since been dominant in this country.

Professor Friedrich Paulsen of the University of Berlin formulated systematically in 1902, in his book on *The German Universities and University Study,* the conception of academic freedom which had arisen in his country during the preceding decades. "It is no longer, as formerly," he wrote,[20]

> the function of the university teacher to hand down a body of truth established by authorities, but to search after scientific knowledge by investigation, and to teach his hearers to do the same. . . . For the academic teacher and his hearers there can be no prescribed and no proscribed thoughts. There is only one rule for instruction: to justify the truth of one's teaching by reason and the facts.

Paulsen, however, introduced a qualification. The professor of philosophy must be absolutely free; but the professor of theology "must assume a positive relation to religion and the church in general," and the professor of political and social science in a state institution must do so toward "the people and the state." The professor "who can find absolutely no reason in the state and in law, who, as a theoretical anarchist, denies the necessity of a state and legal order . . . may try to prove his theory by means of as many good arguments as he can, but he has no call to teach the political sciences at a state institution." The state, for example, is not bound to tolerate adherence to the "principles of the *social-democracy*" on the part of professors of political science. To permit such theories to be taught would indicate that "the authorities regarded the lectures of professors as harmless and insignificant. . . . So long as the state takes the universities seriously, such a form of political science as has been described will be impossible in its institutions of learning."[21]

Paulsen also expressed the view that political partisanship on the part of a faculty member is a disqualification, notwithstanding the fact that professors may be "men of noble discontent" who sow "the thoughts for future acts." The things which universities "are called upon to cultivate transcend the boundaries of countries and nations. . . . The German universities dwell in their own world, outside of politics, and their highest achievements are in science." Hence the professors, "the representatives of science, should not engage in politics, but should reflect upon the state and the law."[22] Academic freedom, in other words, is internal to institutions of higher education, and does not apply to external activities of academic personnel.[23]

The conception of academic freedom which is dominant in American colleges and universities and in other countries today has discarded the limitations that remained in nineteenth century Germany. It accepts, rather, another statement of Paulsen's that "a people," who establish and maintain a university[24]

> cannot as such have an interest in the preservation of false conceptions. Its ability to live depends in no small measure upon its doing that which is necessary from a proper knowledge of actual conditions. And hence the people and the state . . . can have no desire to place obstacles in the way of an honest search for truth in the field of politics and social science, either by forbidding or favoring certain views.

It follows that a society will be strengthened by permitting honest condemnation as well as defense of the state in institutions of higher learning, whether publicly or privately maintained. As to participation by professors in politics, specialization and attention to duty will ordinarily keep the faculty member from an active role; but he cannot be barred from testing his views or gathering data in action, or from urging his conclusions in the world of affairs, whether relevant to his academic subject or not, by joining organizations or by other means. In addition to "full freedom" in research and publication and "freedom in the classroom in discussing his subject," the faculty member in any field of study, speaking or writing as a citizen, "should be free from institutional censorship or discipline."[25]

According to the position taken by some Americans within the academic profession and outside who subscribe to broad principles of academic freedom, certain specific limitations upon that freedom may nevertheless be imposed for reasons of special urgency. During World War I some of the staunchest proponents of academic freedom sanctioned the muzzling of antiwar professors and even of those whose ancestry and utterances gave "reasonable ground for belief that they contemplate[d]" acts to aid the enemy or hamper the war efforts.[26] Many today and during the past thirty years have urged that membership in the Communist Party disqualifies an individual for faculty membership without reference to sincerity or circumstances, because of the Party's discipline and the existence of a basic conflict between its purposes and freedom itself.[27] The professional charter of academic freedom which is currently followed concedes more generally that a college or university may insist upon "limitations of academic freedom because of religious or other aims of the institution," provided the limits are clearly stated in advance.[28] This concession recognizes the church sponsorship of many institutions in this country and the civil liberty of individuals and groups, including those who form academic institutions, to govern their own affairs. At some point in the scale of self-imposed restrictions a college or university that comes under them may, of course, cease to be an institution of higher education according to the prevailing conception;[29] and an institution that does not expressly limit itself assumes an obligation to adhere to the principles inherent in an academic community. As generally understood today, these principles do not sanction the proscription of any ideas or honest means of communicating or effectuating them, on the part of academic personnel, within an institution or outside.

The present American conception of academic freedom did not, of course, spring full-blown from the soil in which higher education grew in this country. It evolved, rather, along with specific protections to academic freedom, from the organizational forms and educational policies that arose in colleges and universities, and from struggles over recurring infringements of freedom or tenure, which sometimes took the form of faculty dismissals. These infringements were committed by governing boards or administrative officers, moved in the typical case by opinion outside the institutions, which the institutional authorities ordinarily shared. At first the pressures that resulted in these incidents were the product of demands for religious conformity;[30] later they involved objections to the economic or political views of faculty members.[31] Most recently, nonconforming utterances in matters of sex, or literary works which have been deemed offensive, have produced faculty dismissals raising issues of freedom.[32]

III. Professional Formulation and Support of Principles of Academic Freedom

Because of concern among professors over dismissals that had taken place, coupled with the belief that it would be desirable to have a national organization of college and university teachers similar to the associations of physicians and lawyers, the American Association of University Professors (AAUP) was formed in 1915 by a group of prominent faculty members in leading institutions. Those who joined as charter members came from sixty institutions. Although the purposes of the new Association were broadly professional, its most noteworthy early pronouncement was the 1915 Declaration of its Committee on Academic Freedom and Tenure, specifically directed to that subject.[33] The officers of the Association quickly became absorbed in efforts to cope with recurring dismissals of faculty members at institutions in various parts of the country.[34] The Association has continued in conjunction with the Association of American Colleges (AAC) to formulate basic principles of academic freedom and tenure.[35] It has also provided means of vindicating these principles by directing professional attention to academic administrations which are found to have violated them,[36] and has spelled out its policies in decisions on particular cases and in annual reports of the Committee on Freedom and Tenure, carrying forward the 1915 Declaration.[37]

These group measures have involved only partial collaboration between the professors, represented by their association, and administrators and trustees. The AAC has shared in what might be called the legislative process; but mediation in on-campus disputes, investigation into challenged dismissals, determinations of whether violations of the principles of freedom and tenure have occurred, and the application of sanctions have fallen to the AAUP acting alone. In its investigations, reports, and use of sanctions, the Association prides itself on proceeding with scrupulous objectivity through processes judicial in character. Its conclusions as to facts have not been challenged, except very rarely by an immediate party.

In the reports it has been necessary to develop through interpretation the rather brief joint statements which underlie the conclusions. As to tenure, for example, the "acceptable academic practice" the 1940 Statement sets forth, of limiting the faculty member's probationary period to seven years, has been translated into a mandatory rule.[38] With respect to academic freedom during the probationary period, for which the 1940 Statement provides, it has been held that the faculty member may not be made to suffer non-renewal of his appointment or denial of tenure because of his exercise of freedom.[39] The freedom of the faculty member to speak as a citizen, which is secured "from institutional censorship or discipline," has been taken to include his privilege of refusing on constitutional grounds to answer questions in an official investigation.[40] The judgment of unfitness to continue in a faculty position, which may be reached in a dismissal proceeding, may not be based merely on conduct, such as simple membership or honest activity in a suspected organization, which is within the ambit of academic freedom.[41] This type of development of the principles of freedom and tenure, although *ex parte,* has implicitly been accepted—in part, no doubt, because of the sheer necessity for it, and to some extent, perhaps, because of the soundness of the interpretations reached.

The extent of the actual acceptance of these interpretations by the academic community as a whole cannot be gauged with precision. The decisions by the AAUP to which they have led—and, indeed, the decisions establishing clear-cut violations of explicit principles—have not secured the reinstatement of faculty members found to have been wrongfully dismissed. The regulations of the offending institutions have, however, typically been made to conform subsequently to the stated principles, as those of many other institutions do, without dissent from the interpretations of the AAUP.[42]

Of central importance in the implementation of the principles of freedom and tenure is the assurance of participation by faculty members in decisions when the dismissal of colleagues is proposed. The 1940 Statement provides that "termination for cause of a continuous appointment, or the dismissal for cause of a teacher previous to the expiration of a term appointment, should, if possible, be considered by both a faculty committee and the governing board of the institution."[43] Often characterized as a means of securing a judgment of the faculty member by his peers in the first instance, this provision draws its chief value from the assurance it gives that academic considerations will enter into decisions and from the likelihood it provides that professionally accepted principles will be given effect. Without such faculty participation, the prospects for thoroughgoing maintenance of academic freedom in American institutions of higher learning would be considerably less than they are.

IV. Legal Impairment and Protection of Academic Freedom

In addition to the contribution which constitutional law has made to the substantive and procedural aspects of academic freedom as professionally defined and maintained, the law of the land may bear directly on academic freedom in at least three ways: through the impairment of freedom by legislative restrictions on it; through judicial enforcement of constitutional barriers to such impairments; and through judicial protection of the right to freedom as against limitation by academic authorities themselves. In rendering decisions in cases arising in any of these areas the courts, especially the Supreme Court of the United States under the Bill of Rights and the fourteenth amendment, may do much to define the effective scope of academic freedom.

Legislation which attaches ideological tests to the eligibility of students or faculty to participate in higher education obviously impairs academic freedom by imposing the alternative of either outward conformity or exclusion for refusal to submit. Statutory oaths of allegiance aroused much opposition among administrators and professors in the 1930's.[44] Even though the required oaths could be taken in good faith and construed according to the subjective loyalties of the takers, they were recognized as efforts to impose conformity on education.[45] These laws remain on the books[46] and have been augmented by a loyalty oath requirement that conditions federal aid to students and scholars under the National Science Foundation and National Defense Education Acts.[47] There have also been added the more recent requirements of disclaimers of subversive associations and beliefs, including such a requirement in the same two federal acts prior to their amendment in 1962.[48] The principal objections to such disclaimers are that they operate somewhat *in terrorem* when their terms are not wholly clear and that the exclusion of any genuinely held ideas whatsoever from colleges and universities is inconsistent with the nature of higher education. In addition, they are invidious when academic personnel are singled out for attention, and can lead easily to inquisitions when false swearing is suspected.[49] Similar in effect are statutory requirements for disclosure of memberships, accompanied by express or implied threats of dismissal if unfavorable affiliations are brought to light.[50] Statutes requiring investigations to ferret out individuals adhering to proscribed organizations or beliefs operate with, if anything, still more drastic effect.[51] Simple prohibitions, enforceable by criminal prosecutions, operate more sporadically. The one which has now replaced the disclaimer requirement in the National Science Foundation and National Defense Education Acts is quite tightly drawn.[52]

Investigations not required by statute and having no prescribed effects under existing law may nevertheless operate *in terrorem* and may lead to a loss of reputation by those who are subject to inquiry, if their beliefs and associations are gone into. Therefore, the possible effect of such investigations in limiting the freedom of students and faculty is recognized, and specific justification for each inquiry must be shown.[53] When justification is shown and the inquiry goes forward, the restriction that may result is a consequence of the conduct of academic institutions in society. Inquiry into the substance of the teaching in an institution seems, however, to be forbidden on constitutional grounds.[54] The character and incidental activities of those who participate in the educational process, in so far as they are deemed relevant to national security, are, on the other hand, subject to scrutiny.[55]

Judicial enforcement of constitutional barriers to the impairment of academic freedom by governmental action, centering in the Supreme Court of the United States, has resulted in predominantly split decisions, falling now on one side of the line separating validity from invalidity and then on the other.[56] Most of the decisions involving faculty members have not turned on issues related specifically to academic affairs, but rather on such questions as whether a dismissal for past invocation of the fifth amendment violated the personal rights of the individual,[57] whether an oath law might require dismissal from any kind of public employment because of innocent membership in a proscribed organization,[58] whether a mandatory oath was invalidly vague in its terms,[59] or whether procedural due process was accorded in a legislative investigation.[60] The permissible scope of governmental inquiries into academic affairs and the permissible bases for excluding persons from teaching positions have, however, been considered; and in the opinions to which these questions have given rise the Justices of the Supreme Court have uttered formulations of academic freedom that will be enduringly influential.

The leading case is *Adler v. Board of Education*,[61] involving the Feinberg Law of New York. The statute and regulations under it by the State Board of Regents required the Board of Education of the city of New York to list organizations found, after hearing, to advocate or teach overthrow of the Government by force or violence or other unlawful means, and further required that persons teaching or advocating overthrow of the Government by these means, or knowingly belonging to organizations so teaching or advocating, should not be appointed or retained as teachers in public institutions. Hearings were to be accorded before denial of appointment or dismissal under the law, with membership in an organization listed by the Board constituting prima facie evidence of disqualification. The Supreme Court sustained the statute in an opinion by Mr. Justice Minton which upholds the authority of the state to exclude from the "sensitive area" of the schoolroom persons of the kind proscribed. The Court cited a decision the preceding year, in which a disclaimer oath requirement for Los Angeles municipal employees was upheld on the ground that public servants may be examined "as to matters that may prove relevant to their fitness and suitability for the public service."[62] Justices Douglas and Black dissented, emphasizing the intimidation caused by such legislation and by the principle of guilt by association of which the New York statute made use. "Where suspicion fills the air," said Mr. Justice Douglas, "and holds scholars in line for fear of their jobs, there can be no exercise of the free intellect."

In *Sweezy v. New Hampshire,* the decision reached by four concurring Justices turned in the end on a denial of due process through failure to show that the questions asked of a visiting lecturer at the University of New Hampshire about his lectures and party affiliations, during an official investigation, came within the authorized scope of the inquiry. The opinion of these four Justices, by Chief Justice Warren, expressed special concern over academic freedom. "The essentiality of freedom in the community of American universities is almost self-evident," he wrote:[63]

No one should underestimate the vital role in a democracy that is played by those who guide and train our youth. To impose any strait jacket upon the intellectual leaders in our colleges and universities would imperil the future of our Nation. No field of education is so thoroughly comprehended by man that new discoveries cannot yet be made. Particularly is that true in the social sciences, where few, if any, principles are accepted as absolutes. Scholarship cannot flourish in an atmosphere of suspicion and distrust. Teachers and students must always remain free to inquire, to study and to evaluate, to gain new maturity and understanding; otherwise our civilization will stagnate and die.

Here, "We believe that there unquestionably was an invasion of petitioner's liberties in the areas of academic freedom and political expression—areas in which government should be extremely reticent to tread."

The same view was elaborated in a concurring opinion by Justices Frankfurter and Harlan, basing the decision on the freedom issue. As a result, in the later *Barenblatt* case,[64] the majority of the Court stated in an opinion by Mr. Justice Harlan that,

. . . broadly viewed, inquiries cannot be made into the teaching that is pursued in any of our educational institutions. When academic teaching-freedom and its corollary learning-freedom, so essential to the well-being of the Nation, are claimed, this Court will always be on the alert against intrusion by Congress into this constitutionally protected domain.

In the eyes of the Court majority in this case, however, the coercive effect of investigations into communist associations and activities of students and teachers is outweighed by the public interest in discovering such conduct, where there is reason to suspect it. A broadscale disclosure of all organizational affiliations cannot, however, be required of teachers in public institutions.[65]

On the frontier of legal protection to academic freedom lies the possible availability of judicial remedies to aggrieved faculty members or students against impairment of their freedoms by actions of the institutions. Breach of contract, violation of an applicable regulation of a public institution, or unconstitutional use of public power (exercised by officers of a public institution as state officials or exercised by a private institution pursuant to delegation) might be the basis of relief. The same analysis as may justify recovery against violation of procedural or tenure rights[66] applies here; but the precise meaning of institutional documents securing the right to freedom is often subject to considerable doubt. The Illinois Court of Appeals has recently rejected a claim that institutional regulations securing faculty freedom provided anything more than due consideration within the university of a claim that freedom had been violated by a dismissal on account of a letter published in the student newspaper.[67] Courts will be reluctant in any event to review the determinations of academic authorities in such matters, and there is no strong demand that they do so.[68] Professional means of vindicating academic freedom against institutional action remain the chief reliance of faculties.

V. By Way of Summary

It should be apparent from even so brief an account as the one in the preceding pages that academic freedom rests on a variety of cultural and institutional factors; that it changes from time to time and from place to place; and that in the United States today it embraces more sweeping claims to independence, as well as a vastly greater range of educational activities, than ever before in history. Originating as a condition of scholarly endeavor in institutions that performed highly specialized functions closely related to philosophy, and restricted until recently to freedom within those institutions, it has been expanded in the United States to cover faculty members in a great variety of institutions "beyond the high school,"[69] and to protect the liberty to participate in extramural as well as intramural activities. To render this expanded academic freedom secure, impressive professional enforcement machinery has been established and the law of the land has been invoked to a significant extent.

The same development as has produced teachers' colleges (now expanded to state colleges and universities), engineering and business education, art institutes, "department store universities," and many other forms of higher education in this country has, of course, brought a far larger portion of the youth of the land into these institutions as students than is or has been the case anywhere else. Popular concern with what goes on there is correspondingly great. The operation of colleges and universities is enmeshed in community affairs at many points. When to this factor is added the direct and immediate dependence of public institutions and many private ones on current appropriations, contributions, or tuition payments for support, the difficulties besetting the maintenance of full academic freedom become apparent.

Also relevant is the form of organization of colleges and universities in this country, which places them, with rare exceptions, legally under the control of lay governing boards. It is this factor which, along with the delegated authority of presidents and other administrators, accounts for the form—namely, contests over the dismissals of faculty members from positions they hold legally as employees—which academic freedom issues have assumed. It accounts, too, for the shape which professional protective measures have taken, opposing faculty judgments within an institution, or marshalled from outside by the national association of faculty members, to those of the legally constituted authorities. Collaboration between employers and employed on a professional basis is growing, however.[70] At the same time, small beginnings have been made at holding in check by legal means the power of the outside community to regulate the beliefs and associations of students and faculty members. On the other hand, litigation as a means of settling internal controversies, which occasionally arises, seems to have extremely limited possibilities.

Academic freedom, however, is by no means wholly or even largely dependent on formal protection for its strength and its survival. To a large extent it exists and is recognized because of professional tradition and because it resides inherently in the functions of teaching, learning, and research. Faculty members in colleges and universities are usually not employed to follow orders but to render instruction and to pursue inquiries in their fields of competence, largely free of supervision and direction, even though there still are exceptions in some small institutions. For students there is much more prescription; but election among an almost bewildering array of course offerings and curricula is quite common. And surely the dominant conception of the student in this country is that, within a given area of subject matter, he is learning to exercise independent judgment and must have his reason appealed to rather than dominated. Hence governing boards, administrative officers, faculty members, students, and the public respect academic freedom almost insensibly; and specific intrusions upon it are relatively rare, even though their absolute number is considerable. Oath laws and similar attempts at control may have persistent insidious effects, nevertheless, and need urgently to be eliminated.

Also badly needed is greater consciousness within the expanded academic community of the importance of academic freedom and of its exercise. The numerous faculty members who are content to perform their specialized work in a manner conducive to pleasant personal relations and to public inconspicuousness contribute little to the ends for which freedom exists.[71] For them and for the general public, which can have the benefits of higher education only by maintaining the conditions in which it grows, judicial formulation of the nature and requirements of academic freedom, such as occasionally takes place in opinions, will (given the American penchant for seeking wisdom from the courts) operate with salutary effect. For the rest, progress is dependent on a developing "spirit of liberty" among academic personnel and in the community at large.

Notes

* A.B., L.L.B. 1922, Washington University; Ph.D. 1925, Robert Brookings Graduate School; J.S.D. 1935, Yale University. Professor of Law, Indiana University. President, American Association of University Professors, 1960–62.

The definition in the first sentence of Part I and the first paragraph of Part II of this article are largely quoted, with the kind permission of the publishers of the *Encyclopaedia Britannica,* from the author's article on Academic Freedom in the current edition of the *Encyclopaedia,* 1 ENCYC. BRIT. 57 (1963). The bibliography attached to that article contains additional references on the subject.

1. *Academic Freedom and Tenure in the Quest for National Security, Report of a Special Committee,* 42 BULLETIN OF THE AMERICAN ASSOCIATION OF UNIVERSITY PROFESSORS [hereinafter cited as A.A.U.P. BULL.] 51, 54–55 (1956).

2. Machlup, *On Some Misconceptions Concerning Academic Freedom,* 41 A.A.U.P. BULL 753 (1955).

3. Rudimentary procedural safeguards are required by the 1940 Statement of Principles on Academic Freedom and Tenure, drafted and supported by educational organizations and published at intervals by the American Association of University Professors (AAUP). See 46 A.A.U.P. BULL. 410 (1960) for the text and a list of supporting organizations, to which several large scholarly associations have since been added. Institutional regulations provide specific procedural rules to a varying extent. See CLARK BYSE & LOUIS JOUGHIN, TENURE IN AMERICAN HIGHER EDUCATION (1959), for the results of a three-state survey of such regulations. A model set of regulations is provided in *Recommended Institutional Regulations on Academic Freedom and Tenure,* approved by the Committee on Academic Freedom and Tenure or the AAUP on August 4, 1957, and published in mimeographed form by the Association. In discussions of academic procedural problems, legal due process of law is often referred to.

4. See *Academic Freedom and Tenure: The University of Illinois,* 49 A.A.U.P. BULL. 25 (1963), for a discussion of the question whether a faculty member's alleged breach of responsibility in public utterance can be a basis of disciplinary proceedings against him.

5. Teacher freedom and student freedom, *Lehrfreiheit* and *Lernfreiheit,* are companion concepts. In Europe the freedom of students to visit other institutions and to govern their own personal conduct is much wider on the whole than in this country. Here the idea has contributed to the policy of elective courses; but no generally recognized code of student freedom has arisen. See RICHARD HOFSTADTER & WALTER P. METZGER, THE DEVELOPMENT OF ACADEMIC FREEDOM IN THE UNITED STATES 383–98 (1955).

6. The United States National Student Association, composed of the student bodies of nearly 400 colleges and universities, the student governments of which have adhered to the organization, devotes a considerable portion of its attention to academic freedom and in particular to student freedom. See its CODIFICATION OF POLICY esp. 28–29, 38–41, 97–112 (1962–63). See also Am. Civil Liberties Union, *Academic Freedom and Civil Liberties of Students in Colleges and Universities* (1961), reprinted in 48 A.A.U.P. BULL. 110 (1962).

7. Dixon v. Alabama State Board of Education, 294 F.2d 150 (5th Cir. 1961), *cert. denied,* 368 U.S. 930 (1961); Knight v. State Board of Education, 200 F. Supp. 174 (M.D. Tenn, 1961). Like some earlier cases, the opinions support rights to due procedure in connection with dismissals for any kind of misconduct. See Byse, *Procedure*

in Student Dismissal Proceedings: Law and Policy, 4 J. COLLEGE STUDENT PERSON-
NEL 130 (1963).

8. Resolution of the Forty-third Annual Meeting, 43 A.A.U.P. BULL. 363 (1957):
"The right to teach and the right to learn are vital and inseparable aspects of academic
freedom. Consequently, free access to every kind of educational opportunity, measured
only by the aptitude and achievement of the individual teacher or student, must be
safeguarded to all Americans, of whatever race. Any interference with such access
imperils the right of the teacher to teach, as well as of the student to learn."

9. Brown v. Board of Education, 347 U.S. 483 (1954); Bolling v. Sharpe, 347 U.S.
497 (1954); Alston v. School Board of Norfolk, 112 F.2d 992 (4th Cir. 1940); Davis
v. Cook, 80 F. Supp. 443 (N.D. Ga. 1948). *Cf.* United Public Workers v. Mitchell, 330
U.S. 75, at 100 (1947).

10. Lennard, *The Threat to Academic Freedom,* Hibbert Journal, Oct. 1948, p. 21.
Robert M. MacIver in his book; ACADEMIC FREEDOM IN OUR TIME (1955), stresses the
autonomy of the faculty within an institution in matters lying within its competence as
basic to academic freedom. See especially pp. 94–95. RUSSELL KIRK, ACADEMIC FREE-
DOM (1955), stresses the inherent right of the academic community to maintain its own
standards in that search for truth which is its reason for being.

11. The AAUP Annual Meeting resolution, *supra* note 8, asserts that individual
rights to teach and to learn are superior to restriction by any authority on ground of
race; and of course judicial judgments which strike down segregation in education are
typically directed against educational authorities. If the policy which excludes a student or faculty member is based on such allowable grounds as competence or prior
training, or perhaps age or sex, the right to maintain it might be claimed as an incident
to institutional academic freedom. In Hamilton v. Regents of the University of California, 293 U.S. 245 (1934), the Regents' policy of excluding male students who would
not submit to compulsory military training was sustained; but in Board of Education
v. Barnette, 319 U.S. 624 (1943), the policy of requiring a salute to the flag (in an
elementary school) had to yield to the right of pupils who refused to take part and
whose parents would be punished for their non-attendance at school if they were ex-
pelled for refusing.

12. See AMERICAN COUNCIL ON EDUCATION, COMMITTEE ON RESEARCH POLICY,
REPORT ON SPONSORED RESEARCH POLICY OF COLLEGES AND UNIVERSITIES (1954);
AM. CIVIL LIBERTIES UNION, STATEMENT CONCERNING THE UNIVERSITY AND CON-
TRACT RESEARCH (1959), reprinted in 46 A.A.U.P. BULL. 52 (1960); HARVARD AND
THE FEDERAL GOVERNMENT: A REPORT TO THE FACULTIES AND GOVERNING BOARDS
OF HARVARD UNIVERSITY (1961); *Twenty-six Campuses and the Federal Government,*
46 EDUCATIONAL RECORD 95, 108–13 (1963); Gosheen, *Federal Financing and
Princeton University, id.* at 168.

13. HOFSTADTER & METZGER, *op. cit. supra* note 5, ch. 1.

14. *Id.* at 393.

15. For examples of successful resistance to attempts of this kind in the face of
strong traditions of academic freedom, see instances reported in RICHARD H. SHYR-
OCK, THE STATUS OF UNIVERSITY TEACHERS 77 (France) and 159 (Egypt) (published

by Int'l Ass'n of Univ. Professors and Lectures, 1961). In India the interaction of administrations, faculty groups, students, and state officials, each invoking political forces in varying degree, gives rise to government intervention from time to time, as it did in the universities of Uttar Pradesh in 1960–61.

16. The latest of the interventions of this variety was that of the Governor of Mississippi in the crisis over admission of a Negro to the University there in September–October 1962, followed by a similar attempt in Alabama. For the response in educational circles, see Resolution adopted by the American Council on Education, Oct. 5, 1962, 44 EDUCATIONAL RECORD 85 (1963), also printed in 48 A.A.U.P. BULL. 318 (1962). An earlier Mississippi episode involving gubernatorial assumptions of the control of state institutions is told about in Hudson, *The Spoils System Enters College,* 64 NEW REPUB. 123 (1930). For the actions of educational organizations in the matter, see 17 A.A.U.P. BULL. 140 (1931). As to the control of Louisiana State University by Governor Huey P. Long a few years later, see Don Wharton, *Louisiana State University,* Scribner's Magazine, Sept. 1937, p. 33. State coercion of private colleges appears in *Academic Freedom and Tenure: Allen University and Benedict College,* 46 A.A.U.P. BULL. 87 (1960).

17. The control of facism over the universities is exemplified by conditions which continue in Spain. See the account by Professor Tierno Galvan in SHYROCK, *op. cit. supra* note 15, at 133. For an account of tight Communist Party control over institutions of higher education in Russia, See I. N. SHUMILIN, SOVIET HIGHER EDUCATION ch. VI (1962).

18. HOFSTADTER & METZGER, *op. cit. supra* note 5, at 383–92.

19. Rockwell, *Academic Freedom—German Origin and American Development,* 36 A.A.U.P. BULL. 225 (1950); Metzger, *The German Contribution to the American Theory of Academic Freedom,* 41 *id.* 214 (1955).

20. Translation by F. Thilly and W. W. Elwang (1906), pp. 228–31.

21. *Id.* at 233–38, 243–54.

22. *Id.* at 254–62.

23. The German university tradition involved a sharp separation between the academic community and the general one, with the former devoted to science and philosophy and hence "utterly indifferent to the turmoils and ambitions of the outer-world." See excerpts from JAMES MORGAN HART, GERMAN UNIVERSITIES: A NARRATIVE OF PERSONAL EXPERIENCE (1874), as printed in 2 RICHARD HOFSTADTER & WILSON SMITH, AMERICAN HIGHER EDUCATION 569, 576 (1961).

24. Paulsen, *supra* note 20, at 244.

25. 1940 Statement of Principles, *supra* note 3.

26. A.A.U.P. Bulletin, Feb.–March 1918, pp. 29, 41.

27. ASSOCIATION OF AMERICAN UNIVERSITIES, THE RIGHTS AND RESPONSIBILITIES OF UNIVERSITIES AND THEIR FACULTIES Pt. IV (1953); Lovejoy, *Communism Versus Academic Freedom,* 18 AMERICAN SCHOLAR 332 (1949); Sidney Hook, *Should Communists Teach?,* N.Y. Times Magazine, Mar. 27, 1959, p. 10; and see Hook & Fuchs, *A Joint Statement on a Matter of Importance,* 42 A.A.U.P. BULL. 692 (1956). For brief accounts of events at the University of Washington and the University of California

which followed the implementation by those institutions of the policy of barring Communist Party members from the faculties, see 42 A.A.U.P. BULL. 61–66, 100–107 (1956).

28. 1940 Statement of Principles, *supra* note 3.

29. The Declaration of Principles formulated in 1915 by the first Committee on Academic Freedom and Tenure of the AAUP distinguished in this regard between "proprietary institutions" espousing particular ideas and those which exercise a "public trust" and "have no moral right to bind the reason or the conscience of any professor." Reprinted in 40 A.A.U.P. BULL. 90, 94–97 (1954).

30. HOFSTADTER & METZGER, *op. cit. supra* note 5, at 155–77, 286–303, 320–45. Views on slavery which were out of accord with those in the academic or surrounding community were also the cause of dismissals or of hostility to individual administrators or faculty members. *Id.* at 253–61.

31. *Id.* ch. IX.

32. *Academic Freedom and Tenure: The University of Illinois, supra* note 4; *Academic Freedom and Tenure: Southwestern Louisiana Institute,* 42 A.A.U.P. BULL. 718 (1956). Instances of dismissal on account of publication of literary works have been the subject of recent complaint to the AAUP. Another recent factor contributing to violations of freedom and tenure has been, of course, a wave of dismissals from institutions in the Deep South because of views or utterances in favor of racial desegregation. For recent summaries, see 48 A.A.U.P. BULL. at 159 and 167–69 (1962). As to the intimidating effect of the climate of opinion in which southern institutions operate today, see Woodward, *The Unreported Crisis in the Southern Colleges,* Harper's, Oct. 1962, p. 82.

33. 1915 Declaration of Principles, *supra* note 29.

34. Metzger, *The First Investigation,* 47 A.A.U.P. BULL. 206 (1961).

35. The two associations formulated a joint statement in 1925, now superseded by the 1940 Statement. See 1925 Conference Statement, 43 A.A.U.P. BULL. 116 (1957). A joint Statement on Procedural Standards in Dismissal Proceedings received final approval in 1957–58. 44 A.A.U.P. BULL. 270 (1958).

36. These means typically consist of an on-the-scene inquiry by a special committee of professors into a challenged dismissal that has not been resolved by negotiation, the publication of its report after approval for publication by the Committee on Academic Freedom and Tenure of the Association, "censure" of the responsible administration (including governing board) where deemed warranted by the Council and an Annual Meeting of the Association, and subsequent negotiations looking to removal of the censure. The list of censured administrations, which originated in 1938 as a substitute for previous removals of institutions from an "eligible list," is regularly published in the *Bulletin.* See, *e.g.,* 49 A.A.U.P. BULL. 4 (1963).

37. These reports are published in the *Bulletin* after their presentation at Annual Meetings. See especially the report for 1950, 37 A.A.U.P. BULL. 72 (1951). The report of the Special Committee on Academic Freedom and Tenure in the Quest for National Security, *supra* note 1, reformulated the applicable general principles with special reference to the issues presented by the national effort to combat communism.

42 A.A.U.P. BULL. at 50–61 (1956). A supplementary statement of the Committee on Academic Freedom and Tenure was published in 1958. 44 A.A.U.P. BULL. 6 (1958).

38. *Academic Freedom and Tenure: Princeton Theological Seminary,* 45 A.A.U.P. BULL. 47 (1959).

39. Alabama Polytechnic Institute, 44 A.A.U.P. BULL. 158 (1958); see also *Academic Freedom and Tenure: Evansville College,* 35 A.A.U.P. BULL. 74 (1949).

40. *The Effects of Refusal to Testify,* 42 A.A.U.P. BULL. 75 (1956).

41. University of Washington, *id.* at 61.

42. The administration is not required to assent affirmatively to an interpretation which is disputable and which does not have the approval of the Association of American Colleges, although it sometimes does assent.

43. Note 3 *supra.*

44. The index to volume 22 of the AAUP *Bulletin* (1936), under the caption "Loyalty Oaths," leads to published accounts of protests against such oaths.

45. See Becker, *In Support of the Constitution,* 21 A.A.U.P. BULL. 327 (1935), reprinted from 140 THE NATION 13 (1935); Angel, address to Yale Alumni, 22 A.A.U.P. BULL. 260 (1936); *Statement on Freedom of Speech—Teachers' Oath Laws,* 23 A.A.U.P. BULL. (1937).

46. WALTER GELLHORN, THE STATES AND SUBVERSION 410–11 (1952).

47. 64 Stat. 156, as amended, 42 U.S.C.A. § 1874(d)(I)(A) (supp. 1963); 72 Stat. 1962, as amended, 20 U.S.C.A. § 581(f) (Supp. 1963).

48. Notes 46 and 47, *supra,* prior to amendment. The requirement of the two acts was that the affiant swear "he does not believe in, and is not a member of and does not support any organization that believes in or teaches, the overthrow of the United States Government by force or violence or by any illegal or unconstitutional methods."

49. Among many published protests against the disclaimer affidavit requirement of the National Defense Education Act, possibly the most eloquent and comprehensive is that written by President A. Whitney Griswold of Yale University and published in the New York Times Magazine of December 20, 1959, at p. 18. For a record of opposition among educators, see *Repealing the Disclaimer Affidavit,* 46 A.A.U.P. BULL. 55 (1960). For the result and a final list of protesting institutions, see Orentlicher, *The Disclaimer Affidavit: A Valedictory,* 48 *id.* 524 (1962).

50. See the Arkansas act involved in Shelton v. Tucker, 364 U.S. 479 (1960). Although the decision invalidating the statue was placed on the ground of undue breadth of the required disclosure (*infra* text at note 65), the legislature of the state was clearly seeking to provide a means of identifying members of the National Association for the Advancement of Colored People (NAACP), and of discouraging membership in that organization. See also NAACP v. Alabama, 357 U.S. 449 (1958); Bates v. Little Rock, 361 U.S. 516 (1960); Louisiana v. NAACP, 366 U.S. 293 (1961).

51. See Adler v. Board of Education, *infra* note 61. The Association of American Law Schools in 1951, dealing also with other aspects of academic freedom in relation to national security. 1951 Proceedings 61–62, 98–101. For comprehensive reports of the Association's Committee on Academic Freedom and Tenure in this area, see *id.* 102–36; 1953 PROCEEDINGS 97–125; 1954 PROCEEDINGS 20–22, 115–20.

52. Under the provision, it becomes a criminal offense for a knowing member of an organization which is registered, or has been required by a final order of the Subversive Activities Control Board to register, under the Internal Security Act, to apply for a federal loan or grant.

53. Sweezy v. New Hampshire, 354 U.S. 234 (1957); see Gibson v. Florida Legislative Investigating Committee, 372 U.S. 539 (1963).

54. *Infra,* text at note 63.

55. Barenblatt v. United States, *infra* note 64.

56. See Carr, *Academic Freedom, the American Association of University Professors, and the United States Supreme Court,* 45 A.A.U.P. BULL. 5 (1959); Fuchs, *The Barenblatt Decision and the Academic Profession, id.* at 333 (1959). For a penetrating discussion of restrictions on the freedom of teachers and the means of combating them, see *Racial Integration and Academic Freedom,* 34 N.Y.U.L. REV. 725, 899 (1959) (Part one of a study by the Arthur Garfield Hays Memorial Fund, School of Law, New York University).

57. Beilan v. Board of Education, 357 U.S. 399 (1958); cf. Nelson v. County of Los Angeles, 362 U.S. 1 (1960).

58. Wieman v. Updegraff, 344 U.S. 183 (1952).

59. Cramp v. Board of Public Instruction, 368 U.S. 278 (1961).

60. Sweezy v. New Hampshire, *supra* note 53.

61. 342 U.S. 485 (1952).

62. Garner v. Los Angeles Board of Public Works, 341 U.S. 716 (1951).

63. 354 U.S. 234, 250 (1957).

64. Barenblatt v. United States, 360 U.S. 109, 112 (1959).

65. Shelton v. Tucker, 364 U.S. 479 (1960).

66. See Nostrand v. Little, 58 Wash. 2d 111, 361 P.2d 551 (1961), *appeal dismissed,* 368 U.S. 436 (1962); Byse, *Academic Freedom, Tenure, and the Law,* 73 HARV. L. REV. 304 (1959).

67. Koch V. Board of Trustees of the University of Illinois, 39 Ill. App.2d 51, 187 N.E.2d 340 (1962).

68. Article 5(3) of the German Constitution reads: "Art and science, research and teaching, shall be free. Freedom of teaching shall not absolve from loyalty to the constitution." Even so explicit a provision might mean only that specified freedoms are guaranteed against interference by non-academic authority. The self-government of academic institutions is included in the guaranty, and is secured as well by state constitutional provisions. 3. ENTSCHEIDUNGEN DES BUNDESVERFASSUNGSGERICHTS 58, 143 (1953); 1 MANGOLDT-KLEIN, DAS BONNER GRUNDGESETZ 253 (2d ed. 1957). It seems unlikely, therefore, that an alleged denial of academic freedom by academic authority would be reached by the guaranty.

69. The German constitutional guaranty of teaching freedom (*Lehrfreiheit*) is not deemed by commentators to extend to instruction that does not depend upon independent investigation. Hence it is confined to academic institutions and does not apply to those that prescribe the content of courses to be taught or the textbooks to be used. I MANGOLDT-KLEIN, *op. cit. supra* note 68, at 257, 258.

70. Faculty participation in college and university government appears to be increasing in the United States. See Report of Committee on the Place and Function of Faculties in College and University Government, 41 A.A.U.P. BULL. 62 (1955).

71. PAUL LAZARSFELD & WAGNER THIELENS, JR., THE ACADEMIC MIND (1958), contains evidence that even in areas of the colleges and universities where considerable independence might be expected a significant portion of faculty members were led by the agitation of the early 1950's to temper their expressions of opinion inside and outside of the classroom.

6

Academic Tenure: An Economic Critique

Robert W. McGee*

Walter E. Block**

I. Introduction

A number of arguments have been put forth in favor of academic tenure, the guarantee of lifetime employment in substantially the same position after some initial probationary period. These arguments have centered around cost effectiveness, academic freedom, and pedagogical quality. They invariably conclude that tenure is good and that horrendous things would happen if tenure were abolished or modified. In fact, it is very difficult to find an academic, especially one with tenure, who is not in favor of tenure.[1] "Tenure is to the academic what the closed shop is to a craft union."[2]

In this Article, we take the position of the devil's advocate. We show that many of the arguments usually offered in favor of tenure do not hold up under close analysis.[3] While tenure can save out-of-pocket expenses, promote independence from outside forces, and increase quality, it also increases overall costs, decreases flexibility, disenfranchises the paying consumer of education, increases dependence on unaccountable insiders, and makes it nearly impossible to remove incompetent and unnecessary professors. While we do not advocate the total abolition of tenure, we would like to see the present tenure practice abolished. We conclude that decisions on the value of tenure should be left to the market. In the absence of the current tenure policy, consumers of education would benefit from lower prices, more choices, and better quality products.

II. A Critical Analysis of Arguments for Tenure

A. *Is Tenure Cost-Effective?*

The argument that tenure is cost-effective is a plausible one on the surface. Just ask this question: If two teaching positions paid the same salary, had identical duties, and were identical in every other way—student body, prestige, geographic location, fringe benefits—but one position carried a guarantee of life-time employment and one did not, which position would one choose? The answer appears obvious. Because most people are risk-averse, they would choose the position that included a guaranteed job for life, other things being equal. Therefore, the possession of tenure has some value.[4] That being the case, professors who have tenure, or who are hired with the possibility of receiving tenure, will work for less money than professors who cannot hope to receive a guarantee of lifetime employment.[5] Consequently, universities can save money by granting tenure.[6] Once tenure exists at an institution, abolishing it would be equivalent to reducing professors' salaries.[7]

Although this argument is true as far as it goes, it is incomplete. There are other factors to consider in evaluating the tenure system besides initial out-of-pocket costs. If guaranteeing workers lifetime employment were cost-effective, wouldn't it make sense for all employers everywhere to grant lifetime employment to all workers? When viewed from this perspective, the cost-effectiveness argument in favor of tenure seems unpersuasive. If it were valid, all employers could reduce labor costs by guaranteeing lifetime employment. Yet the education industry is practically the only American industry that grants lifetime employment security.[8] One might ask why the practice is not more widespread, especially in the private sector where costs are closely scrutinized.

One reason why the idea has not spread throughout the private sector is that lifetime employment guarantees reduce flexibility. If General Motors, Ford, and Chrysler guaranteed their workers lifetime employment, the companies would have gone out of business long ago. To stay solvent, a company must have the flexibility to discard unneeded resources: low-quality or excess machinery, and low-quality or excess employees. The private sector must flexibly comply with the demands of the market in order to survive and prosper.

The education industry need not be so flexible, because it is virtually insulated from competition. Although colleges and universities compete for students, various accreditation agencies and governments dictate much of what they can and cannot do. Colleges and universities cannot compete freely by offering a product that is radically different from what other similar institutions are offering because they must meet the requirements of the accreditation agencies and government regulators, or risk having their accreditation revoked.[9] The insulation from competition in the education industry, and the resulting ability of many educational institutions to survive without being flexible, allows the tenure system to survive. As one academic economist has observed:

> [T]enure is neither necessary nor efficient. Its survival depends upon the absence of private ownership and is also encouraged by subsidization of education by non-customer income sources [(taxpayers and philanthropists)]. Without a private profit-seeking system and without full-cost tuition, the demand for tenure increases and the cost of granting it appears to be cheaper because the full costs are not imposed on those granting it. Competition among schools, teachers, and students provides protection to the search for the truth without tenure.[10]

The inflexibility that results from a policy of guaranteeing lifetime employment means that colleges and universities are not able to fire professors who are either incompetent or no longer needed.[11] If educational consumers—students—want more business or engineering courses, a university might try to meet this demand by hiring additional professors to teach these subjects. But it cannot fire tenured professors in fields not favored by consumers. As a result, classes in unpopular disciplines have fewer students, while classes in popular disciplines grow unwieldy. The quality of the classroom experience could be enhanced if class size in the popular disciplines were reduced, but university budgets are tight. Without extra funds, additional professors in the popular disciplines cannot be hired unless unneeded professors who teach other subjects can be dismissed. If tenure exists, students who study popular subjects must often do so in large classes because universities do not have the flexibility, at least in the short term, to allocate their resources according to consumer demand. Tenure thus prevents efficient resource allocation, to the detriment of consumers.[12] Universities must wait for the faculty in overstaffed departments to retire or die before resources can be reallocated.[13]

Although tenure may allow universities to hire faculty at lower salaries, total salary costs may be higher under a tenure system because universities will be forced to hire more faculty to teach popular disciplines and will not be able to fire unneeded faculty who teach unpopular subjects. If professors in disciplines with small consumer demand were given classes of thirty students instead of ten, two-thirds of them could be fired, and the funds saved could be used to hire professors in disciplines that students want to study, such as business.[14] When this inflexibility factor is considered, one can conclude that tenure actually increases salary costs.[15]

B. *Does Tenure Promote Academic Freedom?*

Another popular argument in favor of tenure is that without it, professors would hesitate to speak out on controversial subjects for fear of being fired.[16] This argument seems plausible on the surface. Certainly, if one need not worry about being fired for speaking out on controversial issues, one will be more likely to speak out than if one fears for his livelihood. We know that many theories that we now recognize as truth were once considered heretical: The world is round, not flat; the earth revolves around the sun, not the other way around; slavery is evil, even though it was thought of as normal and even necessary in the past. Members of the academic profession have been the proponents of these new ideas that have changed our ideas about truth. The argument runs that, in the absence of tenure, professors who speak out on controversial subjects or espouse unpopular views may jeopardize their careers. The free flow of information will be slowed or stopped.

But academics are not the only ones who challenge authority or existing orthodoxy. Novelists, playwrights, editors, news commentators, journalists, song writers, clergy, film producers, actors, cartoonists, and whistleblowers from various walks of life also espouse unpopular views and challenge orthodoxy. Should each of these groups also be given guaranteed jobs for life so that they can feel free to challenge the establishment? In the case of news journalists, tenure is not needed because journalists are motivated by the market. They seek out the truth and try to present it better and faster than the competition, so that their employer can capture a larger audience. Might not the same argument be made for academics? If universities were entrepreneurial, academics who sought the truth would be valued commodities; they would not need to worry about tenure, because their careers would be secure so long as they sought the discovery and dissemination of truth.[17] On the other hand, if teaching the truth offends or harms some individuals or groups, should not these individuals or groups have the right to combat the dissemination of truth by refusing to pay someone to disseminate it? To argue otherwise would be to conclude that professors deserve some special claim to the pocketbooks of the students or taxpayers who pay their salaries.[18]

The academic-freedom argument also suffers from its weak premise—that academics must be completely "free" and "independent." From whom should academics be independent? Academics are always worried about threats from outsiders. But what about the individuals who pay their salaries—education consumers and taxpayers? If a journalist writes something that is unpopular, consumers can exercise their view of the piece by not buying the newspaper that prints the article. Television viewers can turn to another channel if they dislike a commentator's views. Yet taxpayers and consumers of education must often support the careers of academics of whom they disapprove. In effect, those who advocate tenure on the grounds of academic freedom claim that academics have a right to the hard-earned dollars of others even if those who earn the dollars do not support the academics' views. In the view of tenure advocates, academic freedom justifies forcing others to support an academic's views with their cash.

Ironically, a major threat to outspoken professors can be found within the academy itself. Tenured academics decide whether an untenured professor is awarded tenure. Untenured faculty can easily be weeded out if they offend the members of the faculty tenure committee.[19] Unless he can show that racial, ethnic, or gender bias influenced the tenure decision, a professor who is denied tenure has little recourse.[20] Many scholars have had their careers short-circuited by their fellow professors because of their political leanings.[21] If a group of liberals, conservatives, or Marxists wants to exclude those who disagree with their views, all they have to do is deny them tenure. Yale University's president acknowledged this problem in 1972: "In strong universities, assuring freedom from intellectual conformity coerced within the institution is even more of concern than is the protection of freedom from external interference."[22] As another academic observed:

> [It is a] tattered secret that faculty members may devise a pattern of departmental appointments that shuts out significant schools of thought, may enter into a Faustian bargain with the grant-givers that trades off mental independence for a larger bank roll, and may make political judgments when reviewing the professional merits of their peers.[23]

Some academics go even further and prevent individuals from speaking at the university if they espouse views with which they disagree.[24] Officials of the South African government, officials from the Reagan administration, Nicaraguan contras, and other non-liberal types often are the victims of such anti-free speech activists these days.[25] During the 1950s, academics who espoused Communist, Marxist, or collectivist views experienced similar difficulties.[26] Even when an unpopular or "politically incorrect" individual is permitted to speak, he will often pay a price in the form of harassment, heckling, and picketing. Academics who promote cultural diversity often use these disruptions as an excuse to exclude certain individuals from the university and foreclose debate on issues of the day.[27] Academic freedom can be threatened from within the university as well as from without, and the tenure process does not guarantee that untenured professors will be protected from internal assaults on the right to say or write what is on their minds.

C. *Does Tenure Insure a High-Quality Professoriate?*

According to the tenure theory, only those professors who prove themselves through excellent teaching, research, and service are awarded tenure,[28] their weaker brethren fall by the wayside. At some of the "better" universities, however, receiving an award for good teaching is considered the kiss of death for an untenured professor.[29] Anyone who spends so much time preparing for class must somehow be deficient in research, or so the rationale goes.[30] In one recent period, three out of four recipients of Harvard's teaching award were denied tenure.[31] Stephen Ferruolo, a widely known medieval history scholar, won the Dinkelspiel award for outstanding teaching at Stanford in 1982, and was denied tenure shortly thereafter.[32] Bruce Tiffney won Yale's teaching award two weeks after being denied tenure.[33] Faye Crosby won the Yale teaching award in 1982 and was denied tenure three years later.[34] " 'It's extremely unlikely,' says Douglas Kankel, a tenured associate professor in Yale's Biology Department, 'that if you are a professor with an exceptional teaching background, you will survive the tenure process.' "[35] One critic has characterized the trend as systemic: "The pattern extends throughout higher education. Virtually every university in the country has a similar story. These cases are dramatic, irrefutable evidence that the academic culture is not merely indifferent to teaching, it is actively hostile to it. In the modern university, no act of good teaching goes unpunished."[36]

Even if the tenure process serves as a gauntlet that only the excellent survive,[37] that does not mean that the excellent untenured professor will continue to be excellent after receiving tenure. A professor may become out-of-date, lazy, incompetent, or senile after receiving tenure, yet need not fear being fired. Furthermore, the tenure process is marred by favoritism, politicking, and the "good old boy" network. Professors who receive strong tenure recommendations from the department chair and dean have a better chance of receiving tenure than do other, perhaps better-qualified nominees who receive lukewarm recommendations.[38] A majority of the professors who sit on university tenure committees are from fields other than that of the tenure nominee, know little about what the nominee has accomplished in his area of research, and depend heavily on the recommendations of others. When examining a nominee's list of publications, some committee members have even been known to ask which journals are refereed and which are not, because they are totally unfamiliar with the literature in the nominee's field.

Another argument against the present tenure rule of "up-or-out"[39] is that the probationary period is too short to evaluate properly a faculty member's potential.[40] This is especially true whenever the probationary period is short and the faculty member is engaged in a type of research that takes years to complete. The probationary period might end before the professor has published anything, and thus, a professor with excellent potential may be dismissed.[41] The university and the professor lose in such cases. If the professor can find another academic position, one university's loss is another's gain.

But professors who lose their positions must endure the hassle and trauma of finding another position and relocating to another city, often disrupting their family life in the process.

The "up-or-out" policy of tenure also increases turnover rates among untenured faculty. As a result, costs rise as universities engage in constant searches for replacement candidates. The quality of the faculty also generally drops whenever universities fire untenured professors who have a few years experience and replace them with untenured professors who have little or none.[42]

Junior professors who teach such "drill" courses as elementary accounting, beginning French, and freshman English do not need the protection of academic freedom provided by the tenure system as much as professors who teach more theoretical courses.[43] At the same time, many of these young professors face such heavy teaching loads that the burden of a tenure-level research program is at best impracticable. If tenure cannot be completely abolished, at least it should be ended for these junior professors, who stand to lose more from tenure than they can gain. In this way, they can have the opportunity to be employed at the same institution for more than six years and will not have to look for a new job every few years.[44]

As Charles Sykes has noted:

> Tenure corrupts, enervates, and dulls higher education. It is, moreover, the academic culture's ultimate control mechanism to weed out the idiosyncratic, the creative, the nonconformist. The replacement of lifetime tenure with fixed-term renewable contracts would, at one stroke, restore accountability, while potentially freeing the vast untapped energies of the academy that have been locked in the petrified grip of a tenured professoriate.[45]

The argument that tenure insures a high-quality professoriate cannot withstand scrutiny. If tenure cannot provide special benefits in the form of enhanced academic freedom or lower costs—and it appears likely that this is the case—the arguments for its continuation are correspondingly weakened.

III. Additional Reasons for Abolishing Tenure

The tenure system came under increased attack after World War II,[46] and two national commissions cited it as a possible cause of student unrest during the 1960s.[47] The Linowitz Commission called tenure "a shield for indifference and neglect of scholarly duties."[48] The Scranton Commission said that tenure protects "practices that detract from the institution's primary functions, that are unjust to students, and that grant faculty members a freedom from accountability that would be unacceptable for any other profession."[49] The American Association of University Professors (AAUP) and Association of American Colleges (AAC) were understandably upset at these criticisms, but their own commission concluded that the fault was not with the tenure system itself but with its application and administration.[50] The AAUP's commission recommended that

> "adequate cause" in faculty dismissal proceedings should be restricted to (a) demonstrated incompetence or dishonesty in teaching or research, (b) substantial and manifest neglect of duty, and (c) personal conduct which substantially impairs the individual's fulfillment of his institutional responsibilities. The burden of proof in establishing cause for dismissal rests upon the administration.[51]

Other commentators have attacked the tenure system for other reasons. Attorney John Gierak cites Michigan's Teacher Tenure Act[52] as the "single biggest obstacle to correcting the problem of poor teachers in [Michigan] public schools."[53] He gives three compelling reasons for this conclusion:

> [1] The teacher tenure system is wholly unnecessary to protect teachers from arbitrary and capricious actions of school boards, because teachers have more than adequate protection under collective bargaining agreements administered by powerful teachers unions.
>
> [2] Teacher tenure procedures are exorbitantly expensive in terms of both time and money, due in part to the fact that board of education members are required under the system to spend endless hours sitting as a "jury" on charges of teacher incompetency and misconduct.
>
> [3] The enormous amounts of time and money that must be invested in a teacher tenure case are powerful forces built into the tenure system that strongly discourage action against poor teachers. The impact of these cost considerations upon how districts deal with incompetent teachers cannot be overestimated, especially in small districts and those districts experiencing financial difficulties, which include the vast majority of all public school districts in the state.[54]

Times have changed drastically since Michigan passed its teacher tenure law in 1937. Labor law in Michigan and the rest of the nation has evolved to the point where tenure is no longer needed.[55] Teachers are now well-protected against arbitrary dismissal by various teachers' unions, to which the vast majority of teachers belong.[56] Union grievance procedures are much like those afforded by the Teacher Tenure Act. Special legislation is thus no longer needed to protect teachers' rights.[57]

Part of the problem with tenure acts like Michigan's is that they make dismissal of an incompetent teacher exorbitantly expensive. In Michigan, for example, legal fees for an action to discharge an incompetent teacher are typically between $50,000 and $70,000 and in some cases exceed $100,000.[58] Dismissing a teacher is time-consuming—a board of education may have to sit through ten or more hearings before it can take action.[59] In Michigan, if a board of education determines that a teacher should be dismissed, the teacher can request another hearing before the state's Teacher Tenure Commission. If the tenure commission upholds the board's dismissal, the teacher may appeal to the circuit court, then to the appellate court, and finally to the Michigan Supreme Court. In order to pay the legal costs of defending its action, the school board may need to lay off an additional teacher for three or four years.[60] In view of the time required to serve as a board member throughout this process, some school districts may find it difficult to obtain volunteers to sit on their boards of education, especially in large school districts, where several teachers may be attempting to have their dismissals overturned.[61]

With such expensive and drawn-out procedures required to dismiss an incompetent teacher, it is always possible that the school administration will decide that retaining an incompetent teacher is the lesser of two evils.[62] If that happens, the incompetent teacher is left free to damage hundreds or even thousands of students over the course of his career.[63] Allowing incompetent teachers to continue teaching also harms the morale of good teachers and administrators. This problem can be solved by abolishing the Teacher Tenure Act and instead relying upon binding arbitration,[64] which, according to Gierak, offers a number of advantages over the present system:

1. Arbitration is much quicker, which results in less disruption to educational programs, less potential back-pay liability, and increased fairness. . . .
2. Arbitration is much less expensive, for it reduces attorneys fees and costs. . . .
3. Arbitration does not necessarily involve board members. . . .
4. Because arbitrators are mutually selected by the parties, their decisions are generally better received and perceived to be more fair. . . .
5. Arbitration decisions are seldom appealed, which lends greater finality to the process. . . .[65]

Gierak goes on to observe that eliminating the Teacher Tenure Commission and its accompanying overhead would save taxpayers millions of dollars.[66]

While Gierak's arguments do not necessarily apply directly to situations in other states, many states have processes similar to that of Michigan.[67] And, although Gierak aims his attacks at the public primary and secondary school systems, his analysis largely applies to the collegiate level. Unionism is not as rampant at the college level as it is in the primary and secondary public schools, and university trustees do not necessarily become as involved in tenure disputes as do board of education members, but abolishing tenure at the college level can improve the quality of education by ridding the school of incompetent teachers.

IV. Conclusions and Recommendations

Academic tenure has advantages and drawbacks. It may save out-of-pocket expenses, but it also decreases flexibility, and the resulting inflexibility may cost more than the out-of-pocket expenses saved. Tenure enhances independence from outside forces but reduces the influence of those who pay and consume—taxpayers and students—while increasing the influence that tenured professors have on their untenured colleagues. The tenure process might increase the quality of the professoriate if it can truly separate high-quality teachers from those of low quality, but once a professor is tenured, it is difficult for the university to fire him unless he becomes incompetent or unneeded. Indeed, courts have ruled that universities may not fire a tenured professor even for ethical lapses.[68] Moreover, dismissing a tenured professor or teacher who does not want to go can be time-consuming and expensive.

So what is the solution? Is tenure good or bad? Nothing in the discipline of economics allows an unambiguous answer. The question is similar to "What is the optimal allocation of labor and capital in a given plant or industry?" Economics, however, can provide a methodology for answering this question. Let the market determine the worth of tenure. Give buyers and sellers of educational services freedom of choice. Allow colleges and universities the freedom to determine whether they want to offer tenure and how they want their tenure policy to be structured, without fear of losing accreditation.[69] Then, educational consumers would have the option of going to a school that has a tenure policy or one that does not. If tenure is a good management policy, it will tend to show in the consumer's perception of the university's reputation,[70] and that will have an effect on the university's enrollment and the amount of tuition it can charge.

Education consumers' dollar votes will be most effective, however, in rewarding good universities and punishing poor universities only if government is completely removed from the picture.[71] Government tends to reward universities with funding regardless of quality, whereas consumers reward universities (by paying tuition) based on their perceptions of quality. Consumers will have little influence if a university's budget is provided entirely or mostly by government and accredited by a government-approved accreditation agency. Universities can best serve consumers only if they are free to offer the best product they can without artificially-imposed government obstacles and prohibitions. If universities were allowed to become entrepreneurial, they would be forced to serve consumers or suffer a loss of enrollment.[72] Under the present system, universities can thrive while ignoring consumers so long as they continue to receive generous government funding and, at the same time, can prevent other universities from competing effectively by blocking such competitors' innovative courses and delivery systems.[73]

If a consumer-oriented educational system were available, a number of tenure options would likely result. Some universities would probably retain the traditional tenure system. Others would abolish it entirely, thus becoming like every other industry that refuses to guarantee its workers lifetime employment. A number of combinations and permutations would also likely develop. Perhaps five-year renewable contracts would replace tenure in some cases. Through hybrid instruments of this type, professors could be somewhat insulated from external and internal influences but could still be dismissed if their services became unneeded or unwanted. Other universities might decide to grant tenure to some professors and give term contracts to everyone else.[74] The market would discover other options as well, if allowed to operate. Tenure is a management policy. As is the case with all management policies, companies with good policies tend to thrive and companies with poor ones tend to lag behind the competition. The market determines what a good management policy is, and what is not, far better than theoreticians gathered around the fireplace in the faculty lounge.

Notes

* Associate Professor of Business Administration, Seton Hall University. B.A., 1969, Gannon University; M.S.T., 1976, DePaul University; J.D., 1980, Cleveland State University; Ph.D., 1986, University of Warwick.

** Associate Professor of Economics, College of the Holy Cross. B.A., 1964, Brooklyn College; Ph.D., 1972, Columbia University.

1. One journalist scoured North America and could find only one academic who would argue against tenure. *See* Walker, *Tenure Debate Falls Short,* THE PROVINCE, Sept. 4, 1983, at 269, 269. He should have polled primary and secondary school administrators. A 1972 poll of school administrators found that 86 percent wanted tenure either reformed or abolished. *See* E. BRIDGES, MANAGING THE INCOMPETENT TEACHER 3 (1984) (citing Cramer, *How Would Your Faucets Work If Plumbers Were Shielded by Tenure Laws?,* AM. SCH. BD. J., Oct. 1976, at 22, 22–24). In four Gallup polls of parents' attitudes toward public education, more than 50 percent said they opposed tenure. *See* A DECADE OF GALLUP POLLS OF ATTITUDES TOWARD EDUCATION, 1969–1978 (S. Elam ed. 1978).

For a strong defense of tenure, see Machlup, *In Defense of Academic Tenure,* 50 AM. A.U. PROF. BULL. 112 (1964), *reprinted in* ACADEMIC FREEDOM AND TENURE: A

HANDBOOK OF THE AMERICAN ASSOCIATION OF UNIVERSITY PROFESSORS 306–38 (L. Joughin ed. 1969). Professor Machlup's argument is based on the rather curious premise that although tenure harms academics more than it helps them, the benefits to "society" accruing from tenure more than compensate for the loss by academics because tenure encourages the free flow of debate. There is no evidence, however, that tenure improves the flow of debate beyond what already exists as a result of freedom of the press. Professor Machlup does not recognize that other groups are also harmed by tenure: Consumers of education, for example, must be content to endure a number of mediocre and incompetent professors who would be fired in the absence of the protection that tenure affords. Machlup apparently believes that "society" consists of something more than the sum of all individuals, but society as a whole cannot benefit from tenure—only individuals can benefit.

2. Walker, *supra* note 1, at 269.

3. For detailed discussions of tenure and the issues relating to it, see generally THE TENURE DEBATE (B. Smith ed. 1973); and FACULTY TENURE (W. Keast & J. Macy eds. 1973).

4. The United States Supreme Court has held that tenure may create a property right that cannot be taken away without due process. *See, e.g.,* Perry v. Sindermann, 408 U.S. 593 (1972) (a written contract with an explicit tenure provision may be evidence supporting a claim of a property right to continued employment); Connell v. Higginbotham. 403 U.S. 207 (1971) (due-process requirements apply when teacher is hired with clearly implied promise of continued employment); Slochower v. Board of Higher Educ., 350 U.S. 551 (1956) (tenured public college professor has interest in continued employment that is safeguarded by due process); Wieman v. Updegraff, 344 U.S. 183 (1952) (college professors have interest in continued employment that is safeguarded by due process). *Cf.* Board of Regents v. Roth, 408 U.S. 564 (1972) (non-tenured faculty member's property interest in employment was created by the terms of his employment and was insufficient to constitute property interest requiring due-process protections before nonrenewal of contract).

5. *See* Machlup, *supra* note 1, at 323–26. This salary effect is a double-edged sword. On the one hand, it attracts individuals to academia, which increases the supply of professors and lowers salaries generally (as supply increases, price decreases). On the other hand, consumers of education benefit because they can purchase more professors for their money because of the lower unit cost. This raises an interesting point. All professors' salaries tend to be reduced because of tenure. Yet only a minority of professors realistically benefit from the academic freedom that tenure affords. For example, political science professors tend to be shielded more by academic-freedom protections than do mathematicians and French grammarians. Would it not be more equitable, then, to allow those professors who do not see the need for protecting their academic freedom to bargain it away for higher salaries? Allowing this possibility would increase freedom of choice without jeopardizing the positions of those professors who would be content with lower salaries plus tenure.

6. This argument is a pervasive one, one that is always advanced whenever the institution of tenure is attacked or questioned. Twenty-nine economics department fac-

ulty members from the University of British Columbia used this argument when the tenure policy was being challenged in Canada. *See* Block, *Put an End to Academic Tenure*, ECON. AFF., July–Sept. 1984, at 37, 37–38.

7. *See* Milne, *Arthritic Academia: The Problems of Government Universities*, in OCCUPATIONAL REGULATION AND THE PUBLIC INTEREST 193, 198 (R. Albon & G. Lindsay eds. 1984). Of course, if tenure were abolished, professors would tend to demand higher monetary salaries because, as pointed out above, tenure is a form of compensation.

8. The civil service also guarantees lifetime employment, but people rarely argue that providing guaranteed lifetime employment to civil servants reduces labor costs. In fact, there is a widespread perception that the civil service is laden with inefficient or incompetent workers who are underworked and overpaid. Judges often have lifetime tenure, ostensibly so that they will be insulated from political pressure. A problem with lifetime judicial tenure is that it is nearly impossible for the citizenry to remove from the bench an unwanted judge who does not want to resign. The United States Constitution even prevents Congress from reducing judges' pay, although it does not provide that judges must get cost-of-living raises. *See* U.S. CONST. art. III, § 1. Therefore, in the absence of a pay raise, inflation will result in a de facto pay reduction. Such a pay cut, however, would apply to all judges, not just those Congress wished to single out for retribution.

9. Elaboration of this point is beyond the scope of this Article. Accreditation agencies are monopolies. The United States Department of Education places its stamp of approval on only one accreditation agency for each geographic location. For example, all schools in Ohio are accredited by the North Central Association. Any agency other than the North Central Association that accredits schools in Ohio is an unrecognized agency. *See* J. BEAR, HOW TO GET THE DEGREE YOU WANT 32–35 (8th ed. 1982).

The Department of Education also approves accreditation agencies for specific disciplines. For example, business schools are accredited by the American Assembly of Collegiate Schools of Business (AACSB). Much of what the AACSB requires before it will grant accreditation, though, actually decreases the quality of the educational institution. Accreditation pressures force schools to offer courses that are irrelevant and unwanted by educational consumers, and taught by faculty who may not be the best qualified. *See* R. MCGEE, A MODEL PROGRAM FOR SCHOOLS OF PROFESSIONAL ACCOUNTANCY 103–26 (1987) (providing further elaboration).

At least two of the six regional accreditation agencies in the United States are placing pressure on universities to increase ethnic and racial diversity in their faculties and student bodies. This means that schools are being pressured to hire faculty and accept students on the basis of race, ethnic background, and gender, rather than ability. For example, the Middle States Association delayed reaccrediting Baruch College of the City University of New York for three months because of alleged deficiencies in these areas. Critics of this policy say that the accreditation agencies are going too far, but not much can be done because of their monopoly status. *See 2 of 6 Regional Accreditation Agencies Take Steps to Prod Colleges on Racial, Ethnic Diversity*, Chron. Higher Educ., Aug. 15, 1990, at A1, col. 3. *See also Accrediting Quotas*, Wall St. J., Dec. 14, 1990, at A18, col. 1.

10. A. ALCHIAN, *Private Property and the Relative Cost of Tenure,* in ECONOMIC FORCES AT WORK 177, 201 (1977).

11. It is sometimes possible (but expensive) to encourage professors who are no longer needed to leave through early retirement and attractive severance packages. Universities, in effect, buy out the professors' property rights in their tenure agreement. Britain recently used this approach to rid its universities of unwanted faculty. *See* H. FERNS, HOW MUCH FREEDOM FOR UNIVERSITIES? 43 (1982).

12. For a discussion of flexibility and tenure, see Morris, *Flexibility and the Tenured Academic,* HIGHER EDUC. REV., Spring 1974, at 3.

13. *See id.* at 3. Universities have a number of other options in addition to waiting for unneeded faculty to retire or die. They can be given increased courseloads or unwanted administrative duties, which might induce some faculty members to leave. They could deny salary increases, which would decrease their purchasing power as inflation reduces the value of the dollar. Implementing such policies, however, increases animosity and could lead to a strike, which most university officials would rather avoid. Furthermore, such policies often take years to address the problem.

14. Some might argue that the students do not know what is best for them and that college administrators and accreditation agencies are better able to determine what students should study than the students themselves. This assumes that administrators and accreditors have the right to force their views and values on students, who may have far different values and views. Some schools thus require students to take Western civilization courses that consist of works written exclusively by white males. Other schools force students to take "watered down" Western civilization courses that include authors of questionable value just because they happen to be black, hispanic, or female. Some colleges force students to take sensitivity courses or courses that assert a particular political agenda. Many colleges force students to take mathematics, literature, foreign languages, or other courses that many students consider nonessential or a waste of time and money. For example, schools that are accredited by the American Assembly of Collegiate Schools of Business require students to take background "common body of knowledge" courses for the M.B.A. degree that often have little or nothing to do with what the student wants to learn. These courses often comprise up to 50 percent or more of the total coursework required for the M.B.A., thus doubling the cost and the time needed to complete the degree. The requirements for the M.S. degree in taxation are especially outrageous in this regard. In order to take the 10 or so courses needed for the degree, tax students are forced to take many courses totally outside the field of taxation. *See* R. MCGEE, *supra* note 9, at 18–24. Why would an education bureaucrat or committee necessarily know the needs of students better than the students themselves? In what other industry would the providers of a product be able to tell the buyers what they must buy? If the education monopoly were crushed, students could study the subjects that they value and save years of study and thousands of dollars.

15. This does not take into account the possible detrimental effects of the tenure system on the quality of the professoriate. *See infra* pp. 160–62.

16. Some would describe tenure as "the best guarantee of academic freedom." Lo-

vain, *Grounds for Dismissing Tenured Postsecondary Faculty for Cause,* 10 J.C. & U.L. 419, 419 (quoting COMM'N ON ACADEMIC TENURE IN HIGHER EDUC., FACULTY TENURE 21 (1973)). The United States Supreme Court has recognized that academic freedom is a special concern of the First Amendment. *See, e.g.,* Keyishian v. Board of Regents, 385 U.S. 589 (1967) (teachers cannot be dismissed for refusing to sign a certificate that indicates whether or not they had ever been Communists).

17. *See* H. FERNS, *supra* note 11, at 44.

18. *See* A. ALCHIAN, *supra* note 10, at 199.

19. The tenure process works in different ways at different schools. At Seton Hall University, for example, there are three tenure committees, one each at the departmental, school, and university level. At other schools, there is only one committee.

20. Finding proof of discrimination is often difficult. *See generally* Note, *Title VII and the Tenure Decision: The Need for a Qualified Academic Freedom Privilege Protecting Confidential Peer Review Materials in University Employment Discrimination Cases,* 21 SUFFOLK U.L. REV. 691 (1987); Palombi, *The Ineffectiveness of Title VII in Tenure Denial Decisions,* 36 DEPAUL L. REV. 259 (1987); Mahoney, *Title VII and Academic Freedom: The Authority of the EEOC to Investigate College Faculty Tenure Decisions,* 28 B.C.L. REV. 559 (1987).

21. *See, e.g., A Teacher Disillusioned With Utopia,* Boston Globe, Dec. 20, 1990, at 97, col. 3 (professor of comparative literature dismissed from Hampshire College for "his refusal, despite his leftish sympathies, to reduce the European literature he teaches to a one dimensional story of imperialism, colonialism and Third World oppression"); Dershowitz, *Quota System Wrong for Harvard Law,* Boston Herald, May 8, 1990, at 29, col. 1 (female assistant professor denied tenure at Harvard Law School because the "women [faculty members] argued that she, though a woman, was not a feminist"). *See generally* ACADEMIC LICENSE: THE WAR ON ACADEMIC FREEDOM (L. Csorba ed. 1988) [hereinafter ACADEMIC LICENSE]; R. KIMBALL, TENURED RADICALS: HOW POLITICS HAS CORRUPTED OUR HIGHER EDUCATION (1990).

A professor's political opinions often enter into the hiring, firing, and tenure decisions. *See, e.g.,* P. LAZARSFELD & W. THIELENS, THE ACADEMIC MIND 392 (1958); W. BUCKLEY, GOD AND MAN AT YALE 136–90 (1951); E. ROOT, COLLECTIVISM ON THE CAMPUS 289–335 (1955); Menn, *The Tenure Process and Its Invisible Kingmaker,* in How HARVARD RULES 271, 271–78 (J. Trumpdour ed. 1989).

22. Brewster, *On Tenure,* 58 AM. A.U. PROF. BULL. 381, 382 (1972).

23. Metzger, *Academic Freedom: A Symposium,* 13 N.Y.U. EDUC. Q. 4, 5 (1982).

24. The American Association of University Professors (AAUP) takes the position that college and university students have the right to listen to anyone whom they wish to hear, "and affirms its own belief that it is educationally desirable that students be confronted with diverse opinions of all kinds . . . [A]ny person who is presented by a recognized student or faculty organization should be allowed to speak on a college or university campus." *Summary of Forty-Third Annual Meeting,* 43 AM. A.U. PROF. BULL. 359, 363 (1957), *reprinted in* ACADEMIC FREEDOM AND TENURE: A HANDBOOK OF THE AMERICAN ASSOCIATION OF UNIVERSITY PROFESSORS 112–13 (L. Joughin ed. 1969). This position has sometimes been ignored when the person invited to speak has

espoused a conservative position. *See, e.g.,* Silber, *Free Speech and the Academy,* INTERCOLLEGIATE REV., Fall 1990, at 33, 34 (Marxist English professor attacked former contra leader Adolfo Calero at Northwestern University).

25. For a listing of campus free speech abuses, see ACADEMIC LICENSE, *supra* note 21, at 305–12.

26. *See, e.g.,* Keyishian v. Board of Regents, 385 U.S. 589 (1967) (refusal to sign a certificate indicating membership in the Communist Party); Sweezy v. New Hampshire, 354 U.S. 234 (1957) (refusal to answer questions about political beliefs and associations).

27. *See* Chavez, *The Real Aim of the Promoters of Cultural Diversity Is to Exclude Certain People and to Foreclose Debate,* Chron. Higher Educ., July 181, 1990, at B1, col. 2. *See also* Timmons, *Fraudulent Diversity,* NEWSWEEK, Nov. 9, 1990, at 8.

28. A fourth criterion—collegiality—is sometimes added to this list. One court defined collegiality as "the capacity to relate well and constructively to the comparatively small bank of scholars on whom the ultimate fate of the university rests." Mayberry v. Dees, 663 F.2d 502, 514 (4th Cir. 1981), *cert. denied,* 459 U.S. 830 (1982). While personality is not usually an official criterion for tenure, it often plays an indirect role in determining whether a faculty member is awarded tenure. For a discussion of this point, see Zirkel, *Personality as a Criterion for Faculty Tenure: The Enemy It Is Us,* 33 CLEV. ST. L. REV. 223 (1984–85).

A sore spot among those who regard teaching as paramount and everything else as secondary is the rather low esteem in which teaching is held by those in control of promotion and tenure. These persons argue that students are paying tuition to be taught by professors, not graduate assistants, and they are not paying tuition to subsidize faculty research. Yet research is rewarded, and teaching is not. In some universities, it is possible to go through an entire undergraduate program without being taught by a single member of the faculty. The student may be exposed only to a series of graduate assistants. *See* C. SYKES, PROFSCAM: PROFESSORS AND THE DEMISE OF HIGHER EDUCATION 35 (1988) (citing R. DUGGER, OUR INVADED UNIVERSITIES 170 (1974)).

29. *See* C. SYKES, *supra* note 28, at 58 (citing Barol, *The Threat to College Teaching,* NEWSWEEK ON CAMPUS, Oct. 1983).

30. *See id.* at 53.

31. *See id.*

32. *See id.* at 53–54.

33. *See id.* at 54.

34. *See id.*

35. *Id.* (quoting Professor Douglas Kankel).

36. *Id.*

37. Professor Machlup suggests that at least part of the "deadwood" problem is caused not by tenure, but by the inability of university administrations and tenure committees to weed out inefficient and incompetent professors, who also happen to be their friends, before they receive tenure. *See* Machlup, *supra* note 1, at 313–14, 317.

38. One prominent educator has pointed out that this politicking takes valuable time and energy away from teaching. Such politicking, however, is encouraged by the tenure process. *See* G. ROCHE, EDUCATION IN AMERICA 106–07 (1977).

39. In most institutions, professors who do not receive tenure within approximately six years are dismissed.

40. The probationary period varies with the institution. It is generally about six years but may be longer or shorter. Professors who have taught at another institution may have a reduced probationary period at their new institution. The AAUP has recommended a seven-year probationary period. The arbitrariness of this rule has been criticized by a number of commentators, including John R. Silber, now President of Boston University. *See* Silber, *Tenure in Context,* in THE TENURE DEBATE 34, 48–50 (B. Smith ed. 1973).

41. *See* Machlup, *supra* note 1, at 315.

42. *See id.* at 318–19.

43. We do not concede that anyone needs tenure to protect the right to speak and write. We merely assume it here for the sake of argument.

44. Some academic fields are extremely overcrowded. Professors in these fields who are fortunate enough to find one job may not be so lucky if they must find another job after a few years. Some individuals who are good classroom teachers may be forced to leave teaching altogether.

45. C. SYKES, *supra* note 28, at 258.

46. *See* Lovain, *supra* note 16, at 420 (citing COMM'N ON ACADEMIC TENURE IN HIGHER EDUC., FACULTY TENURE 8–10 (1973)).

47. *See id.*

48. *Id.* (quoting SPECIAL COMM. ON CAMPUS TENSIONS, AM. COUNCIL ON EDUC., CAMPUS TENSIONS: ANALYSIS AND RECOMMENDATIONS 42 (1970)).

49. *Id.* (quoting PRESIDENT'S COMM'N ON CAMPUS UNREST, REPORT OF THE PRESIDENT'S COMMISSION ON CAMPUS UNREST 201 (1970)).

50. *See id.* at 421 (citing COMM'N ON ACADEMIC TENURE IN HIGHER EDUC., FACULTY TENURE 20 (1973)).

51. *Id.* (quoting COMM'N ON ACADEMIC TENURE IN HIGHER EDUC., FACULTY TENURE 75 (1973)).

52. MICH. COMP. LAWS § 38.91 (1990) (MICH. STAT. ANN. § 15.1971 (Callaghan (1990)).

53. Gierak, *Abolish the Teacher Tenure Act to Improve the Quality of Public Education,* 68 MICH. B.J. 1098, 1098 (1989). Although Gierak focuses primarily upon primary and secondary schools, his arguments and our subsequent discussion are also applicable to higher education.

Professor Steven Amberg takes a contrary view of the need to abolish the Teacher Tenure Act. *See* Amberg, *Abolish the Teacher Tenure Act? Not While the Need Still Exists,* 68 MICH. B.J. 1104 (1989). However, Amberg ignores Gierak's arguments, does not make any valid arguments of his own, and blames incompetent teachers on administrators who fail to supervise or train them properly.

54. Gierak, *supra* note 53, at 1098.

55. *See id.* at 1099.

56. For a discussion of unions and tenure, see Olswang, *Union Security Provisions, Academic Freedom and Tenure: The Implications of* Chicago Teachers Union v. Hudson, 14 J.C. & U.L. 559 (1988).

57. Almost every state legislature has passed some type of statewide tenure legislation. *See* L. STELZER & J. BANTHIN, TEACHERS HAVE RIGHTS TOO 1 (1980).

58. *See* Gierak, *supra* note 53, at 1100.

59. *See id.* Gierak points out that some hearings take much longer. In Cooper v. Oak Park Public Schools, 624 F. Supp. 515 (E.D. Mich. 1986), board hearings took almost 10 months. *See id.* at 516.

60. *See* Gierak, *supra* note 53, at 1100.

61. *See id.* at 1101.

62. Gierak cites this fact as a major contributing cause to the mediocrity of the public schools. *See id.*

63. Several studies by the American Association of School Administrators found teacher incompetence to be a major problem in public schools. In a 1977 study, school administrators estimated that between 5 and 15 percent of their teachers were unsatisfactory performers. *See* E. BRIDGES, MANAGING THE INCOMPETENT TEACHER I (1984) (citing S. NEILL & J. CUSTIS, STAFF DISMISSAL: PROBLEMS AND SOLUTIONS 5 (1978)).

64. *See* Gierak, *supra* note 53, at 1101–03.

65. *Id.* at 1102. Gierak uses a case-in-point Beebee v. Haslett Public Schools, 406 Mich. 224, 278 N.W.2d 37 (1979), in which "the tenure charges filed with and upheld by the board against a teacher in 1968 were not finally resolved until 1979, a period of litigation spanning 11 years." Gierak, *supra* note 53, at 1103 n. 13. Gierak does not mention how much money was wasted in the course of this litigation or how many students were permanently damaged during the 11 years that this incompetent teacher was in the classroom.

66. *See* Gierak, *supra* note 53, at 1103.

67. As noted above, most other states also have teacher tenure acts. For discussions of Louisiana's Teacher Tenure Act, see Comment, *Louisiana's Teacher Tenure Act,* 34 LOY. L. REV. 517 (1988); and Resetar, *The Louisiana Teachers' Tenure Act— Protection from Dismissal for Striking Teachers?,* 47 LA. L. REV. 1333 (1987).

68. *See* Burton v. Cascade School Dist. Union High School No. 5, 353 F. Supp. 254, 255 (1973), *aff'd,* 512 F.2d 850 (9th Cir.), *cert. denied,* 423 U.S. 839 (1975); Texton v. Hancock, 359 So. 2d 895 (Fla. Dist. Ct. App. 1978). *See also* Magner, *Can't Fire Professor for Ethical Lapses, Rutgers Told,* Chron. Higher Educ., Aug. 15, 1990, at A2, col. 2.

69. For a discussion of how tenure policies may be changed or abolished, and how schools that do not have tenure policies have fared, see R. CHAIT & A. FORD, BEYOND TRADITIONAL TENURE: A GUIDE TO SOUND POLICIES AND PRACTICES (1982).

70. We do not mean to limit our recommendations to universities. The economics of tenure also apply to primary and secondary schools, although the problems and opportunities are somewhat different.

71. Readers may be shocked by the suggestion that education be completely privatized. We have been taught to believe that free public education is desirable and even a right. Discussing this issue in depth is beyond this Article's scope. Fortunately, several books and articles have been written on the benefits of totally private education, which can be much cheaper and qualitatively better than tax-supported education. For discus-

sions of this point, see S. BLUMENFELD, IS PUBLIC EDUCATION NECESSARY? (1985); J. COLEMAN & T. HOFFER, PUBLIC AND PRIVATE HIGH SCHOOLS (1987); J. COONS & S. SUGARMAN, EDUCATION BY CHOICE (1978); S. DENNISON, CHOICE IN EDUCATION (1984); R. FITZGERALD, WHEN GOVERNMENT GOES PRIVATE: SUCCESSFUL ALTERNATIVES TO PUBLIC SERVICES 139–48 (1988); F. FORTRAMP, THE CASE AGAINST GOVERNMENT SCHOOLS (1979); M. PIRIE, PRIVATIZATION: THEORY, PRACTICE AND CHOICE 194–97, 231–35, 283–87 (1988); R. POOLE, CUTTING BACK CITY HALL 172–88 (1980); THE PUBLIC SCHOOL MONOPOLY: A CRITICAL ANALYSIS OF EDUCATION AND THE STATE IN AMERICAN SOCIETY (R. Everhart ed. 1982); E. SAVAS, PRIVATIZING THE PUBLIC SECTOR: HOW TO SHRINK THE GOVERNMENT 102–03 (1982); Spring, *The Public School Movement vs. the Libertarian Tradition,* J. LIBERTARIAN STUD., Spring 1983, at 61; E. WEST, EDUCATION AND THE STATE: A STUDY IN POLITICAL ECONOMY (2d ed. 1970).

72. Professor Armen Alchian suggests that the incidence of tenure is directly correlated to the percentage of university income that comes from endowments and taxpayers. That is, the higher percentage of funding that comes from sources other than consumers (students), the more likely there is to be a high incidence of tenure, because the system is insulated from consumer demand. Such universities can continue to grant tenure, despite its inefficient features, because consumers do not have much clout if the vast majority of university funding comes from other sources. If consumers paid 100 percent of the cost of their education, tenure would be far less likely to exist as a management policy, as evidenced by the fact that at proprietary schools (which are run like businesses), tenure is practically nonexistent. Thus, tenure can best be eliminated by getting government out of education. *See* A. ALCHIAN, *supra* note 10, at 194.

Alchian also points out that teaching will grow in importance as the percentage of total university funding that comes from tuition increases. *See* A. ALCHIAN, *The Economic and Social Impact of Free Tuition,* in ECONOMIC FORCES AT WORK 203, 220 (1977). Students pay tuition to be taught rather than to subsidize faculty research and service, and if they are paying the full cost, they will be able to exercise tremendous influence by threatening to withhold their tuition or take their money to a competing institution. As it stands, tuition covers a small part of total funding, especially at tax-supported institutions. The inescapable conclusion is that teaching will improve if government is removed from the business of funding education. Even if this does not occur, emphasis on teaching could improve if government provided support in the form of vouchers instead of direct funding. A voucher policy still raises a moral question, because under such a policy, the government is still using the force of taxation to make some persons (taxpayers) pay for a benefit that goes to others (students).

73. The accreditation system prevents competition. A university cannot just offer an innovative course whenever and wherever it wants. It must first look over its shoulder to see whether the relevant accreditation agency will permit the new course. The American Assembly of Collegiate Schools of Business (AACSB), for example, routinely prohibits business schools from starting or expanding a new program without its approval—and approval is often denied in advance by telling the business school at the time of its accreditation visit that it may not expand a certain program or start any

new programs unless it first complies with specified conditions and receives AACSB approval. Thus, a business school may be prevented from offering M.B.A. courses at a company's facilities and may be forced by the accreditation agency to phase out such programs already in existence in order to maintain accreditation—even if consumers want the programs to be expanded.

74. Present university policy is either to grant tenure after some period of time, generally about six years, or to give a one-year notice of termination. Thus, professors who do not receive tenure are fired with one year's advance warning. If a termination letter is not received after a certain cut-off date, the professor is often considered tenured. The tenure or term contract option, by contrast, would allow untenured professors to continue teaching without forcing the university to terminate after some arbitrary period of time. Until a few years ago, academics in British schools were generally granted tenure automatically after a one- to five-year probationary period. *See* H. FERNS, *supra* note 11, at 42 n.2.

7

Does Academic Freedom Have Philosophical Presuppositions?

Richard Rorty

As Americans use the term, "academic freedom" names some complicated local folkways which have developed in the course of the past century, largely as a result of battles fought by the American Association of University Professors. These customs and traditions insulate colleges and universities from politics and from public opinion. In particular, they insulate teachers from pressure from the public bodies or private boards who pay their wages.

One way to justify such customs is to start from the premise that the search for objective truth is something quite distinct from politics, and indeed distinct from almost all other cultural activities. So, the argument goes, if politics or passion intrudes on that search, the purposes of colleges and universities—the accumulation of knowledge—will not be served. In particular, if universities are politicized, they will no longer be worthy of trust, just as doctors who care more for their fees than for their patients, or judges who care more about popularity than about justice, are no longer worthy of trust. A politicized university will be likely to produce merely opinion, rather than knowledge.

A number of contemporary philosophers, including myself, do their best to complicate the traditional distinctions between the objective and the subjective, reason and passion, knowledge and opinion, science and politics. We offer contentious reinterpretations of these distinctions, draw them in nontraditional ways. For example, we deny that the search for objective truth is a search for correspondence to reality, and urge that it be seen instead as a search for the widest possible intersubjective agreement. So we are often accused of endangering the traditions and practices which people have in mind when they speak of "academic freedom" or "scientific integrity" or "scholarly standards."

This charge assumes that the relation between a belief about the nature of truth and certain social practices is presuppositional. A practice presupposes a belief only if dropping the belief constitutes a good reason for altering the practice. For example, the belief that surgeons do not perform operations merely to make money for themselves or their hospitals, but do so only if there is a good chance that the operation will be beneficial to the patient, is presupposed by current practices of financing health care. The belief that many diseases are caused by bacteria and viruses, and that few can be cured by acupuncture, is presupposed by current practices of disbursing public funds for medical research.

The question of whether academic freedom rests on philosophical presuppositions raises the general question of whether *any* social practice has *philosophical,* as well as empirical, presuppositions. Beliefs about surgeons' motives and about the causes and curse of diseases are empirical presuppositions. Although the empirical-philosophical distinction is itself pretty fuzzy, it is generally agreed that a belief is on the empirical end of the spectrum to the extent that we are clear about what would falsify it. In the medical examples I have used, we are clear about this. Various specific revelations about the success rate of acupuncture, or about the secret protocols of the American College of Surgeons, could have an immediate, devastating effect on current practices. But when it comes to a philosophical belief like "The truth of a sentence consists in its correspondence to reality," or "Ethical judgments are claims to knowledge, rather than mere expressions of feeling," nobody is very clear about what it would take to make us believe or disbelieve it. Nobody is sure what counts for or against such propositions.

The reasons they are unsure are the same as those why it is unclear whether, if we stopped believing these propositions, we should need to change our practices. Philosophical views are just not tied very closely either to observation and experiment, or to practice. This is why they are sometimes dismissed as merely philosophical, where "merely" suggests that views on these subjects are optional—that most people, for most purposes, can get along without any. But precisely to the extent to which such views are in fact optional, social practices do not have philosophical presuppositions. The philosophical propositions said to be presuppositional turn out to be rhetorical ornaments of practice, rather than foundations of practice. This is because we have much more confidence in the practice in question than in any of its possible philosophical justifications.

In a culture which regards debates among philosophers with appropriate insouciance, purported philosophical foundations would suffer the same fate as has, in the two centuries since the Enlightenment, overtaken theological foundations. As American society has become more and more secular, the conviction has grown that a person's religious beliefs, and perhaps even her lack of any such beliefs, are irrelevant to her participation in most of our social practices. But it was not always that way: Article Six of the Constitution of the United States, which forbids religious tests for office, was hardly uncontroversial. The conservatives who had doubts about Jefferson's Virginia Statue of Religious Freedom were convinced that participation in many of our institutions and practices presupposed Christian belief. They had a plausible case. But Jefferson, we now say with the benefit of hindsight, had a better case.

One useful example of the change in the relation between religious and other social practices is the gradual shift in attitudes toward oath-taking between Jefferson's time and our own. Taking oaths has always been integral to legal practice, but there has been considerable disagreement about what an oath is, what sort of people can take it, and what presuppositions taking it involves. At the beginning of our century the *Encyclopedia Britannica* still defined an oath as "an asseveration or promise made under non-human penalty or sanction". The author of the relevant article offered dozens of instances of the relevance of belief in such sanctions—for example, Siamese Buddhists who made themselves eligible as witnesses in court by praying that, if they lied, they be punished by five hundred reincarnations as a beast and five hundred more as an hermaphrodite.

Nowadays most of us who are called upon to be witnesses in court, atheists and theists alike, solemnly and sincerely swear to tell the whole truth without giving much thought to the existence or nature of non-human penalties or sanctions. We atheists no longer even bother to distinguish between swearing and affirming, although that distinction was of great concern to the British House of Commons when the atheist Charles Bradlaugh asked to be seated, and was written into British law in 1888 only after anguished debate. No bailiff asks us about our religious beliefs before administering the oath. The suggestion that she do so would be regarded by the court as an absurd waste of time. Truthfulness under oath is, by now, a matter of our civic religion, our relation to our fellow-Americans, rather than of our relation to a nonhuman power. The relation between belief in the existence of a certain kind of God and the practice of oathtaking used to be presuppositional, but now it is not.

As I see it, it is with truth as it is with truthtelling: philosophical debates about the nature of truth should become as irrelevant to academic practices as debates about the existence and forms of post-mortem punishment are to present-day judicial practices. Just as we have much more confidence in our judicial system than we do in any account of the after-life, or the workings of

Divine Providence, so we have, or at least should have, much more confidence in our colleges and universities than we do in any philosophical view about the nature of truth, or objectivity, or rationality.

More specifically, I shall argue in what follows that philosophers who deny that there is any such thing as the correspondence of a belief to reality, and thus seem to many nonphilosophers to have denied the existence of truth, are no more dangerous to the pursuit of truth than theologians who deny the existence of hellfire. Such theologians put neither morality nor Christianity in danger, and such philosophers endanger neither the university nor society. Those theologians did, however, change our sense of what Christianity was—of what it takes to be a good Christian. We now have a conception of Christianity which would have seemed perverse and outrageous to many of our eighteenth-century ancestors, though not to Jefferson. Analogously, these philosophers may gradually change our sense of what a university is, and what its role in society is. We may wind up with a conception of the university and its social role which would have seemed outrageous to Ranke, to Weber, and to Nicholas Murray Butler, though not to John Dewey.

I view it as a mark of moral and intellectual progress that we are more and more prepared to judge institutions, traditions and practices by the good they seem to be doing than by the philosophical or theological beliefs invoked in their defense. More generally, I view it as a mark of such progress that we are coming to think of such beliefs as abbreviations of practices rather than as foundations for practices, and that we are becoming able to see many different beliefs as equally good abbreviations for the same practice. My view of the nonpresuppositional relation of any given set of philosophical convictions to academic freedom is of a piece with President Eisenhower's famous dictum that America is firmly founded in religious belief, and that it doesn't matter which religion it is. I think that there are a lot of different philosophical beliefs about the nature of truth and rationality which can be invoked to defend the traditions and practices which we call "academic freedom," and that in the short run, at least, it does not greatly matter which ones we pick.[1]

A distinguished fellow-philosopher, John Searle, sharply disagrees with me on this point. Outside of philosophy, Searle and I agree on a great deal. We are equally suspicious of the mannered posturing, and the resentful self-righteousness, of the academic left in the United States. We are equally suspicious of attempts to require courses which will shape students sociopolitical attitudes, the sort of courses which students at Berkeley now refer to as "compulsory chapel." We are equally nostalgic for the days when leftist professors concerned themselves with issues in real politics (such as the availability of health care to the poor, or the need for strong labor unions) rather than with

academic politics. But Searle and I disagree over the relevance of our professional specialty—philosophy—to the phenomena we both dislike.

In an article entitled "Rationality and Realism, What Is at Stake?"[2], Searle
describes what he calls "the Western Rationalistic Tradition," and says that it
is under attack from such philosophers as Thomas Kuhn, Jacques Derrida and
myself. Searle goes on to say that the biggest single consequence of the rejection of the Western Rationalistic Tradition is that it makes possible an abandonment of traditional standards of objectivity, truth, and rationality, and
opens the way for an educational agenda one of whose primary purposes is to
achieve social and political transformation.[3]

Searle lists a number of philosophical positions that he regards as central
to the Western Rationalistic Tradition, but I shall discuss only two: the claim
that, in Searle's words, "knowledge is typically of a mind-independent reality,
and the claim that knowledge is expressed in "propositions which are true
because they accurately represent that reality". I disagree with both claims. I
agree with Kuhn that we should deny all meaning to claims that successive
scientific beliefs become more and more probable or better and better approxi-
mations to the truth and simultaneously suggest that the subject of truth claims
cannot be a relation between beliefs and a putatively mind-independent or
"external" world."[4]

I agree with Hilary Putnam that elements of what we call "language" or
"mind" penetrate so deeply into what we call "reality" that the very project of representing ourselves as being "mappers" of something "language-
independent" is fatally compromised from the start. Like Relativism, Realism
is an impossible attempt to view the world from Nowhere.[5]

Kuhn, Putnam, Derrida and I would all, I think, agree with Donald Davidson that it is futile either to reject or accept the idea that the real and the true
are "independent of our beliefs." The only evident positive sense we can make
of this phrase, the only use that derives from the intentions of those who
prize it, derives from the idea of correspondence, and this is an idea without
content.[6]

The detailed arguments which go on between philosophers like Davidson,
Putnam, Derrida, Kuhn, and myself—philosophers who think that "correspondence to reality" is a term without content—and philosophers like Searle,
are as baffling to nonspecialists as those between theologians who debate tran-
substantiation, or who ask whether it is worse to be reincarnated as a hermaphrodite than as a beast. The technical, nit-picking, character of both sets of
arguments is itself a reason for suspecting that the issues debated are not very
closely tied in with our social practices.

If what Searle calls "traditional standards of objectivity, truth and rationality" are simply the normal practices of the academy—or, to give Searle the

benefit of the doubt, those practices as they were before people like Kuhn, Derrida and I began to muddy the waters—then I see no more reason to think that abandoning a belief in correspondence will make one a less honest scholar than to think that abandoning a belief in God will make one a less honest witness. The loyalty of philosophers on both sides of the argument about correspondence to these "traditional standards" is much greater than their attachment to the significance, or the insignificance, of the idea of "correspondence."

Searle is right, however, that the bad guys tend to favor my side of the argument. There really are people around who have no qualms about converting academic departments and discipline into political power bases. These people do not share Searle's and my reverence for the traditions of the university, and they would like to find philosophical support for the claim that such reverence is misplaced. Here is an example of the kind of rhetoric which Searle quotes with relish as an illustration of the evil influence of views like mine: "As the most powerful modern philosophies and theories have been demonstrating, claims of disinterest, objectivity and universality are not to be trusted, and themselves tend to reflect local historical conditions".[7] I have to admit to Searle that the committee which produced that dreadful sentence actually did include people who really do believe that the philosophical views I share with Kuhn and Derrida entail that the universities have no further use for notions like "disinterest" and "objectivity."

But these people are wrong. What we deny is that these notions can be explained or defended by reference to the notion of "correspondence to mind-independent reality." Philosophers on my side of the argument think that we can only explain what we mean when we say that academic research should be disinterested and objective by pointing to the ways in which free universities actually function. We can only defend such universities by pointing to the good which these universities do, to their role in keeping democratic government and liberal institutions alive and functioning.

The distinction I am drawing is analogous to that between saying "we have no further use for Christianity" and saying "we cannot explain the Eucharist by reference to Aristotelian notions of substance and accident." At the time of the Council of Trent, many intelligent people thought that if we gave up on the Aristotelian-Thomistic account of the Eucharist, the Christian religion, and thus the stability of the European socio-political order, would be endangered. But they were mistaken. Christianity survived the abandonment of this account, and survived in what Protestants think of as a desirably purified form.

Philosophers on my side of the argument think that if we stop trying to give epistemological justifications for academic freedom, and instead give socio-political justifications, we shall be both more honest and more clearheaded.

We think that disinterested, objective inquiry would not only survive the adoption of our philosophical views, but might survive in a desirably purified form. One result of the adoption of our views might be, for example, that physics-envy will become less prevalent, and that distinctions between disciplines will no longer be drawn in phallogocentric terms, such as "hard" and "soft." Biologists and historians might stop looking down their noses at colleagues in other departments who cannot produce experimental or archival data in support of their conclusions. We might stop debating the pointless and tiresome question of whether doctoral dissertations in English literature constitute contributions to knowledge, rather than being merely expressions of opinion. Sociologists and psychologists might stop asking themselves whether they are following rigorous scientific procedures, and start asking themselves whether they have any suggestions to make to their fellow-citizens about how our lives, or our institutions, should be changed.

The crucial move made by people on my side of the argument about the nature of objectivity is that, just as the only difference between unconsecrated and consecrated bread is in the social practices appropriate to each, so the only difference between desirable objectivity and undesirable politicization is the difference between the social practices conducted in the name of each. The point, we say, is not whether Christ is Really Present in the bread, but whether we should treat a consecrated Host as we would a snack. The point is not whether disinterested and objective inquiry will lead to correspondence to mind-independent reality, but how to keep the Old Guard from freezing out the Young Turks while simultaneously preventing the Young Turks from wrecking the university.

A healthy and free university accommodates generational change, radical religious and political disagreement, and new social responsibilities, as best it can. It muddles through. There are no rules for this muddling through, any more than there are rules which our appellate judges follow when they accommodate old constitutional provisions to new socio-political situations. Debate at English Department faculty meetings is no less, and no more, rational than at the conferences where justices of the Supreme Court discuss pending cases. As philosophers of law, from Cardozo to Dworkin, have advised us, attempts to draw nice clean lines between law and morality, or between jurisprudence and politics, have met with little success. The question whether the judges of the higher courts explain what the law already was, or instead make new law, is as idle as the philosophical question about whether literary criticism produces knowledge or opinion. But recognizing the idleness of the first question does not make philosophers of law, or the rest of us, value the ideal of a free and independent judiciary any the less. Nor does it make us less able to tell good judges from bad judges, any more than our lack of an epistemology of literary criticism makes us less able to tell good critics from bad critics, boring pedants from original minds.

More generally, the experience that each of us in this room has had with decisions about curriculum and appointments should persuade us that the distinction between academic politics and the disinterested pursuit of truth is pretty fuzzy. But that fuzziness does not, and should not, make us treasure free and independent universities any the less. Neither philosophers nor anyone else can offer us nice sharp distinctions between appropriate social utility and inappropriate politicization. But we have accumulated a lot of experience about how to keep redrawing this line, how to adjust it to meet the needs of each new generation. We have managed to do so in ways which have kept our colleges and universities healthy and free.

One of the things this accumulated experience has taught us is that universities are unlikely to remain healthy and free once people outside the universities take a hand in redrawing this line. The one thing that has proved worse than letting the university order its own affairs—letting its members quarrel constantly and indecisively about what shall count as science or as scholarship—is letting somebody else order those affairs. As long as we keep this lesson in mind, and manage to keep the traditions of civility alive within the academy, what Searle calls "traditional standards of objectivity, truth and rationality" will take care of themselves. These standards are not under the guardianship of the philosophers, and changes in opinion among the philosophy professors will not cause us to abjure, or change, them. As Nelson Goodman said about logic, all the logician can do is tell you what deductive arguments people usually accept as valid, she cannot correct their notions of deductive validity. Similarly, all we philosophers can do when asked for standards or methods of disinterested and objective inquiry is to describe how the people we most admire conduct their inquiries. We have no independent information about how objective truth is to be obtained.

So much for the Overall Argument I should like to offer you. I want to turn now to the more technical aspects of the disagreement between myself and Searle. The central question which Searle raises is whether, if we do not believe in mind-independent reality, you can still believe in, and insist upon, objectivity?[8] Philosophers on my side of the argument answer that objectivity is not a matter of corresponding to objects but of getting together with other subjects—that there is nothing to objectivity except intersubjectivity. So when Searle says "If there is no such thing as objective truth and validity, then you might as well discuss the person making the statement and his motives for making it," we rejoin that nobody ever said there was no such thing as objective truth and validity. What we say is that you gain nothing for the pursuit of such truth by talking about the mind-dependence or mind-independence of reality. All there is to talk about are the procedures we use for bringing about agreement between inquirers.

One reason that the question of mind-independent reality is so vexed and confusing is an ambiguity in the notion of "independence." Searle sometimes writes as if philosophers who, like myself, do not believe in "mind-independent reality" must deny that there were mountains before people had the idea of "mountain" in their minds, or the word "mountain" in their language. But nobody denies that. Nobody thinks that there is a chain of causes which makes mountains an effect of thoughts or words. What people like Kuhn, Derrida and I believe is that it is pointless to ask whether there really are mountains or whether it is merely convenient for us to talk about mountains.

We also think it pointless to ask, for example, whether neutrinos are real entities or merely useful heuristic fictions. This is the sort of thing we mean by saying that it is pointless to ask whether reality is independent of our ways of talking about it. Given that it pays to talk about mountains, as it certainly does, one of the obvious truths about mountains is that they were here before we talked about them. If you do not believe that, you probably do not know how to play the usual language-games which employ the word "mountain." But the utility of those language-games has nothing to do with the question of whether Reality as It Is In Itself, apart from the way it is handy for human beings to describe it, has mountains in it. That question is about the other, non-causal, sense of "independence." My side thinks nothing could possibly turn on the answers to questions of independence in that sense, and that therefore we can get along quite nicely without the notion of Reality as It Is In Itself.

Davidson says that the question of whether the real is "independent of our beliefs" should not be asked because he thinks that the only relevant sense of independence is not "causal antecedence" but "existence in itself." He thinks that the notion of "correspondence to reality" is useless because the relevant reality is reality "as it is in itself." We who agree with Davidson think that the whole project of distinguishing between what exists in itself and what exists in relation to human minds—the project shared by Aristotle, Locke, Kant and Searle—is no longer worth pursuing.[9] This project, like the project of underwriting the sanctity of the Eucharist, once looked interesting, promising, and potentially useful. But it did not pan out. It has turned out to be a dead end.

Another semi-technical point I need to make concerns an ambiguity lurking in the notion of "accurate representation." Searle says, you recall, that the Western Rationalistic Tradition holds that knowledge is expressed in "propositions which are true because they accurately represent that [mind-independent] reality." We Davidsonians want to distinguish between two senses of the term "represent accurately." In the non-philosophical sense of this term, to ask a witness if she has accurately represented a situation is to ask about her truthfulness, or her carefulness. When we say that good historians accurately represent what they find in the archives, we mean that they look hard for relevant documents, do not discard documents tending to discredit the historical thesis they are propounding, do not misleadingly quote passages out of context, tell the same historical story among themselves that they tell us, and so on. To assume that a historian accurately represents the facts as she knows them is to assume that she behaves in the way in which good, honest, historians behave. It is not to assume anything about the reality of past events, or the truth-conditions of statements about such events, or about the necessarily hermeneutical character of the *Geisteswissenschaften,* or about any other philosophical topic.[10]

But when philosophers discuss the question of whether knowledge consists in accuracy of representation, they are not concerned with honesty or carefulness. The question at issue between representationalists like Searle and anti-representationalists like me is merely this: can we pair off parts of the world with parts of beliefs or sentences, so as to be able to say that the relations between the latter match the relations between the former? Can true beliefs or sentences be treated on the model of realistic portraiture? There are obviously some cases which can be so treated, such as the immortal "The cat is on the mat." There are lots of other cases, such as the sentence "neutrinos have no mass" or "the pursuit of scholarly truth requires academic freedom," to which the notion of "parts of the world" has no evident application. We philosophers haggle endlessly about whether the notions of "correspondence" and "representation"' can be extended to these harder cases. When we are tired of haggling about that, we start haggling over whether there is any criterion for whether a belief accurately represents reality other than its coherence with the rest of our beliefs, and if not, whether we should distinguish between the *criterion* of true belief and the *nature* of true belief.

Searle's claim that the correspondence theory of truth has moral or social importance runs together the philosophical and nonphilosophical senses of "accurate representation." If we anti-representationalists and anti-correspondentists ever win our argument with Searle, that will give historians and physicists no reason to behave differently than they presently do. Nor, I suspect, will their morale or their efficiency improve if Searle and his fellow representationalists should win. Honesty, care, truthfulness, and other moral and social virtues are just not that closely connected with what we philosophy professors eventually decide to the least problematic way of describing the relationship between human inquiry and the rest of the universe.

The claim about a lack of close connection which I have just made is not put forward as a philosophical truth about the necessary, a historical, relation of philosophy to the rest of culture. It is simply a sociological truth about the lack of interest which most people, intellectuals as well as nonintellectuals, currently have in philosophy. It is like the truth that the adoption of the ethics of love suggested by St. Paul does not depend upon the Orthodox, as opposed to the Arian, position on the relation between the First and Second Persons of the Trinity. That is a sociological truth about contemporary Christians, not an a historical truth about the relation between ethics and theology. Things were otherwise in the days when not only your physical safety, but your choice of which charioteers to cheer for in the hippodrome, depended upon your theological allegiance.

If Searle has his way—if he succeeds in persuading us (or even in persuading funding agencies) that the relation between the Western Rationalistic Tradition and current academic practices is in fact presuppositional, and that refuting Kuhn, Derrida, and me is an urgent social need—then the academy will divide up into those who cheer for the representationalist philosophical team and those who (selflessly sacrificing grants for the sake of philosophical correctness) cheer for their opponents. Scholars and scientists will go around asking each other, and being asked by grant-givers, "Which side are you on?"

I think that would be unfortunate, if only because it would be a waste of people's time, and of their emotional energy. It would be better to distinguish the ethics of the academy—the customs and practices which help to determine the attitude of students to books, faculty to students, administrators to faculty and donors, and so on—from the private theological or philosophical convictions of any of the persons involved. To help keep the academy free and de-politicized, we should, for example, make sure that professors do not mock the beliefs of their fundamentalist students, that donors do not designate particular persons to fill the chairs they endow, and that a scholar's conclusions about controversial issues within her field, or about political or philosophical matters, continue to be irrelevant to her membership in the university. But we should not worry about whether truth sentences accurately represent mind-independent reality.

So far I have been arguing that philosophy does not make much difference to our practices, and that it should not be allowed to do so. But this may seem a strange position for somebody who calls himself a pragmatist. We pragmatists say that every difference must make a difference to practice. Yet we think it important to argue that the Western Rationalistic Tradition, as Searle defines it, is *wrong*. We insist on trying to develop another, better, tradition. So how can we, without dishonesty, say that philosophical controversies do not matter all that much?

We pragmatists can make our position consistent, I think, by saying that although they don't matter much in the short run, they may well matter a lot in the long run. The Christian who believes that God will punish him with hell-fire if he lies under oath and the atheist who believes that he will be unable to live with himself if betrays the social compact by committing perjury will, in the short run, do the same thing. But in the long run it may make a lot of difference whether a society is regulated by its members' fear of non-human sanctions or by secular sentiments of pride, loyalty, and solidarity. The physicist who describes himself as uncovering the absolute, intrinsic, in itself character of reality and his colleague who describes herself as assembling better instruments for prediction and control of the environment will, in their race for the glittering prizes of their profession, do much the same things. But in the long run physicists whose rhetoric is pragmatist rather than Western Rationalist might be better citizens of a better academic community.

Deep emotional needs are fulfilled by the Western Rationalist Tradition, but not all such needs should be fulfilled. Deep emotional needs were fulfilled by belief in a non-human judge and non-human sanctions. These were the needs which Dostoevski evinced when he said that if God did not exist, everything would be permitted. But these needs should be, and to some extent have been, sublimated or replaced, rather than gratified. I have pressed the analogies between theological and philosophical belief because I see the Western Rationalist Tradition as a secularized version of the Western Monotheist Tradition—as the latest twist on what Heidegger calls "ontotheology." We pragmatists take the same dim view of Absolute Truth, and of Reality as it is in Itself, as the Enlightenment took of Divine Wrath and Divine Judgment.

John Dewey once quoted G. K. Chesterton's remark that "Pragmatism is a matter of human needs and one of the first of human needs is to be something more than a pragmatist."[11] Chesterton had a point, and Dewey granted it. Dewey was quite aware of what he called "a supposed necessity of the 'human mind' to believe in certain absolute truths." But he thought that this necessity had existed only in an earlier stage of human history, a stage which we might now move beyond. He thought that we had reached a point at which it might be possible, and helpful, to wrench ourselves free of it. He recognized that his suggestion was counter-intuitive, and would meet the kind of opposition which Searle mounts. But he thought that the long-run good done by getting rid of outdated needs would outweigh the temporary disturbance caused by attempts to change our philosophical institutions.

As Dewey saw it, the need to distinguish between the pursuit of truth "for its own sake" and the pursuit of what Bacon called "the improvement of man's estate," arose out of particular social conditions.[12] These conditions prevailed in ancient Greece, and made it useful to draw certain distinctions which became, in the course of time, part of our common sense. These included, for example, the distinctions between theory and practice, mind and body, objective and subjective, morality and prudence, and all the others which Derrida groups together as "the binary oppositions of Western metaphysics."

Dewey was happy to admit that these distinctions had, in their time, served us well. In their time, they were neither confusions, nor repressive devices, nor mystifications. On the contrary: they were instruments which Greek thinkers used to change social conditions, often for the better. But over a couple of millennia these instruments outlived their usefulness. Dewey thought that, just as many Christians have outgrown the need to ask whether the sentences of the Creed correspond to objective reality, so civilization as a whole might outgrow the supposed necessity to believe in absolute truths.

Dewey learned from Hegel to historicize everything, including Hegel's own picturesque, but outdated, story of the union of subject and object at the end of History. Like Marx, Dewey dropped Hegel's notion of Absolute Spirit, but kept his insight that ideas and movements which had begun as instruments of emancipation (Greek metaphysics, Christianity, the Rise of the Bourgeoisie, the Hegelian System) had typically, over the course of time, turned into instruments of repression—into parts of what Dewey called "the crust of convention." Dewey thought that the idea of "absolute truths" was such an idea, and that the pragmatic theory of truth was "true in the pragmatic sense of truth: it works, it clears up difficulties, removes obscurities, puts individuals into more experimental, less dogmatic, and less arbitrarily skeptical relations to life." "The pragmatist," he continued, "is quite content to have the truth of his theory consist in its working in these various ways, and to leave to the intellectualist the proud possession of [truth as] a unanalyzeable, unverifiable, unworking property."[13]

Dewey said that Chesterton's remark "has revealed that the chief objection of absolutists to the pragmatic doctrine of the personal (or "subjective") factor in belief is that the pragmatist has spilled the personal milk in the absolutist's coconut."[14] His point was that Chesterton had implicitly admitted that the best, and perhaps the only argument, for the absolutist view of truth was that it satisfied a human need. Dewey saw that need as one we could outgrow. Just as the child outgrows the need for parental care, and the need to believe in parental omnipotence and benevolence, so we may in time outgrow the need to believe in divinities which concern themselves with our happiness, and in the possibility of allying ourselves with a non-human power called The Intrinsic Nature of Reality. In doing so, we might outgrow both the need to see ourselves as deeply sinful and guilty, and the need to escape from the relative to the absolute. Eventually, Dewey thought, the subjective-objective distinction and relative-absolute distinctions might become as obsolete as the distinction between the soul and the body, or between natural and supernatural causes.

Dewey was quite aware, however, that the good work still being done by old distinctions would have to be taken over by new distinctions. He was also quite aware of what Berkeley called the need to "speak with the vulgar and think with the learned," to apply different strokes to different folks. So his writings are a sometimes confusing mixture of invocations of familiar distinctions with counter-intuitive, philosophical, reinterpretations of those distinctions. His reformulations were often, at least to the vulgar, merely bewildering. So we should not be surprised to find Dewey, at the same time that he was energetically defending the pragmatic theory of truth against his absolutist opponents, writing such sentences as "The university function is the truth-function" and "The one thing that is inherent and essential [to the idea of the university] is the idea of truth." [15]

The non-philosophers who read these sentences, which appeared in 1902 in an article called "Academic Freedom," probably took "the idea of truth" to mean something like "the idea of an accurate representation of the intrinsic nature of reality." Most people still take it to mean something like that. They automatically contrast the attempt to get such representations—to attain objective truth—with the attempt to make people happy, to fulfill human needs. The latter, they say, involves an element of subjectivity which should be excluded from science and scholarship. When such people are told by Searle and others that Kuhn, Derrida and I deny that true beliefs represent anything, and that reality has an intrinsic nature, they may well believe that the university is endangered, and that the need to preserve academic freedom may require the refutation of these dangerous philosophers. [16]

Dewey, I think, would say that if it should ever come down to a choice between the practices and traditions which make up academic freedom and anti-representationalist theories of truth and knowledge, we should go for academic freedom. We should put first things first. Change in philosophical opinion is, on Dewey's view, in the service of socio-political progress. He would have had no interest in sacrificing free universities to his philosophical convictions. But, of course, he did not think that it would ever come down to any such choice. He saw no tension between his philosophical and his political work. I think that he would have accepted my distinction between the short run and the long run effects of change in philosophical opinion.

Nothing, including the nature of truth and knowledge, is worth worrying about if this worry will make no difference to practice. But there are all sorts of ways of making a difference. One of them is by slowly, over a long period of time, changing what Wittgenstein called the pictures which hold us captive.

We shall always be held captive by some picture or other, for we shall never escape from language or from metaphor—never see either God or the Intrinsic Nature of Reality face to face. But old pictures may have disadvantages which can be avoided by sketching new pictures. Escape from prejudice and superstition, Dewey thought, is not escape from Appearance to Reality, but escape from the satisfaction of old needs into the satisfaction of new needs. It is a process of maturation, not a progress from darkness to light. On his view, escape from the Western Rationalist Tradition will indeed be an escape from error to truth, but it will not be an escape from the way things appear to the way things really are. It will merely be an escape from immature needs: the needs Chesterton felt and Dewey did not.

By way of conclusion, I shall put Dewey aside and come back to Searle. Searle sees the difference between him and me as the difference between someone with a decent respect for hard fact, and other associated intellectual virtues, and someone who relishes, and helps encourage, what he calls "the general air of vaguely literary frivolity that pervades the Nietzscheanized Left."[17] He sees as presuppositional the relationships which I see as largely ornamental. He says that the only argument for his own realist, representationalist, view is that

> it forms the presupposition of our linguistic and other sorts of practices: You cannot coherently deny realism and engage in ordinary linguistic practices, because realism is a condition of the normal intelligibility of those practices. You can see this if you consider any sort of ordinary communication. For example, suppose I call my car mechanic to find out if the carburetor is fixed. . . . Now suppose I have reached a deconstructionist car mechanic and he tries to explain to me that a carburetor is just a text anyway, and that there is nothing to talk about except the textuality of the text . . . Whatever else is clear about such situations, one thing is clear: communication has broken down. . . . Give me the assumption that these sorts of communication are even possible between human beings and you will see that you require the assumption of an independently existing reality.[18]

I do not think that this frivolously literary car mechanic is a plausible product of the overthrow of the Western Rationalistic Tradition. The deconstructionist Ph.D.s in English who, after finding themselves unemployable in the academy, lucked into jobs as car mechanics have no trouble telling where their job stops and their philosophy begins. They would presumably say, as I would, that the difference deconstruction has made to their lives is, like the difference Methodism or atheism made to their ancestors' lives, atmospheric and spiritual. They might even quote Dewey and say, as I myself would, that they have found Derrida's writings useful for getting "into more experimental, less dogmatic, and less arbitrarily skeptical relations to life."[19]

The more serious question, however, is, as I said earlier, the one about presuppositions. I can go some way with Searle on this question. Thus I agree with him when he makes the Wittgensteinian point that

> For those of us brought up in our civilization, especially the scientific portions of our civilization, the principles that I have just presented as those of the Western Rationalistic Tradition do not function as a *theory*. Rather, they function as part of the taken for-granted background of our practices. The conditions of intelligibility of our practices, linguistic and otherwise, cannot themselves be demonstrated as truths within those practices. To suppose they could was the endemic mistake of foundationalist metaphysics.[20]

I break off from Searle only at the point where he suggests that our practices would somehow become unintelligible if we described what we are doing in different ways—and in particular if we described them in the non-realist, non-representationalist, terms commended by philosophers like Davidson and Derrida.

Searle and I recognize that certain propositions are intuitively obvious, indemonstrable, and taken for granted. But whereas he sees them as incapable of being questioned without questioning the practices themselves (or, at least, their "intelligibility"), I see them as optional glosses on those practices. Where he sees conditions of intelligibility, presuppositions, I see rhetorical flourishes designed to make practitioners feel that they are being true to something big and strong: The Intrinsic Nature of Reality. On my view, the comfort derived from this feeling is, at this stage in the maturation of Western humanity, as unnecessary, and as potentially dangerous, as the comfort derived from the conviction that one is obeying the Will of God.

It is unnecessary and dangerous because our maturation has consisted in the gradual realization that, if we can rely on one another, we need not rely on anything else. In religious terms, this is the Feuerbachian thesis that God was just a protection of the best, and sometimes of the worst, of humanity. In philosophical terms, it is the thesis that anything talk of objectivity can do to make our practices intelligible can be done equally well by talk of intersubjectivity. In political terms, it is the thesis that if we can just keep democracy and reciprocal tolerance alive, everything else can be settled by muddling through to some reasonable sort of compromise.

To adopt these various theses, it helps to reflect that nothing in your practices requires you to distinguish an intrinsic from an extrinsic feature of reality.[21] If you give up the intrinsic-extrinsic distinction, the distinction between what things are like apart from human needs and interests and what they are like in relation to those needs and interests, you can also give up the idea that there is a great big difference between seeking for human happiness and seeking for scholarly or scientific truth. For now you will not think of the latter search as the attempt to represent the intrinsic features of reality, without regard to human needs, but as finding descriptions of reality which satisfy certain particular human needs—those which your fellow scientists and scholars have agreed need to be satisfied. The difference between bad subjectivity and sound scholarship will now be glossed as that between the satisfaction of private, idiosyncratic, and perhaps secret, needs and the satisfaction of needs which are widely shared, well-publicized, and freely debated.

This substitution of objectivity-as-intersubjectivity for objectivity-as-accurate representation is the key pragmatic move, the one that lets pragmatists feel that they can have moral seriousness without "realist" seriousness. For moral seriousness is a matter of taking other human beings seriously, and not taking anything else with equal seriousness. It turns out, pragmatists say, that we can take each other very seriously indeed without taking the intrinsic nature of reality seriously at all. We shall not change our practices—either political or academic—merely because we have ceased to concern ourselves with epistemology, or because we have adopted non-representationalist philosophies of language and mind. But we may change our attitudes toward these practices, our sense of why it is important to carry them out. Our new sense of what we are doing will be itself as indemonstrable, and as intuitive, as was the Western Rationalistic Tradition. But pragmatists think it will be better, not just because it will free philosophers from perpetual oscillation between skepticism and dogmatism, but because it will take away a few more excuses for fanaticism and intolerance.

Notes

1. Eisenhower might have added that any religion that is dubious about American democratic institutions must have something wrong with it. I should claim that any philosophy that is dubious about the folkways which we call "academic freedom" must have something wrong with it.

2. *Daedalus,* volume 122, no. 4 (Fall 1992), pp. 55–84 (this volume, pp. 197–220).

3. "Rationality and Realism . . . ," p. 72.

4. T.S. Kuhn, "Afterwords" in Paul Horwich, ed., *World Changes: Thomas Kuhn and the Nature of Science* (Cambridge, Mass.: MIT Press, 1993), p. 330.

5. Putnam, *Reality with a Human Face* (Cambridge, Mass.: Harvard University Press, 1990), p. 28. For my differences with Putnam, who considers me a "cultural relativist," and has some sympathy with Searle's criticisms of me and Derrida, if not those of Kuhn, see my "Putnam and the Relativist Menace," *Journal of Philosophy,* vol. xc, no. 9 (September 1993), pp. 443–461.

6. Davidson, "The Structure and Content of Truth," *Journal of Philosophy,* vol. lxxxvii, no. 6 (June 1990), p. 305.

7. The American Council of Learned Societies, *Speaking for the Humanities,* ACLS Occasional Paper, No. 7, 1989, p. 18—quoted by Searle at p. 69 of "Rationality and Realism . . ."

8. Compare Thomas Haskell's remark, in his essay in this volume: "If there is no respectable sense in which we are entitled to say that there is a 'nature of things' for inquirers to 'get right,' then one cannot help wondering what the community of inquirers is for."

Later in his essay Haskell describes me as differing from Peirce, Lovejoy, and Dewey in that I am unable to say, as they did, that some interpretations were better than others, "better in a strong sense that did not depend on correspondence and yet was not reducible to perspective." But all I am interested in is getting rid of correspondence, and the notion of the "intrinsic nature" of things which is needed to make sense of correspondence. I do not want to reduce anything to perspective, and would not know how to do so. See my remarks on relativism in "Solidarity or Objectivity?" in my *Objectivity, Relativism and Truth* (Cambridge: Cambridge University Press, 1991) and in "Putnam and the Relativist Menace," *Journal of Philosophy* 90 (1993), pp. 443–461.

9. For Searle's clearest statement of this distinction, see his *The Rediscovery of the Mind* (Cambridge, Mass.: MIT Press, 1992), p. 211: ". . . it is essential to understand the distinction between features of the world that are *intrinsic* and features that are *observer relative.* The expressions "mass," "gravitational attraction," and "molecule" name features of the world that are intrinsic. If all observers and users cease to exist, the world still contains mass, gravitational attraction and molecules. But expressions such as "nice day for a picnic" ". . . name objects by specifying some feature that has been assigned to them, some feature that is relative to observers and users."

For pragmatists like me, the feature of being a molecule is just as much or as little "relative to observers and users" as the suitability of a day for picnic. So we are not sure whether, as Searle goes on to say, ". . . if there had never been any users or observers, there would be no such features as being a nice day for a picnic . . ." We see no useful purpose served by this attempt to distinguish intrinsic from observer-relative features of reality. "Essential," we ask Searle, "for what?"

10. Here I find myself in disagreement with Joyce Appleby, Lynn Hunt, and Margaret Jacob, in their *Telling the Truth about History* (New York: Norton, 1994). They say that "The most distinctive of historians' problems is that posed by temporality itself. . . . The past, insofar as it exists at all, exists in the present; the historian too is stuck in time present, trying to make meaningful and accurate statements about time past. Any account of historical objectivity must provide for this crucial temporal dimension." (p. 253) I am not sure who has had the "debilitating doubts that the past is knowable" (p. 270) of which they speak, nor why we should take such doubts more seriously than Descartes' doubt about the existence of matter. I do not think that there is something called "temporality" which poses a big problem, nor that we require either "a theory of objectivity for the twenty-first century" (p. 254) or a "revitalized and transformed practice of objectivity" (p. 237).

One of the morals of what Kuhn says about the difference between textbook accounts of inquiry, written by people with philosophical axes to grind, and the actual processes of initiation into a disciplinary matrix (such as historiography) seems to me to be that we never have had much of a "theory of objectivity," and that we do not need a new one now. What we have had, and will with luck continue to have, is what Thomas Haskell (following Francis Abbot) calls "communities of the competent," communities which can muddle their way through an unending process of self-transformation without philosophical assistance.

Appleby and her colleagues think philosophy does help, and so they offer, as part of a "combination of practical realism and pragmatism," an "epistemological position that claims that people's perceptions of the world have some correspondence with that world." Philosophers like me think that "correspondence to reality" is just an uncashable and obsolete metaphor. So for us the term "some correspondence" is like "somewhat pregnant"; we do not do not think the issue is about *how much* correspondence perception, or historiography might have. The epistemological position these three historians propose seems to us to fall between two irreconcilable philosophical alternatives, rather than providing a happy synthesis or compromise.

11. John Dewey, "A Short Catechism Concerning Truth," *The Middle Works of John Dewey,* vol. 6 (Carbondale, Illinois: Southern Illinois University Press, 1978), p. 11.

12. See, on this point, the opening chapters of Dewey's *The Quest for Certainty.*

13. Ibid., p. 9.

14. Ibid., p. 11. Robert Westbrook (*John Dewey and American Democracy* (Ithaca: Cornell University Press, 1991), pp. 137–8) cites this passage and points out that it applies to Bertrand Russell's criticisms of pragmatism as well as to Chesterton's. Pragmatism's radicalism and originality are nicely instanced by its ability to question a presupposition common to Chesterton and Russell, writers who had very little else in common.

15. "Academic Freedom," *The Middle Works of John Dewey,* vol. 2 (Carbondale, Illinois: Southern Illinois University Pres, 1976), p. 55.

16. Searle is of course only one of a great number of philosophers who take this line. John Silber, president of Boston University and a well known Kant scholar, reported to his trustees that "Some versions of critical theory, radical feminism and multiculturalism, among other intellectual positions, are ideological in character and inhospitable to free intellectual inquiry" and that "We [at Boston University] have resisted relativism as an official intellectual dogma, believing that there is such a thing as truth, and if you can't achieve it, at least you can approach it." (See "New Eruption at Boston U.," *The Chronicle of Higher Education,* December 8, 1993, p. A27.) Nineteen philosophers signed a letter to the *Times* of London saying that Derrida should not receive an honorary degree from Cambridge because his work offers "little more than semi-intelligible attacks upon the values of reason, truth, and scholarship" (*The Times,* May 9, 1992).

It is instructive to compare such assaults to those written, in the 1930s and 1940s, against logical positivism by C. E. M. Joad, Mortimer Adler, Brand Blandshard, and other philosophers. In its brief heyday, logical positivism was as fanatical, intolerant, and brutal as any intellectual movement has ever been, but by now the cries of "civilization in danger!" which were raised against it seem a bit overwrought. Many of the slogans of "poststructuralism" now current in our universities, the slogans which Searle sees as exemplifying literary frivolity and dangerous politicization, will come to seem as patently silly and self-righteously snotty as the youthful excesses of the first generation of logical positivists now seem to us. But the brief reign of post-structuralism will probably do a bit of good, just as the brief reign of logical positivism did. Post-structuralism claims far too much for literature and for politics, just as positivism claimed far too much for science and for philosophy. But intellectual progress is often made by just such violent pendulum swings.

17. Searle, "Rationality and Realism . . .", p. 78.

18. "Rationality and Realism . . .", p. 81. Searle goes on to say that "One interesting thing about the present theorists who claim to have shown that reality is a social construct, or that there is no independently existing reality, or that everything is really a text, is that they have denied one of the conditions of intelligibility of our ordinary linguistic practices without providing an alternative conception of that intelligibility." Pragmatists do not think there are such things as conditions of intelligibility. There are only tacit agreements to continue with certain social practices.

19. Searle's phrase "literary frivolity," like his reference (quoted below) to "the more scientific portions of our civilization" is characteristic of the traditional alliance of analytic philosophy with the sciences against the humanities. In the 1930s, the heyday of logical positivism and the seedtime of analytic philosophy, the contrast between Carnap's respect for scientists and Heidegger's respect for poets was seen as a contrast between responsibility and frivolous irresponsibility.

If you say that "the university function is the truth function," and if you think of truth as something about which you can expect to get a consensus, then, as Louis Menand points out in this volume, "the criticism of literature has the weakest case for inclusion in the professional structure of the research university." The books of F. R. Leavis or Harold Bloom are not happily described as "contributions to knowledge." But this apparent weakness is a product of the mistaken idea that consensus among inquirers—consensus of the sort which Leavis and Bloom knew better than to hope for—is the goal of any responsible intellectual activity.

I hope that this latter idea, and the resulting split between Snow's "two cultures," will sooner or later become obsolete. We might hasten the process of obsolescence by reflecting that we are much more certain of the value of departments of English literature than we are about the nature of the research university, or of knowledge. English departments can always be made to look silly by asking them what they have contributed to knowledge lately. But humanists can make biology or mathematics departments look bad by asking what they have done lately for human freedom. The best thing about our universities is the live-and-let-live spirit which lets us wave such pointless questions aside. When, however, outside pressure makes us nervous and self-conscious, we start asking bad questions like "What is a university, anyway?" That question is almost certain to be answered by invidious comparisons between disciplines, and especially between the sciences and the humanities.

20. "Rationality and Realism . . . ," p. 80.

21. But you can still happily agree with common sense that there were dinosaurs and mountains long before anybody described them as dinosaurs and mountains, that thinking doesn't make it so, and that bank accounts and gender roles are social constructions in a sense in which giraffes are not. There would have been no bank accounts or gender roles had there been no human societies, whereas there would have been giraffes, but that is not to say that giraffes are part of Reality as it is in Itself, apart from human needs and interests. In a wider sense of "social construction," everything, including giraffes and molecules, is socially constructed, for no vocabulary (e.g., that of zoology or physics) cuts reality at the joints. Reality has no joints. It just has descriptions—some more socially useful than others.

8

Rationality and Realism, What Is at Stake?

John R. Searle

Debates about the nature of higher education have been going on in American research universities for decades. There is nothing new about passionate controversies over the curriculum, over academic requirements, and even over the aims of higher education itself. But the current debates are in certain respects unusual. Unlike earlier academic reformers, many of the present challengers to the academic tradition have an explicitly leftist political agenda, and they seek explicit political goals. Furthermore, and more interestingly, they often present a challenge not just to the content of the curriculum but to the very conceptions of rationality, truth, objectivity, and reality that have been taken for granted in higher education, as they have been taken for granted in our civilization at large. I would not wish to exaggerate this point. The challengers of the tradition present a wide variety of different viewpoints and arguments. They are by no means united. But there has been a sea change in discussions of the aims of education in that the ideals which were previously shared by nearly everyone in the disputes—ideals of truth, rationality, and objectivity, for example—are rejected by many of the challengers, *even as ideals.* This is new.

In some of the disciplines in the humanities and social sciences, and even in some of the professional schools, there now are developing two more or less distinct faculty subcultures, one might almost say two different universities. The distinction between the two subcultures cuts across disciplinary boundaries, and it is not sharp. But it is there. One is that of the traditional university dedicated to the discovery, extension, and dissemination of knowledge as traditionally conceived. The second expresses a much more diverse set of attitudes and projects, but just to have a label, I will describe it as the subculture of "postmodernism." I do not mean to imply that this concept is well-defined or even coherent, but when describing any intellectual movement it is best to use terms the adherents themselves would accept, and this one appears to be accepted as a self-description by many of the people I will be discussing.

I referred above to "debates," but that is not quite accurate. There really is not much in the way of explicit debate going on between these two cultures over the central philosophical issues concerning the mission of the university and its epistemic and ontological underpinnings. There are lots of debates about specific issues such as multiculturalism and affirmative action, but not much in the way of a debate about the presuppositions of the traditional university and the alternatives. In journalistic accounts, the distinction between the traditional university and the discourse of postmodernism is usually described in political terms: the traditional university claims to cherish knowledge for its own sake and for its practical applications, and it attempts to be apolitical or at least politically neutral. The university of postmodernism thinks that all discourse is political anyway, and it seeks to use the university for beneficial rather than repressive political ends. This characterization is partly correct, but I think the political dimensions of this dispute can only be understood against a deeper dispute about fundamental philosophical issues. The postmodernists are attempting to challenge certain traditional assumptions about the nature of truth, objectivity, rationality, reality, and intellectual quality.

In what follows, I will try to identify some of the elements of the Western conceptions of rationality and realism that are now under challenge. My aim is not so much to resolve the disputes but to identify (at least some of) what exactly is in dispute. I will also briefly discuss some of the consequences different conceptions of rationality and realism have for higher education. These are not the only issues underlying the disputes in current debates about higher education, nor are these the only theoretical and philosophical issues in higher education, but they are worth discussing and as far as I know have not been addressed in quite these terms before.[1]

The Western Traditions: Some Preliminaries

There is a conception of reality, and of the relationships between reality on the one hand and thought and language on the other, that has a long history in the Western intellectual tradition. Indeed, this conception is so fundamental that to some extent it defines that tradition. It involves a very particular conception of truth, reason, reality, rationality, logic, knowledge, evidence, and proof. Without too much of an exaggeration one can describe this conception as "the Western Rationalistic Tradition." The Western Rationalistic Tradition takes different forms but it underlies the Western conception of science, for example. Most practicing scientists simply take it for granted. In the simplest conception of science, the aim of science is to get a set of true sentences, ideally in the form of precise theories, that are true because they correspond, at least approximately, to an independently existing reality. In some other areas, such as the law, the Western Rationalistic Tradition has undergone some interesting permutations and it is certainly no longer in its pure form. For example, there are rules of procedure and evidence in the law which are adhered to even in cases where it is obvious to all concerned that they do not produce the truth. Indeed, they are adhered to even in cases when it is obvious that they prevent arriving at the truth. The Western Rationalistic Tradition is not a unified tradition in either its history or in its present application.

Two forms of disunity need special emphasis. First, at any given time the most cherished assumptions of the Western Rationalistic Tradition have been subject to challenge. There has seldom been unanimity or even consensus within it. Second, over time those assumptions have evolved, typically in response to challenges. For example, the role of sacred texts such as Scriptures in validating claims to knowledge, the role of mystical insight as a source of knowledge, and the role of the supernatural generally have declined spectacularly with the demystification of the world that began, roughly speaking, with the advent of the modern era in the seventeenth century. Any attempt to characterize the Western Rationalistic Tradition, therefore, inevitably suffers from some degree of oversimplification or even distortion. Furthermore, any attempt such as I am about to make to describe its present form is inevitably from the point of view of a particular thinker at a particular time and place—how it seems to him or her, then and there. And, by the way, the recognition of this limitation—that accuracy and objectivity are difficult to attain because of the fact that all representation is *from a point of view* and *under some aspects and not others*—is one of the central epistemic principles of the Western Rationalistic Tradition in its current incarnation.

I believe a decisive step in the creation of the Western Rationalistic Tradition was the Greek creation of the idea of a *theory*. It is important to state this point precisely. Many features of the Western Rationalistic Tradition—the presupposition of an independently existing reality, and the presupposition that language, at least on occasion, conforms to that reality—are essential to any successful culture. You cannot survive if you are unable to cope with the real world, and the ways that human beings characteristically cope with the real world essentially involve representing it to themselves in language. But

the introduction of the idea of a theory allowed the Western tradition to produce something quite unique, namely systematic intellectual constructions
that were designed to describe and to explain large areas of reality in a way
that was logically and mathematically accessible. Euclid's *Elements* provides
a model for the kind of logical relationships that have been paradigmatic in
the Western tradition. Indeed, the Greeks had almost everything necessary for
theory in the modern sense. One essential thing they lacked and which Europe
did not get until the Renaissance was the idea of systematic experiments. The
Greeks had logic, mathematics, rationality, systematicity, and the notion of a
theoretical construct. But the idea of matching theoretical constructs against
an independently existing reality through systematic experimentation really
did not come in until much later. However, I am getting ahead of my story.

Another feature of Western Rationalistic Tradition is its self-critical quality.
Elements within it have always been under challenge; it was never a unified
tradition. The idea of *critique* was always to subject any belief to the most
rigorous standards of rationality, evidence, and truth. Socrates is the hero of
the intellectual branch of the Western Rationalistic Traditional tradition in
large part because he accepted nothing without argument and was relentlessly
critical of any attempts at solving philosophical problems. Recently, however,
the self-critical element in the Western Rationalistic Tradition has had a peculiar consequence. If the point of the criticisms is to subject all beliefs, claims,
prejudices, and assumptions to the most rigorous scrutiny through the magni-
fying glass of rationality, logic, evidence, etc., then why should the criticisms
eventually not be directed at rationality or logic or evidence themselves? The
heroic age of the Western Rationalistic Tradition came during and after the
Renaissance when the faiths and dogmas of the Middle Ages were subjected
to ever more savage criticisms, until finally we reached the European Enlightenment and the skepticism of Hume and Voltaire, for example. But now, why
should we not also be skeptical of rationality, logic, evidence, truth, reality,
etc., themselves? If the uncritical acceptance of a belief in God can be demol-
ished, then why not also demolish the uncritical acceptance of the belief in
the external world, the belief in truth, the belief in rationality, indeed, the
belief in belief? At this point, the Western Rationalistic Tradition becomes not
merely self-critical, but self-destructive. Nietzsche, on one possible interpretation, can be regarded both as diagnosing and exemplifying this self-destructive
element. Nietzsche is a philosopher of considerable variety, but at his worst
he exhibits a distinct shortage of argument and a tendency to substitute rhetoric for reason. For the present discussion, the interesting point is that he has
come back into fashion. I believe this is, in large part, because of his attacks
on various aspects of the Western Rationalistic Tradition. It is not easy to
locate any arguments, much less proofs, in his attacks.

The Western Rationalistic Tradition:
Some Basic Principles

Now I want to try to articulate some essential features of the Western Rationalistic Tradition in its contemporary incarnation. What is in dispute? What is under attack? What is presupposed by the intellectual tradition that stretches back to the Greeks? For example, the Western Rationalistic Tradition is sometimes accused of "logocentrism"; a few decades ago, the same style of objection was made to something called "linear thinking." What exactly does one accept when one is "logocentric," i.e., when one accepts the Greek ideal of "logos" or reason? What is one committed to when one engages in "linear thinking," i.e., when one tries to think straight? If we can understand the answers to these questions, we will know at least something of what is at stake in the current debates in higher education.

It might seem impossible to make even the crudest summary of the Western Rationalistic Tradition because of the enormous variety I mentioned earlier, but there is a simple test for distinguishing the center from the periphery, namely what do the attackers of the tradition feel it necessary to attack, what do the challengers feel it necessary to challenge. For example, there are lots of theories of truth, but anyone who wants to challenge the tradition has to attack the correspondence theory of truth. The correspondence theory is the norm, the default position; other positions are defined in relation to it. Similarly, there are lots of versions of realism as well as of idealism, but anyone who wants to attack the accepted view in this domain has to attack the idea that there is a mind-independent reality, a real world that exists entirely independently of our thought and talk.

We cannot discover the essential elements of the Western Rationalistic Tradition just by studying the doctrines of the great philosophers. Often the important thing is not what the philosopher said but what he took for granted as too obvious to need saying. Some of the best known philosophers became famous for attacking central elements of the Western Rationalistic Tradition—the Irish philosopher George Berkeley, Hume, and Kant, for example.

For the sake of simplicity, I will state what I take to be some of the basic tenets of the Western Rationalistic Tradition as a set of propositions.

Reality exists independently of human representations. This view, called "realism," is the foundational principle of the Western Rationalistic Tradition. The idea is that though we have mental and linguistic representations of the world in the form of beliefs, experiences, statements, and theories, there is a world "out there" that is totally independent of these representations. This has the consequence, for example, that when we die, as we will, the world will in large part go on unaffected by our demise. It is consistent with realism to recognize that there are large areas of reality that are indeed social constructs. Such things as money, property, marriage, and governments are created and maintained by human cooperative behavior. Take away all of the human representations and you have taken away money, property, and marriage. But it is a foundational principle of the Western Rationalistic Tradition that there are also large sections of the world described by our representations that exist completely independently of those or any other possible representations. The elliptical orbit of the planets relative to the sun, the structure of the hydrogen atom, and the amount of snowfall in the Himalayas, for example, are totally independent of both the system and the actual instances of human representations of these phenomena.

This point needs to be stated carefully. The vocabulary or system of representation in which I can state these truths is a human creation, and the motivations that lead one to investigate such matters are contingent features of human psychology. Without a set of verbal categories I cannot make any statements about these matters or about anything else. Without a set of motivations, no one would bother. But the actual situations in the world that correspond to these statements are not human creations, nor are they dependent on human motivations. This conception of realism forms the basis of the natural sciences.

At least one of the functions of language is to communicate meanings from speakers to hearers, and sometimes those meanings enable the communication to refer to objects and states of affairs in the world that exist independently of language. The basic conception of language in the Western Rationalistic Tradition contains both the communicative and the referential character of language. The speaker can succeed in communicating thoughts, ideas, and meanings generally to a hearer; and language can be used by speakers to refer to objects and states of affairs that exist independently of the language and even of the speaker and the hearer. Understanding is possible because the speaker and the hearer can come to share the same thought, and that thought, on occasion at least, concerns a reality independent of both.

The philosophy of language has a curious history in the Western tradition. Though it is currently at or near the center of attention, especially in English-speaking countries, the forms of our present interests and preoccupations with language are fairly recent. The philosophy of language, in the contemporary sense of that expression, begins with the German mathematician and philosopher Gottlob Frege in the nineteenth century. Previous philosophers often wrote philosophically about language, but none had a "philosophy of language" in the contemporary sense. Even such traditional topics on "the problem of universals" and "the nature of truth" were transformed by the post-Fregean movement.

I think part of the reason for this is that for many centuries most thinkers simply took it for granted that words communicate ideas, and they referred to objects by way of ideas. John Locke describes the accepted view, in contrast to his own, as follows:

> But though words, as they are used by men, can properly and immediately signify nothing but the ideas that are in the mind of the speaker, yet they in their thoughts give them a secret reference to two other things.
>
> *First, To the ideas in other men's minds.*—First, they suppose their words to be marks of the ideas in the minds also of other men, with whom they communicate: for else they should talk in vain, and could not be understood, if the sounds they applied to one idea were such as by the hearer were applied to another, usually to examine whether the idea they and those they discourse with have in their minds to be the same: but think it enough that they use the word, as they imagine, in the common acceptance of that language; which they suppose, that the idea they make it a sign of is precisely the same to which the understanding of men of that country apply that name.
>
> *Secondly, To the reality of things.*—Secondly, because men would not be thought to talk barely of their own imaginations, but of things as really they are; therefore they often suppose their words to stand also for the reality of things.[2]

With Frege the philosophical tradition did not abandon the two principles but rather came to see them as immensely problematic. How does it work? How is it possible that communication can take place? How is it possible that words and sentences relate? In the twentieth century, the philosophy of language became central to philosophy in general, both because of its own intrinsic interest and because it was central to other problems in philosophy such as the nature of knowledge and truth.

Truth is a matter of the accuracy of representation. In general, statements attempt to describe how things are in the world that exists independently of the statement, and the statement will be true or false depending on whether things in the world really are the way that the statement says they are.

So, for example, the statement that hydrogen atoms have one electron, or that the earth is 93 million miles from the sun, or that my dog is now in the kitchen are true or false depending on whether or not things in the hydrogen atom, solar system, and domestic canine line of business, respectively, are really the way these statements say that they are. Truth, so construed, admits of degrees. The statement about the sun, for example, is only *roughly true.*

In some versions, this idea is called the "correspondence theory of truth."

It is often presented as a definition of "true" thus: *A statement is true if and only if the statement corresponds to the facts.*

In recent centuries, there has been a lot of debate among professional philosophers over the correspondence theory of truth. Much of this debate is about special problems concerning the notions of fact and correspondence. Does the notion of correspondence really *explain* anything? Are facts really independent of statements? Does every true statement really correspond to a fact? For example, are there moral facts? And if not, does that mean that there are no true statements in morals? I hold definite opinions on all these issues, but since I am now unveiling the Western Rationalistic Tradition and not expounding my own views, I will confine myself to the following.

The concept of truth as it has evolved over the centuries contains two separate strands, and the two strands do not always entwine together. Sometimes it seems we have two different conceptions of truth. Truth is an obsession of the Western Rationalistic Tradition, so this apparent ambiguity is important. The ambiguity is between truth as correspondence and truth as disquotation. On the correspondence theory, statement *p* is true if and only if *p* corresponds to a fact. For example, the statement that the dog is in the kitchen is true if and only if it corresponds to the fact that the dog is in the kitchen. On the disquotational theory, for any statement *s* that expresses a proposition *p*, *s* is true if and only if *p*. So, for example, the statement "the dog is in the kitchen" is true if and only if the dog is in the kitchen. This is called "disquotation" because the quotation marks on the left-hand side of "if and only if" are simply dropped on the right-hand side.

These two criteria for truth do not always appear to give the same result. The second makes it look as if the word "true" does not really add anything. Saying that it is true that the dog is in the kitchen is just another way of saying that the dog is in the kitchen, so it seems that the word "true" is redundant. For this reason, the disquotation criterion has inspired the "redundancy theory of truth." The first criterion, the correspondence criterion, makes it look as if there is a genuine relation between two independently identified entities—the statement and the fact. The difficulty, however, with this conception is that the two entities are not independently identifiable. You cannot answer the question, "which fact does the statement correspond to?," without stating a true statement. So, once I have identified the statement, "the dog is in the kitchen," and then I have identified the fact that the dog is in the kitchen, there is not anything else for me to do by way of comparing the statement to the fact to see if they really do correspond. The alleged correspondence relation has already been established by the very identification of the fact.

Is there any way to explain the correspondence theory which overcomes this difficulty, and is there any way to resolve the tension between the disquotation criterion and the correspondence criterion and overcome the apparent ambiguity in the concept of truth? I think that there is.

The word "fact" has evolved out of the Latin "facere" in such a way that it has come to mean that which corresponds to a true statement in virtue of which the statement is true. So the correspondence theory—a statement is true if and only if it corresponds to a fact—is a truism, a tautology, an analytic statement. But the grammar of the language then misleads us. We think that because "fact" is a noun, and nouns typically name things, and because "corresponds" typically names a relation between things, that therefore there must be a class of complicated objects, the facts, and a relation that true statements bear to these complicated objects, correspondence. But this picture does not work. It sounds plausible for the statement that the dog is in the kitchen but what about the true statement that the dog is not in the kitchen? Or the true statement that three-headed dogs have never existed? What complicated objects do they correspond to?

The mistake is to think that facts are a class of complicated objects, and that to find the truth we must first find the object and then compare it with a statement to see if they really do correspond. But that is not how language works in this area. The fact that the dog is not in the kitchen, or the fact that three-headed dogs have never existed are as much facts as any other, simply because the corresponding statements are true, and "fact" is *defined as* whatever it is that makes a statement true.

For this reason, because of the definitional connection between fact and true statement, there could not be an inconsistency between the correspondence criterion of truth and the disquotational criterion. The disquotational criterion tells us that the statement, "the dog is in the kitchen," is true if and only if the dog is in the kitchen. The correspondence criterion tells us that the dog is in the kitchen is true if and only if it corresponds to a fact. But which fact? The only fact it could correspond to, if true, is the fact that the dog is in the kitchen. But that is precisely the result given by the disquotational criterion, because that is the fact stated by the righthand side of the equation: the statement, "the dog is in the kitchen," is true if and only if the dog is in the kitchen. So both the correspondence theory and the disquotational theory are true and they are not inconsistent. The correspondence theory is trivially true and thus misleads us because we think correspondence must name some very general relation between language and reality, whereas in fact, I am suggesting, it is just a shorthand for all of the enormous variety of ways in which statements can accurately represent how things are. Statements are typically true in virtue of, or because of, features of the world that exist independently of the statement.

The upshot of this discussion, as far as the Western Rationalistic Tradition is concerned, is this: for the most part the world exists independently of language and one of the functions of language is to represent how things are in the world. One crucial point at which reality and language make contact is marked by the notion of truth. In general, statements are true to the extent that they accurately represent some feature of reality that exists independently of the statement.[3]

There are various important philosophical problems about correspondence and disquotation, but if we mind our p's and q's we can see that none of these problems threatens our basic conception of truth as the accuracy of representation.

Knowledge is objective. Because the content of what is known is always a true proposition, and because truth is in general a matter of accurate representation of an independently existing reality, knowledge does not depend on nor derive from the subjective attitudes and feelings of particular investigators. All representation is, as I said earlier, from a point of view and under certain aspects and not others. Furthermore, representations are made by particular investigators, subject to all the usual limitations of prejudice, ignorance, stupidity, venality, and dishonesty; they are made for all sorts of motives on the parts of the makers, some benign, some reprehensible, including desires to get rich, to oppress the oppressed, or even to get tenure. But if the theories put forward accurately describe an independently existing reality, none of this matters in the least. The point is that the objective truth or falsity of the claims made is totally independent of the motives, the morality, or even the gender, the race, or the ethnicity of the maker.

It is worth pausing to state the significance of this principle to some of the present debates. A standard argumentative strategy of those who reject the Western Rationalistic Tradition is to challenge some claim they find objectionable, by challenging the maker of the claim in question. Thus, the claim and its maker are said to be racist, sexist, phono-phallo-logocentric, and so forth. To those who hold the traditional conception of rationality, these challenges do not impress. They are, at best, beside the point. To those within the Western Rationalistic Tradition, these types of challenge have names. They are commonly called argumentum ad hominem and the genetic fallacy. Argumentum ad hominem is an argument against the person who presents a view rather than against the view itself, and the genetic fallacy is the fallacy of supposing that because a theory or claim has a reprehensible origin, the theory or claim itself is discredited. I hope it is obvious why anyone who accepts the idea of objective truth and therefore of objective knowledge thinks this is a fallacy and that an argumentum ad hominem is an invalid argument. If someone makes a claim to truth and can give that claim the right kind of support, and if that claim is indeed true, then that person genuinely knows something. The fact that the whole enterprise of claiming and validating may have been carried out by someone who is racist or sexist is just irrelevant to the truth of the claim. That is part of what is meant by saying that knowledge is objective. It is less obvious, but I hope still apparent, why anyone who denies the possibility of objective truth and knowledge might find *these* sorts of arguments appealing. If there is no such thing as objective truth, then the criteria for assessing claims have no essential connection with truth or falsity, and may as well be concerned with the maker of the argument, his or her motives, the consequences of making the claim, or other such issues.

Logic and rationality are formal. In the Western Rationalistic Tradition, there are traditionally supposed to be two kinds of reason: theoretical reason, which aims at what is reasonable to believe, and practical reason, which aims at what is reasonable to do. But it is, I believe, an essential part of the Western conception of rationality, reason, logic, evidence, and proof that they do not *by themselves* tell you what to believe or what to do. According to the Western conception, rationality provides one with a set of procedures, methods, standards, and canons that enables one to assess various claims in light of competing claims. Central to this view is the Western conception of logic. Logic does not by itself tell you what to believe. It only tells you what must be the case, given that your assumptions are true, and hence what you are committed to believing, given that you believe those assumptions. Logic and rationality provide standards of proof, validity, and reasonableness but the standards only operate on a previously given set of axioms, assumptions, goals, and objectives. Rationality as such makes no substantive claims.

Where practical reason is concerned, this point is sometimes made by saying that reasoning is always about means not about ends. This is not quite right, given the Western conception, because one can reason about whether or not one's ends are proper, appropriate or rational, but only in the light of other ends and other considerations such as consistency. The formal character of rationality has the important consequence that rationality as such cannot be "refuted' because it does not make any claim to refute.

On a natural interpretation, the previous five principles have the following consequence.

Intellectual standards are not up for grabs. There are both objectively and intersubjectively valid criteria of intellectual achievement and excellence. The previous five principles imply, in a fairy obvious way, a set of criteria for assessing intellectual products. Given a real world, a public language for talking about it, and the conceptions of truth, knowledge, and rationality that are implicit in the Western Rationalistic Tradition, there will be a complex, but not arbitrary, set of criteria for judging the relative merits of statements, theories, explanations, interpretations, and other sorts of accounts. Some of these criteria are "objective" in the sense that they are independent of the sensibilities of the people applying the criteria; others are "intersubjective" in the sense that they appeal to widely shared features of human sensibility. An example of objectivity in this sense is the criterion for assessing validity in propositional calculus. An example of intersubjectivity is the sort of criteria appealed to in debating rival historical interpretations of the American Civil War. There is no sharp dividing line between the two, and in those disciplines where interpretation is crucial, such as history and literary criticism, intersubjectivity is correspondingly central to the intellectual enterprise.

There are endless debates in the history of Western philosophy about these issues. In my own view, for example, even objectivity only functions relative to a shared "background" of cognitive capacities and hence is, in a sense, a form of intersubjectivity. However, for the present discussion what matters is that according to the Western Rationalistic Tradition there are rational standards for assessing intellectual quality. Except in a few areas, there is no algorithm that determines the standards and they are not algorithmic in their application. But all the same they are neither arbitrarily selected nor arbitrarily applied. Some disputes may be unsettleable—but that does not mean that anything goes.

For the traditional conception of the university this principe is crucial. For example, in the traditional university, the professor assigns Shakespeare and not randomly selected comic strips, and she does so in the belief that she could demonstrate that Shakespeare is better. No principle of the Western Rationalistic Tradition is more repulsive to the culture of postmodernism than this one, as we will soon see.

Some Consequences of Higher Education

One could continue this list of the essential claims of the Western Rationalistic Tradition for a long time. But even these six theses express a massive and powerful conception. Together they form a coherent picture of some of the relations between knowledge, truth, meaning, rationality, reality, and the criteria for assessing intellectual productions. They fit together. Knowledge is typically of a mind-independent reality. It is expressed in a public language, it contains true propositions—these propositions are true because they accurately represent that reality—and knowledge is arrived at by applying, and is subject to, constraints of rationality and logic. The merits and demerits of theories are largely a matter of meeting or failing to meet the criteria implicit in this conception.

All six of these principles are currently under attack in different forms, and I now want to explore some of the consequences, both of the principles and of the attacks. It is no exaggeration to say that our intellectual and educational tradition, especially in the research universities, is based on the Western Rationalistic Tradition. The scholarly ideal of the tradition is that of the *disinterested* inquirer engaged in the quest for *objective* knowledge that will have *universal* validity. Precisely this ideal is now under attack. In a pamphlet issued by the American Council of Learned Societies, authored by six heads of prominent humanities institutes and designed to defend the humanities against charges that they have abandoned their educational mission, we read: "As the most powerful modern philosophies and theories have been demonstrating, claims of disinterest, objectivity and universality are not to be trusted, and themselves tend to reflect local historical conditions." They go on to argue that claims to objectivity are usually disguised forms of power seeking.[4]

In most academic disciplines it is fairly obvious how acceptance of the Western Rationalistic Tradition shapes both the content and the methods of higher education. As professors in research universities, we traditionally take ourselves as trying to advance and disseminate human knowledge and understanding, whether it be in physical chemistry, microeconomics, or medieval history. It is less obvious, but still intelligible, how standards of rationality, knowledge, and truth are supposed to apply to the study of fictional literature or the visual arts. Even in these areas the traditional assumptions by which they were studied and taught were of a piece with the rest of the Western Rationalistic Tradition. There were supposed to be intersubjective standards by which one could judge the quality of literary and artistic works, and the study of these works was supposed to give us knowledge not only of the history of literature and art but of the reality beyond to which they refer, if only indirectly. Thus, for example, it was commonly believed, at least until quite recently, that the study of the great classics of literature gave the reader insights into human nature and the human condition in general. It was, in short, something of a cliché that you could learn more about human beings from reading great novels than you could from most psychology courses. Nowadays, one does not hear much talk about "great classics of literature," and the idea of intersubjective standards of aesthetic quality is very much in dispute.

If the relation of the Western Rationalistic Tradition to the traditional ideals of the university is—more or less—obvious, the relation between attacks on the Western Rationalistic Tradition and proposals for educational reform is much less obvious. It is simply a fact that, in recent history, rejection of the

Western Rationalistic Tradition has gone hand in hand with the proposals for politically motivated changes in the curriculum. So, what is the connection? I think the relationships are very complex, and I do not know of any simple answer to the question. But underlying all the complexity there is, I believe, this simple structure: those who want to use the universities, especially the humanities, for leftist political transformation correctly perceive that the Western Rationalistic Tradition is an obstacle in their path. In spite of their variety, most of the challengers to the traditional conception of education correctly perceive that if they are forced to conduct academic life according to a set of rules determined by constraints of truth, objectivity, clarity, rationality, logic, and the brute existence of the real world, their task is made more difficult, perhaps impossible. For example, if you think that the purpose of teaching the history of the past is to achieve social and political transformation of the present, then the traditional canons of historical scholarship—the canons of objectivity, evidence, close attention to the facts, and above all, truth—can sometimes seem an unnecessary and oppressive regime that stands in the way of achieving more important social objectives.

In my experience at least, the present multiculturalist reformers of higher education did not come to a revised conception of education from a refutation of the Western Rationalistic Tradition; rather they sought a refutation of the Western Rationalistic Tradition that would justify a revised conception of education that they already found appealing. For example, the remarkable interest in the work of Thomas Kuhn on the part of literary critics did not derive from a sudden passion in English departments to understand the transition from Newtonian Mechanics to Relativity Theory. Rather, Kuhn was seen as discrediting the idea that there is any such reality. If all of "reality" is just a text anyway, then the role of the textual specialist, the literary critic, is totally transformed. And if, as Nietzsche says, "There are not facts, but only interpretations," then what makes one interpretation better than another cannot be that one is true and the other false, but, for example, that one interpretation might help overcome existing hegemonic, patriarchal structures and empower previously underrepresented minorities.

I think in fact that the arguments against the Western Rationalistic Tradition used by a Nietzscheanized Left[5] are rather weak, but this does not matter as much as one might suppose because the refutation of the Western Rationalistic Tradition is not the primary goal. It is only necessary that the refutation have enough respectability to enable one to get on with the primary social and political goal. Historically, part of what happened is that in the late 1960s and 1970s a number of young people went into academic life because they thought that social and political transformation could be achieved through educational and cultural transformation, and that the political ideals of the 1960s could be achieved through education. In many disciplines, for example, analytic philosophy, they found the way blocked by a solid and self-confident professorial establishment committed to traditional intellectual values. But in some disciplines, primarily those humanities disciplines concerned with literary studies—English, French, and Comparative Literature especially—the existing academic norms were fragile, and the way was opened intellectually for a new academic agenda by the liberating impact of the works of authors such as Jacques Derrida, Thomas Kuhn, and Richard Rorty, and to a lesser extent by Michel Foucault and the rediscovery of Nietzsche. Notice that the postmodernist-cultural Left differs from the traditional leftwing movements such as Marxism in that it makes no claims to being "scientific." Indeed it is, if anything, antiscientific, and Marxist-inspired philosophers who accept the Western Rationalistic Tradition, such as Jurgen Habermas, are much less influential in postmodernist subculture than, say, Derrida or Rorty.

There are now departments in some research universities that are ideologically dominated by antirealist and antirationalist conceptions, and these conceptions are beginning to affect both the content and the style of higher education. In cases where the objective is to use higher education as a device for political transformation, the usual justification given for this is that higher education has always been political anyway, and since the claim of the universities to impart to their students a set of objective truths about an independently existing reality is a sham hiding political motives, we should convert higher education into a device for achieving beneficial rather than harmful social and political goals.

So far I have argued that the biggest single consequence of the rejection of the Western Rationalistic Tradition is that it makes possible an abandonment of traditional standards of objectivity, truth, and rationality, and opens the way for an educational agenda, one of whose primary purposes is to achieve social and political transformation. I now want to explore the specific forms that this transformation is supposed to take. Most visibly in the humanities, it is now widely accepted that the race, gender, class, and ethnicity of the student defines his or her identity. On this view it is no longer one of the purposes of education, as it previously had been, to enable the student to develop an identity as a member of a larger universal human intellectual culture. Rather, the new purpose is to reinforce his or her pride in and self-identification with a particular subgroup. For this reason, *representativeness* in the structure of the curriculum, the assigned readings, and the composition of the faculty becomes crucial. If one abandons the commitment to truth and intellectual excellence that is the very core of the Western Rationalistic Tradition, then it seems arbitrary and elitist to think that some books are intellectually superior to others, that some theories are simply true and others false, and that some cultures have produced more important cultural products than others. On the contrary, it seems natural and inevitable to think that all cultures are created intellectually equal. In literary studies some of these features are indicated by a change in the vocabulary. One does not hear much about "the classics," "great works of literature," or even "works"; rather the talk nowadays is usually of "texts" with its leveling implication that one text is as much of a text as any other text.

Another form of transformation is this: we now commonly hear in the research universities that we must accept new and different conceptions of academic "excellence." We are urged to adopt different criteria of academic achievement. An argument sometimes given in favor of altering the traditional conception of academic excellence is that changes in the university brought about by changes in the larger society require new standards of excellence. A number of new faculty members were not recruited according to the traditional standards and did not enter the university with the idea of succeeding by those standards. Often they have been recruited for various social, political, or affirmative action needs. For these new interests and needs, new criteria of excellence have to be designed. However, the Western Rationalistic Tradition does not give you much room to maneuver where intellectual excellence is concerned. Intellectual excellence is already determined by a set of preexisting standards. In order to redefine excellence, you have to abandon certain features of the Western Rationalistic Tradition.

The connection between the attack on rationality and realism and curricular reform is not always obvious, but it is there to be found if you are willing to look closely enough. For example, many of the multiculturalist proposals for curricular reform involve a subtle redefinition of the idea of an academic subject from that of a *domain to be studied* to that of a *cause to be advanced.* Thus, for example, when Women's Studies departments were created some years ago, many people thought these new departments were engaged in the ("objective," "scientific") investigation of a domain, the history and present condition of women, in the same way that they thought that the new departments of Molecular Biology were investigating a domain, the molecular basis of biological phenomena. But in the case of Women's Studies, and several other such new disciplines, that is not always what happened. The new departments often thought of their purpose, at least in part, as advancing certain moral and political causes such as that of feminism.

And this shift from the territorial conception of an academic department to the moral conception in turn has further consequences down the line. Thus, traditionally the commitment to objectivity and truth was supposed to enable the scholar to teach a domain, whatever his or her moral attitudes about the domain. For example, you do not have to be a Platonist to do a good scholarly job of teaching Plato or a Marxist to do a good job of teaching Marx. But once the belief in objectivity and truth are abandoned and political transformation is accepted as a goal, then it seems that the appropriate person to teach Women's Studies would be a politically active feminist woman. On the traditional conception, there is no reason why Women's Studies should not be taught by a scholar who is male, even by a male who is unsympathetic with contemporary feminist doctrines; but in most Women's Studies departments in the United States that would now be out of the question. I hope it is obvious that analogous points could be made about Chicano Studies, Gay and Lesbian Studies, African American Studies, and other elements of the recent attempts at curricular reform.

Furthermore, the shift from domain-to-be-investigated to moral-cause-to-be-advanced is often not made explicit. When making the case to the general academic public for multiculturalist curriculum, the advocates often cite the uncharted academic territories that need to be investigated and taught, and the educational needs of a changing student population. Among themselves, however, they tend to emphasize the political transformations to be achieved, and these transformations include undermining certain traditional conceptions of the academic enterprise. Traditional "liberal" scholars are easily persuaded that new domains need to be investigated and new sorts of students need to be taught; they are often unaware that the main purpose is to advance a political cause.

I realize that the introduction of curricular reforms and even new academic departments to satisfy political demands is nothing new in the history of American universities. However, there is a difference between the traditional reforms and the new conception of education. Traditionally, the idea was that a new *science* of a particular area would help to solve some pressing political or social problem. For example, the development of political economy as a discipline was built in part around the conception of developing a scientific theory of economy and society that would help solve social problems. Part of the difference that I am pointing to is this: On the new conception, the very idea of "science"—is itself regarded as repressive. The idea of developing a rigorous science to investigate, for example, gender and racial differences, is precisely the sort of thing that is under attack. In short, the idea is not to build a new policy on the basis of new scientific theory. Rather, the policy is given in advance and the idea is to develop a departmental and curricular base where that policy can be implemented in the university and extended to the society at large.

I do not wish these remarks to be misunderstood. There are many hard-working men and women engaged in solid traditional scholarship in these new disciplines, and they are committed to the highest standards of truth and objectivity as traditionally conceived. My point here is that they have a significant number of colleagues who do not share these values, and their rejection of these values is connected to their rejection of the Western Rationalistic Tradition.

The introduction of new academic departments is a visible sign of change. Less visible, but much more pervasive, is the change in the self-definition of the individual scholar. I mentioned earlier that there was an increase in the use of ad hominem arguments and genetic fallacies. If there is no such thing as objective truth and validity, than you might as well discuss the person making the argument and his motives for making it, as discuss its claims to validity and the alleged "truth" of its conclusions. But this is only the tip of the iceberg of a much larger shift in sensibility. The new sensibility is usually described (and excoriated) as "relativism," but I think a better term for it might be "politically motivated subjectivism." Previous scholars tried to overcome the limitations of their own prejudices and points of view. Now these are celebrated. For example, funding agencies such as the National Endowment for the Humanities (NEH) receive an increasing number of applications in which it is obvious that the scholar wants to write a book about his or her *politically motivated subjective reactions to, feelings about, and general "take on"* the Renaissance, the plight of women in the Middle Ages, minority novelists of the Pacific Northwest, transvestites in the eighteenth century.

Another scarcely noticed consequence of the rejection of the Western Rationalistic Tradition is the blurring of the distinction between high culture and popular culture in the teaching of the humanities. Traditionally, the humanities thought of themselves as conserving, transmitting, and interpreting the highest achievements of human civilization in general and Western civilization in particular. This view is now regarded as elitist, and there has now been a general abandonment of the idea that some works are qualitatively better than others. There is, rather, the assumption that all works are simply texts and can be treated as such.

On the traditional conception, the distinction between high culture and popular culture manifested itself in the fact that works of high culture were celebrated whereas works of popular culture were, if studied at all, treated as objects of sociological study or investigation. They were treated as symptomatic or expressive, but not themselves as achievements of the highest order. In the subtle shift that has been taking place, no works are celebrated as such. Rather, some works are regarded as important, significant, or valuable because of a political or social message that they convey.

Some Attacks on the Western Rationalistic Tradition

There are really too many kinds of attacks on the Western Rationalistic Tradition, and I am too unfamiliar with many of them, so I can only offer the briefest of surveys. There are deconstructionists, such as Derrida, inspired by Nietzsche and the later works of the German philosopher Martin Heidegger, who think that they can "deconstruct" the entire Western Rationalistic Tradition. There are some feminists who think that the tradition of rationality, realism, truth, and correspondence is essentially a kind of a masculinist device for oppression. There are some philosophers who think that we should stop thinking of science as corresponding to an independently existing reality. Rather, we should think that science in particular, and language in general, just gives us a set of devices for coping. On this view, language is for "coping," as opposed to "matching" or "corresponding." Thus according to Richard Rorty, the pragmatist "drops the notion of truth as correspondence with reality altogether, and says that modern science does not enable us to cope because it corresponds, it just plain enables us to cope."[6]

These attacks on the Western Rationalistic Tradition are peculiar in several respects. First, the movement in question is for the most part confined to various disciplines in the humanities, as well as some social sciences departments and certain law schools. The antirationalist component of the contemporary scene has—so far—had very little influence in philosophy, the natural sciences, economics, engineering, or mathematics. Though some of its heroes are philosophers, it has, in fact, little influence in American Philosophy departments. One might think that since the points at issue are in a very deep sense philosophical, the debates about the curriculum that are connected to the desire to overthrow the Western Rationalistic Tradition must be raging in philosophy departments. But at least in the major American research universities, this, as far as I can tell, is not so. Professional philosophers spend a lot of time fussing around the edges of the Western Rationalistic Tradition. They are obsessed by such questions as: "What is the correct analysis of truth?," "How do words refer to objects in the world?," and "Do the unobservable entities postulated by scientific theories actually exist?" Like the rest of us, they tend to take the core of the Western Rationalistic Tradition for granted even when they are arguing about truth, reference, or the philosophy of science. The philosophers who make an explicit point of rejecting the Western Rationalistic Tradition, such as Richard Rorty or Jacques Derrida, are much more influential in departments of literature than they are in philosophy departments.

A second, and perhaps more puzzling, feature is that it is very hard to find any clear, rigorous, and explicit arguments against the core elements of the Western Rationalistic Tradition. Actually, this is not so puzzling when one reflects that part of what is under attack is the whole idea of "clear, rigorous, and explicit arguments." Rorty has attacked the correspondence theory of truth, and Derrida has claimed that meanings are undecidable, but neither in their works, nor in the works of other favorites of the postmodernist subculture, will you find much by way of rigorous arguments that you can really sharpen your wits on. Somehow or other, there is the feeling that the Western Rationalistic Tradition has become superseded or obsolete, but actual attempts at refutations are rare. Sometimes we are said to be in a postmodern era, and have thus gone beyond the modern era that began in the seventeenth century; but this alleged change is often treated as if it were like a change in the weather, something that just happened without need of argument or proof. Sometimes the "arguments" are more in the nature of slogans and battlecries. But the general air of vaguely literary frivolity that pervades the Nietzscheanized Left is not regarded as a defect. Many of them think that is the way you are supposed to conduct intellectual life.

Two of the most commonly cited authors by those who reject the Western Rationalistic Tradition are Thomas Kuhn and Richard Rorty. I will digress briefly to say a little about them. Kuhn, in *The Structure of Scientific Revolutions,* is supposed to have shown that the claims of science to describe an independently existing reality are false, and that, in fact, scientists are more governed by crowd psychology than by rationality, and tend to flock from one "paradigm" to another in periodic scientific revolutions. There is no such thing as a real world to be described by science; rather each new paradigm creates its own world, so that, for example, as Kuhn says, "after a revolution scientists work in a different world."[7]

I think this interpretation is something of a caricature of Kuhn. But even if it were a correct interpretation, the argument would not show that there is no real world independent of our representations, nor would it show that science is not a series of systematic attempts, in varying degrees successful, to give a description of that reality. Even if we accept the most naive interpretation of Kuhn's account of scientific revolutions, it does not have any such spectacular ontological consequences. On the contrary, even the most pessimistic conception of the history of science is perfectly consistent with the view that there is an independently existing real world and the objective of science is to characterize it.

Rorty has many discussions of truth and correspondence and I could not attempt to do them justice here, but I will pick up on only one or two crucial aspects. He says repeatedly that "true" is just a term of commendation that we use to praise those beliefs that we think it is good to believe, and that truth is made and not discovered.[8] The difficulty with the first of these views is that in the ordinary sense of the word, there are lots of things that for one reason or another one thinks it is good to believe that are not true, and lots of things that are true but it would be better if they were not generally believed. I think, for example, that it is good that mothers believe the best of their children even though such beliefs often turn out false. Likewise, the persistence of religious beliefs is on balance a good thing, though most such beliefs are probably false. Rorty's claim suffers from the usual difficulty of such philosophical reductions: it is either circular or obviously false. On the one hand, the criterion of goodness can be defined as truth or correspondence to reality, in which case the analysis is circular. On the other hand, if one does not redefine "truth," there are lots of counterexamples, lots of propositions that it is good for one reason or another for people to believe but which are not true in the ordinary sense of the word; and there are propositions that for one reason or another it would be bad to believe but which are nonetheless true.

There is an ambiguity in Rorty's claim that truth is made and not discovered. Since truth is always in the form of true *statements* and true theories, then indeed true statements and true theories have to be made and formulated by human beings. But it does not follow from this fact that there is no independently existing reality to which their statements and theories correspond. So there is a sense in which truth is made—namely true statements are made. But there is also a sense, consistent with this, in which truth is discovered. What one discovers is that which makes the statements true (or false, as the case might be). In a word, true *statements* are made, but the truth of statements is not made, it is *discovered.*

Rorty's argument is typical of these discussions in that more is *insinuated* than is actually argued for. What is claimed, I guess, is that true statements, like all statements, are made by human beings. What is insinuated is much more serious: there are no facts in the real world that make our statements true, and perhaps the "real world" is just our creation.

The Status of the Western Rationalistic Tradition

I have not found any attacks on the Western Rationalistic Tradition—not in Rorty or Kuhn, much less in Derrida or Nietzsche—that seem to me at all convincing or even damaging to any of the basic principles I have enunciated. But the question naturally arises: is there anything to be said in *defense* of the Western Rationalistic Tradition? Is there any proof or argument that this is one possible right way to think and act? Certainly, alternative visions are possible, so why accept this one?

There is something puzzling about demanding an argument in favor of, or a proof of, the validity of a whole mode of sensibility and framework of presuppositions in which what we count as a proof and as an argument take place. The situation is a bit like the common occurrence of the 1960s in which one was asked to justify rationality: "What is your argument for rationality?" The notion of an argument already presupposes standards of validity and hence rationality. Something only counts as an argument given that it is subject to the canons of rationality. Another way to put this same point is: You cannot justify or argue for rationality, because there is no content to rationality as such, in a way that there is a content to particular claims made within a framework of rationality. You might show that certain canons of rationality are self-defeating or inconsistent, but there is no way to "prove" rationality.

It might seem that with realism the situation is different. Surely, one might say, the claim that reality exists independently of human representations is a factual claim and, as such, can be true or false. I want to suggest that in the actual operation of our linguistic, cultural, and scientific practices, all six principles function quite differently from ordinary empirical or scientific theses. Since realism is the foundation of the entire system, I will say a few words about it. I have presented the Western Rationalistic Tradition as if it consisted of a series of theoretical principles, as if it were simply one theory we might hold along with a number of others. Those of us brought up in our intellectual tradition find this mode of exposition almost inevitable, because our model of knowledge, as I remarked earlier, comes from the presentation of well-defined theses in systematic theoretical structures. But in order that we should be able to construct theories at all, we require a set of background presuppositions that are prior to any theorizing. For those of us brought up in our civilization, especially the scientific portions of our civilization, the principles that I have just presented as those of the Western Rationalistic Tradition do not function as *a theory*. Rather, they function as part of the taken-for-granted background of our practices. The conditions of intelligibility of our practices, linguistic and otherwise, cannot themselves be demonstrated as truths within those practices. To suppose they could was the endemic mistake of foundationalist metaphysics.

In "defense" of realism, the only thing that one can say is that it forms the presupposition of our linguistic and other sorts of practices. You cannot coherently deny realism and engage in ordinary linguistic practices, because realism is a condition of the normal intelligibility of those practices. You can see this if you consider any sort of ordinary communication. For example, suppose I call my car mechanic to find out if the carburetor is fixed; or I call the doctor to get the report of my recent medical examination. Now, suppose I have reached a deconstructionist car mechanic and he tries to explain to me that a carburetor is just a text anyway, and that there is nothing to talk about except the textuality of the text. Or suppose I have reached a postmodernist doctor who explains to me that disease is essentially a metaphorical construct. Whatever else one can say about such situations, one thing is clear: communication has broken down. The normal presuppositions behind our practical everyday communications, and a fortiori, behind our theoretical communications, require the presupposition of a preexisting reality for their normal intelligibility. Give me the assumption that these sorts of communication are even possible between human beings and you will see that you require the assumption of an independently existing reality. A public language presupposes a public world.

Realism does not function as a thesis, hypothesis, or supposition. It is, rather, the condition of the possibility of a certain set of practices, particularly linguistic practices. The challenge, then, to those who would like to reject realism is to try to explain the intelligibility of our practices in light of that rejection. Philosophers in the past who cared seriously about these matters, and who rejected realism, actually tried to do that. Berkeley, for example, tries to explain how it is possible that we can communicate with each other, given that on his view there are no independently existing material objects, but only ideas in minds. His answer is that God intervenes to guarantee the possibility of human communication. One interesting thing about the present theorists who claim to have shown that reality is a social construct, or that there is no independently existing reality, or that everything is really a text, is that they have denied one of the conditions of intelligibility of our ordinary linguistic practices without providing an alternative conception of that intelligibility.

Conclusion

There are many debates going on in the research universities today and many proposals for educational change. I have not tried to explain or even describe most of what is going on. I have been concerned with only one issue: the philosophical presuppositions of the traditional conception of higher education and the educational consequences of accepting or denying those presuppositions. I have claimed that a deeper understanding of at least some of the headline issues can be gained by seeing them in their philosophical content.

However, there is one danger endemic to any such presentation. You are almost forced to present the issues as clearer and simpler than they really are. In order to describe the phenomena at all, you have to state them as more or less clear theses on each side: the subculture of the traditional university and the subculture of postmodernism. However, in real life people on both sides tend to be ambivalent and even confused. They are often not quite sure what they actually think. In light of this ambivalence, it is perhaps best to think of the present account not so much as a characterization of the thought processes of the participants in the current debates but as a description of what is at stake.

Acknowledgments

I have benefitted from discussion of these issues with various colleagues and friends. I would especially like to express my gratitude to my fellow authors in this volume who participated with me in the *Dædalus* authors' conference in Cambridge and made valuable suggestions for improving the article. I have also been helped by Hubert Dreyfus, Jennifer Hudin, Dagmar Searle, and Charles Spinosa.

Notes

1. I have discussed some related issues in two other articles. See John R. Searle, "The Storm Over The University," *New York Review of Books* XXVII (19) (6 December 1990): 34–42, and John R. Searle, "Is There a Crisis in American Higher Education?," *The Bulletin of the American Academy of Arts and Sciences* XLVI (4) (January 1993): 24–47.

2. John Locke, *Locke on Human Understanding* (London: Routledge and Sons, 1909), 324–25.

3. I say "in general" because, for example, sometimes statements are self-referential; for example, "This sentence is in English."

4. The American Council of Learned Societies, *Speaking for the Humanities,* ACLS Occasional Paper, No. 7, 1989, 18.

5. I believe this expression was coined by Allan Bloom.

6. Richard Rorty, *Consequences of Pragmatism* (Minneapolis, Minn.: University of Minnesota Press, 1982).

7. Thomas S. Kuhn, *The Structure of Scientific Revolutions,* 2d ed. (Chicago, Ill.: University of Chicago Press, 1970), 135.

8. See especially Richard Rorty, *Objectivity, Relativism and Truth,* Philosophical Papers Vol. 1 (Cambridge and New York: Cambridge University Press, 1991.)

Bibliography

American Association of University Professors. *AAUP Policy Documents & Reports.* Washington, D.C.: AAUP, 1995.

Arden, Eugene. "Is Tenure 'Obsolete'?" *Academe* (January–February 1995), 38–42.

Atherton, Margaret, Sidney Morgenbesser, and Robert Schwartz. "On Tenure." *The Philosophical Forum* X, 2–4 (1978–79), 341–59.

Baade, Hans W., ed. *Academic Freedom: The Scholar's Place in Modern Society.* Dobbs Ferry, N.Y.: Oceana Publications, 1964.

Benjamin, Ernst, and Donald R. Wagner, eds. *Academic Freedom: An Everyday Concern.* San Francisco: Jossey-Bass, 1994.

Berman, Paul, ed. *Debating P.C.: The Controversy over Political Correctness on College Campuses.* New York: Dell, 1992.

Bernstein, Richard. "Guilty If Charged." *New York Review of Books* (January 13, 1994), 11–14.

Brown, Ralph S., and Jordan E. Kurland. "Academic Tenure and Academic Freedom." *Law and Contemporary Problems* 53 (Summer 1990), 325–55.

Cahn, Steven M. *Morality, Responsibility, and the University: Studies in Academic Ethics.* Philadelphia: Temple University Press, 1990.

Cahn, Steven M. *Saints and Scamps: Ethics in Academia.* Lanham, Md.: Rowman & Littlefield, 1986.

Chait, Richard. *Beyond Traditional Tenure: A Guide to Sound Policies and Practices.* San Francisco: Jossey-Bass, 1982.

Commission on Academic Tenure in Higher Education. *Faculty Tenure.* San Francisco: Jossey-Bass, 1973.

Cotter, William R. "Why Tenure Works." *Academe* (January–February 1996), 26–29.

Curry, Barbara K., and James Earl Davis. "Representing People: The Obligations of Faculty as Researchers." *Academe* (September–October 1995), 40–43.

Daniel, John, Frederiek de Vlaming, Nigel Hartley, and Manfred Nowak, eds. *Academic Freedom 2: A Human Rights Report.* London: Zed Books, 1993.

De George, Richard T. *The Nature and Limits of Authority.* Lawrence: University Press of Kansas, 1985.

Dewey, John. "Academic Freedom." *Educational Review* 23 (1902), 1–14.

Dewey, John. "Address of the President." *Bulletin of the American Association of University Professors* (December 1915), 9–13.

Dickman, Howard, ed. *The Imperiled Academy.* New Brunswick, N.J.: Transaction, 1993.

Dworkin, Ronald. "Objectivity and Truth: You'd Better Believe It," *Philosophy and Public Affairs* 25, 2 (1996), 87–139.

Dworkin, Ronald. "We Need a New Interpretation of Academic Freedom." *Academe* (May–June 1996), 10–15.

Fernando, Laksiri, Nigel Hartley, Manfred Nowak, and Theresa Swinehart, eds. *Academic Freedom 1990: A Human Rights Report.* Geneva: World University Service, 1990.

Fish, Stanley. *There's No Such Thing as Free Speech and It's a Good Thing, Too.* New York: Oxford University Press, 1994.

Fox-Genovese, Elizabeth, and Larry Scanlon. "Debating Political Correctness." *Academe* (May–June 1995), 8–15.

Fuchs, Ralph F. "Academic Freedom—Its Basic Philosophy, Function, and History." *Academic Freedom: The Scholar's Place in Modern Society,* Hans W. Baade, ed. Dobbs Ferry, N.Y.: Oceana Publications, 1964.

Galle, William P., Jr., and Clifford M. Koen Jr. "Tenure and Promotion after *Penn v. EEOC.*" *Academe* (September–October 1993), 19–26.

Gates, Henry Louis, Jr. "Truth or Consequences: Putting Limits on Limits." *The Limits of Expression in American Intellectual Life.* American Council of Learned Societies Occasional Papers, no. 22, 1993, 15–28.

Gregory, John DeWitt. "Secrecy in University and College Tenure Deliberations: Placing Appropriate Limits on Academic Freedom." *U.C. Davis Law Review* 16 (1983), 1023–46.

Grexa, Thomas. "Title VII Tenure Litigation in the Academy and Academic Freedom—A Current Appraisal." *Dickinson Law Review* 96 (Fall 1991), 11–36.

Hentoff, Nat. " 'Speech Codes' on the Campus and Problems of Free Speech." *Dissent* (Fall 1991), 546–49.

Hook, Sidney. *Academic Freedom and Academic Anarchy.* New York: Cowles, 1970.

Hook, Sidney, Paul Kurtz, and Miro Todorovich, eds. *The Idea of a Modern University.* Buffalo: Prometheus Books, 1974.

Huer, Jon. *Tenure for Socrates: A Study in the Betrayal of the American Professor.* New York: Bergin & Garvey, 1991.

Joughin, Louis, ed. *Academic Freedom and Tenure: A Handbook of the American Association of University Professors.* Madison: University of Wisconsin Press, 1967.

Keller, Evelyn Fox. "Science and Its Critics." *Academe* (September–October 1995), 10–15.

Kimball, Roger. *Tenured Radicals: How Politics Has Corrupted Our Higher Education.* New York: Harper & Row, 1990.

Ladenson, Robert F. "Is Academic Freedom Necessary?" *Law and Philosophy* 5 (1986), 59–87.

Leap, Terry L. *Tenure, Discrimination and the Courts,* 2d ed. Ithaca: Cornell University Press, 1995.

Leiser, Burton M., ed. "Academic Freedom and Tenure Symposium." *Pace Law Review* 15, 1 (Fall 1994).

Machlup, Fritz. "In Defense of Academic Tenure." *AAUP Bulletin* 50 (Summer 1964), 112–24.

Mann, Patricia S. "Hate Speech, Freedom, and Discourse Ethics in the Academy." *Radical Philosophy of Law,* David S. Caudill, ed. Atlantic Highlands, N.J.: Humanities Press, 1995.

McGee, Robert W. "Academic Tenure: Should It Be Protected By Law?" *Western State University Law Review* 20, 2 (Spring 1993), 593–602.

McGee, Robert W., and Walter E. Block. "Academic Tenure: An Economic Critique." *Harvard Journal of Law & Public Policy* 14, 2, 545–63.

Menand, Louis. "The Future of Academic Freedom." *Academe* (May–June 1993), 11–17.

Metzger, Walter P., ed. *The American Concept of Academic Freedom in Formation: A Collection of Essays and Reports.* New York: Arno Press, 1977.

Metzger, Walter P., ed. *The Constitutional Status of Academic Freedom.* New York: Arno Press, 1977.

Metzger, Walter P., ed. *The Constitutional Status of Academic Tenure.* New York: Arno Press, 1977.

Meyers, Diana Tietjens. "Rights in Collision: A Non-Punitive, Compensatory Remedy for Abusive Speech." *Law and Philosophy* 14, 2 (1995), 203–43.

O'Neill, Robert M. "Academic Freedom and the Constitution." *Journal of College and University Law* 11 (1984), 275–92.

O'Neill, Robert M. "Scientific Research and the First Amendment: An Academic Privilege." *U.C. Davis Law Review* 16 (Summer 1983), 837–55.

Pellegrino, Edmund D., Robert M. Veatch, and John P. Langan, eds. *Ethics, Trust and the Professions: Philosophical and Cultural Aspects.* Washington, D.C.: Georgetown University Press, 1991.

Perley, James E. "Tenure, Academic Freedom, and Governance." *Academe* (January–February 1995), 43–47.

Pincoffs, Edmund L., ed. *The Concept of Academic Freedom.* Austin: University of Texas Press, 1972.

Rashdall, Hastings. *Universities of Europe in the Middle Ages,* F. M. Powicke and A. B. Emden, eds. Oxford: Clarendon Press, 1987, 3 vols.

Rogers, Carl R. *Freedom to Learn.* Columbus: Merrill, 1969.

Rorty, Richard. "Does Academic Freedom Have Philosophical Presuppositions." *Academe* (November–December 1994), 52–63.

Rosovsky, Henry. *The University: An Owner's Manual.* New York: Norton, 1990.

Scott, Joan Wallach. "Academic Freedom as an Ethical Practice." *Academe* (July–August 1995), 44–48.

Searle, John. "Rationality and Realism: What Is at Stake?" *Daedalus* 122, 4 (Fall 1993), 55–84.

Searle, John. "The Storm over the University." *New York Review of Books,* 37 (December 6, 1990), 43–42.

Sunstein, Cass R. "Liberalism, Speech Codes, and Related Problems." *Academe* (July–August 1993), 14–25.

Van Alstyne, William W., ed. *Freedom and Tenure in the Academy.* Durham, N.C.: Duke University Press, 1993.

Weingartner, Rudolph H. "Ethics in Academic Personnel Processes: The Tenure Decision." *Morality, Responsibility, and the University: Studies in Academic Ethics,* Steven M. Cahn, ed. Philadelphia: Temple University Press, 1990.

Worgul, George S., Jr., ed. *Issues in Academic Freedom.* Pittsburgh: Duquesne University Press, 1992.

Index

AAC. *See* Association of American Colleges

AACSB. *See* American Assembly of Collegiate Schools of Business

AAUP. *See* American Association of University Professors

AAUP Bulletin, 122

Abbot, Francis, 194n10

Academe, 121

academic freedom, 9, 10, 11, 13–14, 15, 16, 22, 24, 27–28, 29, 30, 32, 39, 47, 55, 108, 118, 132–35, 156, 159–60; attacks on, ix, x, 86–94, 111–13, 160; Basic Philosophy, Function, and History, 136–55; development of, 138–41; faculty, 55, 74–84, 110–11, 137, 140; and freedom of speech, 80, 86 (*see also* freedom of speech); justification of, 53–84; and law, 143–47; narrow version, 85, 86; obligation to protect, 16–17, 22, 48; philosophical presuppositions, 176–96; professional formulation, 141–43; restrictions on, 78–79, 83, 91; scope, 136–38; student, 68–74, 99, 132–33 (*see also* freedom to learn); in a technological age, 104–11; untenured faculty, 24, 50

academic tenure. *See* tenure, academic

accountability, 14, 25, 29, 30, 162–63; of committees, 82; definition, 61; of faculty, 79–80; institutional, 61, 62, 65–67. *See also* evaluation

ad hominem argument, 206–7, 214

Adler, Mortimer, 194n16

Adler v. Board of Education, 145

Age of Reason, 136

Alabama, 151n16

Alabama Polytechnic Institute, 153n39

Albany, 100

Alchian, Armen, 174n72

Amberg, Steven, 172n53

Amendments to U. S. Constitution: Fifth Amendment, 145; First Amendment, 98, 99, 101, 121; Fourteenth Amendment, 99, 101, 143

American Assembly of Collegiate Schools of Business (AACSB), 168n9, 174n73

American Association of Law Schools, 153n51

American Association of School Administrators, 173n63

American Association of University Professors (AAUP), x, 4, 6, 9, 27, 31, 34, 44, 52n, 117, 119, 120, 121, 123, 132, 135, 141, 142, 143, 152n29, 163, 170n24, 176

American College of Surgeons, 177

American Council of Learned Societies, 209

American Philosophical Society, 31

Appleby, Joyce, 193n10

appointment, initial, 4

arbitration, 164

argumentum ad hominem. *See* ad hominem argument

Aristotle, 184

Arkansas, 153n50

assistants, teaching. *See* teaching assistants

Association of American Colleges (AAC), 27n1, 31, 34, 117, 119, 120, 123, 142, 163

225

Dostoevski, F. M., 187
Douglas, Justice, 145
downsizing, 19–20
Dreyfus, Hubert, 220
Dworkin, Ronald, 28n9, 182

education: liberal, 105–6; traditional conception of, 219
Egypt, 150n15
Eisenhower, Dwight D., 179, 192n1
Elements, 200
Empire Black Arts Council Festival, 100
employment, continuous, 4, 7, 22
employment-at-will, 4, 28n2
Encyclopedia Britannica, 178
Enlightenment, 178, 200
ethics, 7, 22, 23, 29–52, 41, 43–45, 49–51, 71–72, 83, 124, 129–35; professional, 129. *See also* responsibility
Euclid, 200
evaluation: post-tenure, 39–43; by students, 79. *See also* review, academic
excellence, academic, 212
exigency, financial, 33, 41, 43–45, 47–48, 81, 118; definition, 44

faculty: evaluation, 31–32; part-time, 26, 45–49, 82–84; responsibility of, 71–72, 83
fallacy, genetic, 206, 214
Feinberg Law, 145
Ferruolo, Stephen, 161
financial exigency. *See* exigency, financial
Ford Motor Corp., 157
Foucault, Michel, 211
France, 150n15
Frankfurter, Justice Felix, 146
freedom, academic. *See* academic freedom
freedom, faculty. *See* academic freedom, faculty
freedom of speech, 14, 55, 72, 73, 85, 127; and academic freedom, 80; civil

right, 85, 86; in classroom, 80; student, 132–33 (*see also* freedom to learn)
freedom to learn, 55, 68–74, 130, 137, 149n5; definition, 70; European, 68
Frege, Gottlob, 202, 203
friendship, 50–51
Fuchs, Ralph F., 136–155

General Motors Corp., 157
German Universities and University Study, The, 139
Germany, 55, 139, 140, 151n23, 154n68, 154n69
Gierak, John, 163, 164, 172n53, 173n59
Goodman, Nelson, 183
governance, university, 70, 80–82, 86, 130, 155n70
Greece, 136, 187
Griswold, A. Whitney, 153n49

Habermas, Jurgen, 211
Hampshire College, 170n21
harassment, sexual, 91
Harlan, Justice, 146
Harleston, Bernard W.. 97, 98, 100, 102–4
Harvard Crimson, 102
Harvard Law School, 170n21
Haskell, Thomas, 193n8, 194n10
hate speech, 94–97, 126
Hegel, Georg W. F., 188
Heidegger, Martin, 187, 215
Himalays, 202
Hirsch, E. D., 97
Hollywood, 100
Holmes, Justice Oliver Wendell, 128
House of Commons (British), 178
Hudin, Jennifer, 220
humanities, 54, 58, 76, 77, 109, 197, 210, 214; knowledge in, 88–89
Hume, David, 200, 201
Hunt, Lynn, 193n10

About the Author

RICHARD T. DE GEORGE is University Distinguished Professor of Philosophy and of Russian and East European Studies and Director of the International Center for Ethics in Business at the University of Kansas. He has written widely in the field of applied ethics and he is the author of over 150 articles and the author or editor of seventeen books, including *Ethics, Free Enterprise, and Public Policy; Business Ethics* (now in its fourth edition and also available in Japanese); and *Competing With Integrity in International Business.*

He has been the president of several academic organizations, including the American Philosophical Association, the Society for Business Ethics, and the International Society of Business, Economics, and Ethics. He received his B.A. from Fordham University and his Ph.D. from Yale University. He has been a research fellow at Yale University, Columbia University, and Stanford University, and he was awarded a Doctor Honoris Causa by Nijenrode University (The Netherlands) in 1996.